GEDDES&GROSSET

Dictionary of
Abbreviations
& Acronyms

pocket reference digest

This edition published 1999 by Geddes & Grosset, an imprint of
Children's Leisure Products Limited

© 1999 Children's Leisure Products Limited,
David Dale House, New Lanark ML11 9DJ, Scotland

ISBN 1 85534 217 0

Printed and bound in India

A

A absolute, as in temperature; ampere; area; Associate; alcohol; argon (chemical element).

Å Ångstrom (unit of measurement).

a acre; *anno*, Latin ' in the year'; *annus*, Latin 'year'; *ante*, Latin 'before'; anterior; *atto*, Latin '110⁻¹⁸'.

a. *anno*, Latin 'in the year'; *ante*, Latin 'before'; *aqua*, Latin 'water'.

A1 first-class.

AA Alcoholics Anonymous; Analogue Addicts; Architectural Association; Automobile Association; anti-aircraft.

AAA Action Against Abuse of Women and Girls; Action Against Allergy; Amateur Athletic Association; American Academy of Achievement; American Academy of Art; Anglo-Albanian Association; Association for Applied Artists; Association of Authors Agents; Association of Average Adjusters; Association of Attenders and Alumni of the Hague Academy of International Law.

AAAA Association for the Abolition of the Aberrant Apostrophe; Australian Advertising Advisory Agency.

AAAD American Athletic Association for the Deaf.

AAAI American Association for Artificial Intelligence.

AAAofE Amateur Athletic Association of England.

AAB Association of Applied Biologists; Attendance Allowance Board.

AABB American Association of Blood Banks; Association for the Advancement of British Biotechnology; Australian Association of Bush Regenerators.

AABDF Allied Association of Bleachers, Printers, Dyers and Finishers.

AABL Associated Australasian Banks in London.

AABM Australian Association of British Manufacturers.

AABR Association for the Advancement of the Blind and Retarded.

AABS Association for the Advancement of Baltic Studies.

AABTL Amalgamated Association of Beamers, Twisters and Drawers (Hand and Machine).

AABTT Association for Analytic and Bodymind Therapy & Training.

AAC Agricultural Advisory Council for England and Wales; Amateur Athletic Club; American Archery Council; Anglo-American Corporation; *anno ante Christum*, Latin 'in the year before Christ'.

AACB Associate of the Association of Certified Book-keepers.

AACBC American Association of College Baseball Coaches.

AACBP American Association of Crown and Bridge Prosthodontics.

AACE Association for the Advancement of Computing in Education.

AACP Anglo-American Council for Productivity; Associate of the Association of Computer Professionals.

AACPA Autoclaved Aerated Concrete Products Association.

AACS Aberdeen-Angus Cattle Society; Association of Art Centres in Scotland.

AADW Association of Artists and Designers in Wales.

AAE Association for Adult Education.

AAEW Atlantic Airborne Early Warning.

AAH Association for Applied Hypnosis; Association of Art Historians.

AAHC Association of Agricultural and Horticultural Colleges (Eire).

AAI Alternatives to Abortion International; Architectural Association of Ireland; Association of Advertisers in Ireland; Association of Alabaster Importers; Association of Art Institutions; Association of Artists in Ireland.

AAIA Associate of the Association of International Accountants.

AAIB Aircraft Accident Investigation Board.

7

AAIP Association of American Indian Physicians.

AAM Anglican Association of Musicians; air-to-air missile.

AAMC Association for the Advancement of Maternity Care.

AAMRH Association of Agricultural Medicine and Rural Health.

AAMS Associate Member of the Association of Medical Secretaries, Practice Administrators and Receptionists.

A & A additions and amendments.

A & E accident and emergency (as in a hospital department).

A & I accident and indemnity.

A & M Ancient and Modern (hymn book).

A & N Army and Navy (club); Army and Navy (stores).

A & R Artist and Repertoire.

AAO Anglo-Australian Observatory.

aaO *am angeführten Orte*, German 'at the place quoted'.

aar average annual rainfall; against all risks.

AARG Aerial Archaeology Research Group.

AARM Association of Aquatic and Recreation Management.

AART Action Against Racism in Training.

AASC Anglo-American Sporting Club.

AASI Associate of the Ambulance Service Institute.

AASM Association of Aviation and Space Museologists.

AASP Associate Member of the Association of Sales Personnel.

AAU Amateur Athletic Union.

AB Advisory Board; able-bodied seaman; *Artium Baccalaureus*, Latin 'Bachelor of Arts'.

Ab antibody; alabamine (chemical element).

ABA Amateur Boxing Association; Antiquarian Booksellers Association; Association of British Archaeologists.

ABBA Amateur Basketball Association.

ABAC Association of Business and Administrative Computing.

ABACUS Association of Bibliographic Agencies of Britain, Australia, Canada and the United States.

ABAS Amateur Basketball Association of Scotland; Association of Business Administration Studies.

ABC Active Birth Centre; Advance Booking Charter; Associated British Cinemas; Association of British Climatologists; Association of British Companies; Association of British Parking Enforcement Companies; Association of Building Centres; Association of Business Communicators; Audit Bureau of Circulations; automatic binary computer.

ABCAT Association of British Cutlers & Allied Trades.

ABCB Association of British Consortium Banks.

ABCC Association of British Chambers of Commerce; Association of British Correspondence Colleges.

ABCD Association for Bridge Construction and Design; Association of British Choral Directors.

ABCHI Association of British Health-Care Industries.

ABCL Association of British Container Lessors.

ABCM Association of Building Component Manufacturers.

ABCN Association of British Clinical Neurophysiologists.

ABCO Association of British Conference Organisers.

ABCOC Advance Booking Charter Operators Council.

ABCP Association of Butter and Cheese Packers.

ABCS Association of British Chick Sexers.

ABCUL Association of British Credit Unions Limited.

ABD Association of British Detectives; Association of British Drivers.

ABDO Association of British Dispensing Opticians.

ABDP Association of British Directory Publishers.

ABDS Associate of the British Display Society.

ABDSA Association of British Dental Surgery Assistants.

ABE Association of British Editors; Association of Building Engineers; Association of Business Executives.

ABEng Associate Member of the Association of Building Engineers.

ABES Association for Broadcast Engineering Standards.

ABET Advisory Board on Educational Technology.

ABF Actors' Benevolent Fund; Army Benevolent Fund.

abf absolute bloody final.

ABFD Association of British Factors and Discounters.

ABFL Association of British Foam Laminators.

ABH Association of British Hairdressers; Association of Hispanists of Great Britain and Ireland; actual bodily harm.

ABHA Associate of the British Hypnotherapy Association.

ABI Association of British Insurers; Association of British Investigators.

ABID Associate of the British Institute of Interior Design.

ABIH Association of British and International Hairdressers and Hairdressing Schools.

ABIM Associate of the British Institute of Management; Association of British Insecticide Manufacturers.

ab init. *ab initio*, Latin 'from the beginning'.

ABIOEC Association of British Independent Oil Exploration Companies.

ABIPP Associate of the British Institute of Professional Photography.

ABIS Association of Burglary Insurance Surveyors.

ABLE Action for Better Limb Engineering.

ABM Association of Board Makers; Association of Breastfeeding Mothers; Association of British Maltsters; Association of British Music; Association of Button Merchants; anti-ballistic missile.

ABMEC Association of British Mining Equipment Companies.

ABMEWS anti-ballistic missile early warning system.

ABMP Association of British Meat Processors.

ABMPCAE Association of British Manufacturers of Photographic, Cine & Audio Equipment.

ABMPM Association of British Manufacturers of Printers Machinery.

ABMRC Association of British Market Research Companies.

ABMSAC Association of British Mountaineering Societies and Climbers.

ABN Association of British Neurologists.

ABNA Anorexia Bulimia Nervosa Association.

ABO Association of British Orchestras; antigen-based bloodgroup-classification.

A-bomb atomic bomb.

ABP arterial blood pressure; Archbishop.

ABPC Associated British Picture Corporation; Association of British Packing Contractors; Association of British Pewter Craftsmen.

ABPCO Association of British Professional Conference Organisers.

ABPI Association of the British Pharmaceutical Industry.

ABPMM Association of British Preserved Milk Manufacturers.

ABPN Association of British Paediatric Nurses.

ABPS Association of British Philatelic Societies.

ABPT Association of Blind Piano Tuners.

ABPVM Association of British Plywood and Veneer Manufacturers.

ABRC Advisory Board for Research Councils; Association of British Research Councils; Advisory Board for Redundant Churches.

ABRFM Association of British Roofing Felt Manufacturers.

ABRO Animal Breeding Research Organization; Army Base Repair Organization.

ABRP Advisory Board on Restricted Patents.

ABRRM Association of British Reclaimed Rubber Manufacturers.

ABRS Association of British Riding Schools.

ABRSM Associated Board of the Royal Schools of Music.

ABS Architects' Benevolent Society; Associate of the Building Societies Institute; Association of British Sailmakers; Association of British Spectroscopists; Association of Broadcasting Staff; Association of Business Schools; *antiblockiersystem* (car brake; German 'anti-lock system').

ABSA Association for Business Sponsorship of the Arts.

ABSFAM Association of British Solid Fuel Appliance Manufacturers.

ABSFCE Association of British Salted Fish Curers and Exporters.

ABSI Association of the Boot and Shoe Industry.

ABSM(TTD) Diploma of the Birmingham School of Music.

ABSO Association of British Security Officers.

ABSSG Associate of the British Society of Scientific Glassblowers.

ABSTD Association of Basic Science Teachers in Dentistry.

ABSW Association of British Science Writers.

ABSWAP Association of Black Social Workers and Allied Professions.

ABT American Board of Trade; Australian Broadcasting Tribunal.

ABTA Allied Brewery Traders Association; Association of British Travel Agents.

ABTAC Australian Book Trade Advisory Committee.

ABTAPL Association of British Theological and Philosophical Libraries.

ABTCM Association of British Textured Coating Manufacturers.

ABTM American Board of Tropical Medicine; Association of British Transport Museums.

ABTT Association of British Theatre Technicians.

ABVA Association of British Veterinary Acupuncture.

ABVT American Board on Veterinary Toxicology.

ABWAK Association of British Wild Animal Keepers.

ABYA Association of Brokers and Yacht Agents.

ABYC American Boat and Yacht Council.

ABZ Association of British Zoologists.

AC Air Command Air Corps; Alpine Club; Alpine Convention; Appeal Court; Arts Council; Assistant Commissioner; Athletic Club; alternating current (used in physics); *appellation contrôlée*, French 'regulated naming', used in the origin of wines; aircraftman; *ante Christum*, Latin 'before Christ'.

Ac actinium (chemical element).

ac *ante cibum*, Latin 'before food'.

a/c account; account current.

ACA Acoustic Corporation of America; Advertisement Contractors Association; Advisory Committee on Advertising; Afro-Caribbean Association; Agricultural Council of America; Aircrewmen Association; Aluminium Costings Association; American Cartographic Association; Anglers Co-operative Association; Architectural Cladding Association; Associate of the Institute of Chartered Accountants in England and Wales; Asian Christian Association; Associate of the Institute of Chartered Accountants in Ireland; Association for Continence Advice; Association of Canadian Archivists; Association of Consultant Architects; Association of Consulting Actuaries; Association of County Archivists; Australian Coal Association.

ACAA Asian Christian Art Association.

ACAAI Air Cargo Agents Association of India.

ACAC American Christian Action Council; Arab Civil Aviation Authority; Australian Chemicals Advisory Committee.

ACACHE Association of Career Advisers in Colleges of Higher Education.

ACADS Association for Computer Aided Design.

ACAE Australian Commission on Advanced Education.

ACAF Aero-Club Air France.

ACAHA Association of Chief Administrators of Health Authorities.

ACAI Accademia Archeologica Italiana.

ACAIP Advisory Committee on Animal Import Priorities.

ACAN Action Committee Against Narcotics.

ACANZ Agricultural Council of Australia and New Zealand.

ACAO Association of Chief Ambulance Officers.

ACAQ Advisory Committee on Air Quality.

ACARD Advisory Council for Applied Research and Development.

ACARMA Agricultural Chemical and Animal Remedies Manufacturing Association of New Zealand.

ACAS Advisory, Conciliation and Arbitration Service; Association of Concerned African Scholars.

ACASLA Association of Chief Architects of Scottish Local Authorities.

ACASS Association of Chartered Accountant Students Societies.

ACASSI Association of Chartered Accountants Students Societies in Ireland.

ACAST Advisory Committee on the Application of Science and Technology to Development.

ACAT Action de Chrétiens pour l'Abolition de Torture; African Cooperative Action Trust.

ACATCM All-China Association of Traditional Chinese Medicine.

ACATS Association of Civil Aviation Technical Staffs.

ACAV Agence Centrafrique de Voyage; American Committee on Arthropod-borne Viruses.

ACAVA Association for Cultural Advancement through Visual Art.

ACAVC Advisory Committee on Agricultural and Veterinary Chemicals.

ACB Agricultural Cooperatives Bank of Iran; American Council of the Blind; Arab Central Bank; Associación Costarricense de Bibliotecarios; Association Canadienne des Bibliothèques; Association of Certification Bodies; Association of Clinical Biochemists.

ACBA Aggregate Concrete Block Association.

ACBB American Council for Better Broadcasts.

ACBC Australian Catholic Bishops' Conference.

ACBM Association of Cartonboard Makers.

ACBSI Associate of the Chartered Building Societies Institute.

ACC Aboriginal Coordinating Council; Academy of Canadian Cinema; Action for the Crippled Child; Afghan Cart Company; Agricultural Credit Corporation, (Eire, Jordan); American Cars Corporation (Ivory Coast); American Catholic Committee; Anglican Consultative Council; Animal Christian Concern; Anti-Animal Carcass Campaign; Anti-Consumerism Campaign; Antique Collectors Club; Asian Coconut Community; Asian Cultural Council (USA); Asmara Chamber of Commerce (Ethiopia); Associated Cement Companies (India); Associated Communications Corporation; Association of Clinical Competence; Association of Computer Clubs; Association of Conservative Clubs; Association of County Councils; Army Catering Corps; Australian Chamber of Commerce.

ACCA Air Charter Carriers Association; American Cotton Cooperative Association; Animal Clinical Chemistry Association; Associate of the Chartered Association of Certified Accountants.

ACCAD Advisory Committee for the World Climate Applications and Data Programmes.

ACCART Australian Council for Care of Animals in Research and Teaching.

ACCBD Advisory Committee on Conservation of Biological Diversity.

ACCC Advisory Committee to the Canada Centre for Inland Waters; American Council of Christian Churches; Association of Classic Car Clubs.

ACCDU African Caribbean Community Development Unit.

ACCE Association of Christian Centres in Europe (Germany); Association of County Chief Executives.

accel. *accelerando*, Italian 'more quickly' (in music).

ACCEPT Addictions Community Centre for Education, Prevention & Treatment.

ACCET Asian Centre for Comparative Education.

ACCF Asian Christian Communications Fellowship.

ACCI Association of Chambers of Commerce of Ireland; Australian Chamber of Commerce and Industry.

ACCM Advisory Council for the Church's ministry.

ACCME Accreditation Council for Continuing Medical Education.

ACCO Association of Child Care Officers; Australian Council of Consumer Organisations.

ACCT Association of Cinematograph, Television and Allied Technicians.

ACCTVS Association of Closed Circuit Television Surveyors.

ACD Advisory Committee on National Health Service Drugs; Association for Curriculum Development.

AC/DC alternating current/direct current.

ACDP Advisory Committee on Dangerous Pathogens.

ACDS Advisory Committee on Dangerous Substances; Anglo-Continental Dental Society.

ACE Access Committee for England; Advisory Centre for Education; Age Concern England; Agricultural Communicators in Education; Alliance for everage Cartons and the Environment; American College of Ecology; Association for Coal in Europe; Association for Cultural Exchange; Association for the Conservation of Energy; Association of Children's Entertainers; Association of Circulation Executives; Association of Comics Enthusiasts; Association of Conference Executives; Association of Consulting Engineers; Association of Cost Engineers; Athens Centre of Ekistiks; Australian Christian Endeavour Union.

ACEA Associate of the Association of Cost and Executive Accountants.

ACEG Afghan Carpet Exporters' Guild.

ACEI Association of Consulting Engineers of Ireland.

ACENVO Association of Chief Executives of National Voluntary Organisations.

ACEO Association of Chief Education Officers.

ACER Advisory Committee on Environmental Resources; Afro-Caribbean Education Resource Centre; Australian Council for Educational Research.

ACERT Advisory Committee for the Education of Romany and other Travellers.

ACertCM The Archbishop of Canterbury's Certificate in Church Music.

ACES American Catholic Esperanto Society; Applied Computational Electromagnetics Society; Arab Centre for Energy Studies.

ACESW Association of Chief Education Social Workers.

ACET AIDS Care Education and Training; Association of Consultants in Education and Training.

ACF Active Citizen Force (South Africa); Agricultural Co-operative Federation; Anarchist Communist Federation; Army Cadet Force; Association of Charitable Foundations; Australian Cotton Foundation; Automobile Club de France.

ACFA Air Charter Forwarders Association; American Council for Free Asia; Army Cadet Force Association; Association of Cystic Fibrosis Adults.

ACFAI All-China Federation of Automobile Industry.

ACFHE Association of Colleges for Further and Higher Education.

ACFI Associate of the Clothing and Footwear Institute.

ACFM Advisory Committee on Fisheries Management; Association of Cereal Food Manufacturers.

ACFSS Aged Christian Friend Society of Scotland.

ACG Anti-Counterfeiting Group; Arts Centre Group; automatic control gear.

ACGA American Cricket Growers' Association.

ACGB Aircraft Corporation of Great Britain; Arts Council of Great Britain.

ACGF Australian Citrus Growers Foundation.

ACGI Associate of the City and Guilds of London Institute (at City and Guilds College, Imperial College, London).

ACGM Advisory Committee on Genetic Manipulation.

ACGME Accreditation Council for Graduate Medical Education.

ACH Association for Comparative Haematology; Association of Clinical Hypnotherapists; Association of Community Homes; Association of Contemporary Historians.

ACh acetylcholine.

ACHAS Acoustical Commission of the Hungarian Academy of Sciences.

ACHCEW Association of Community Health Councils for England and Wales.

ACHE Action on Child Exploitation.

ACHRO Asian Coalition of Human Rights Organisations.

ACHSTS African Council for the Training and Promotion of Health Sciences Teachers and Specialists.

ACHSWW American Committee on the History of the Second World War.

ACIA Associate of the Corporation of Insurance Brokers.

ACIArb Associate of the Chartered Institute of Arbitrators.

ACIB Associate of the Chartered Institute of Bankers.

ACIBS Associate of the Chartered Institute of Bankers in Scotland.

ACIBSE Associate of the Chartered Institution of Building Services Engineers.

ACIF Agricultural Construction Industry Association.

ACIG Animal Cruelty Investigation Group.

ACII Associate of the Chartered Insurance Institute.

ACIF African Caribbean Institute of Jamaica.

ACILA Associate of the Chartered Institute of Loss Adjusters.

ACIOB Associate of the Chartered Institute of Building.

ACIS African Church Information Service; American Committee for Irish Studies; American Council for International Stud-

ies; Associate of the Institute of Chartered Secretaries; Association of Contemporary Iberian Studies.

ACIUCN Australian Committee for the International Union for the Conservation of Nature and Natural Resources.

ACJA All-China Journalists' Association; American Criminal Justice Association.

ACLM American College of Legal Medicine; Antigua Caribbean Liberation Movement; Association of Contact Lens Manufacturers.

ACLS Automatic Carrier Landing System.

ACM Air Chief Marshal; American council on Marijuana and other Psychoactive Drugs; Arab Common Market; Association for College Management; Association of Clinical Microbiologists; Australian Chamber of Manufacturers.

ACMA Agricultural Co-operative Managers Association; Aluminium Coin Manufacturers' Association; American Cutlery Manufacturers Association; Associate of the Institute of Cost and Management Accountants; Association of Cost and Management Accountants (South Africa); Athletic Clothing Manufacturers Association.

ACMC Advanced Composites Manufacturing Centre; American Common Market Club; Association of Canadian Medical Colleges.

ACMD Advisory Council on the Misuse of Drugs.

ACME Advisory Council on Medical Establishments (Scotland); Association of Cotton Merchants in Europe.

ACML Anti-Common Market League; Arab Centre for Medical Literature (Kuwait); Association of Canadian Map Libraries.

ACN Aid to the Church in Need; Action Christian National Party (Namibia); *ante Christum natum*, Latin 'before the birth of Christ'.

ACO African Curriculum Organisation; American College of Orgonomy; Association of Charity Officers; Association of Conservation Officers.

ACOLF Advisory Committee on Live Fish.

ACOP Advisory Committee on Pilotage; Association of Chief Officers of Police; Association of Chief Officers of Probation.

ACOPS Advisory Committee on Oil Pollution of the Sea; Advisory Committee on Protection of the Sea.

ACORBAT Association for Co-operation in Banana Research in the Caribbean and Tropical America.

ACORD Advisory Council on Research and Development For Fuel and Power; Agency for Cooperation and Research in Development (India); Agency for Cooperation in Rural Development (Switzerland); Asian Centre for Organisation, Research and Development; Euro Action-Agency for Cooperation and Research and Development.

ACORN automatic checkout and recording network (computing).

ACOST Advisory Committee on Science and Technology.

ACOSVO Association of Chief Officers of Scottish Voluntary Organisations.

ACOT Associated Committee on Tribology (Canada); Council for Development in Agriculture (Eire).

ACP American College of Prosthodontics; Associate of the College of Preceptors; Association of Canadian Publishers; Association of Cheese Processors; Association of Child Psychotherapists; Association of Circus Proprietors of Great Britain; Association of Clinical Pathologists; Association of Computer Professionals; Australian College of Paediatrics.

ACPA American Capon Producers Association; American Cleft Palate Association; Association of Christians in Planning and Architecture.

ACPM Advisory Committee on Programme Management; Associate of the Confederation of Professional Management; Association of Corrugated Paper Makers.

ACPO Association of Chief Police Officers.

ACPP Association for Child Psychology and Psychiatry.

ACPSM Association of Chartered Physiotherapists in Sports Medicine; Australasian College of Physical Scientists in Medicine.

ACQS Association of Consultant Quantity Surveyors.

ACR Association for Consumer Research; Association of Clinic Research; Association of Countryside Rangers; Australian Catholic Relief.

ACRA Aluminium Can Recycling Association; Aontacht Cumann Riartha Aitreabhthoiri; Association of College Registrars and Administrators; Association of Company Registrations Agents; Australian Cultivar Registration Authority.

ACRE Action with Communities in Rural England; Association for Consumer Research; Association of Community Councils in Rural England.

ACRR Advisory Council on Race Relations.

ACS Additional Curates Society; Age Concern Scotland; American Camellia Society; Armstrong Clan Society; Association of Certified Secretaries of South Africa; Association of Commonwealth Students; Association of Consulting Scientists; Association of Cricket Statisticians; Australian Customs Service.

ACSA Associate of the Institute of Chartered Secretaries and Administrators.

ACSHEE Advisory Committee on the Safety of Household Electrical Equipment.

ACSI Association of Christian Schools International.

ACSIL Admiralty Centre for Scientific Information and Liaison.

ACSIR Advisory Council for Scientific and Industrial Research.

ACSO Association of County Supplies Officers.

ACT Action by Christians Against Torture; Agricultural Central Trading; Aid for Children with Tracheostomies; Arts Counselling Trust; Asian Confederation of Teachers; Association of Career Teachers; Association of Christian Teachers; Associate in Corporate Treasury Management; Association of Cycle Traders; Association of Cytogenetic Technologists; Australian Capital Territory; Northern Ireland Advisory Com-

ACTA Animal Consultants and Trainers' Association; Association of Cardiothoracic Anaesthetists; Association of Chart and Technical Analysts; Australian City Transit Authority.

ACTAC Association of Community Technical Aid Centres.

ACTAF Association of Community Trusts and Foundations.

ACTH Association for Cushing's Treatment and Help; adrenocorticotropic hormone (medical).

ACTHCM Associate Member of the Confederation of Tourism, Hotel and Catering Management.

ACTION Active Citizens To Improve Our Neighbourhood.

ACTO Association of Camping Tour Operators; Association of Chief Technical Officers.

ACTR American Council of Teachers of Russian.

ACTRAM Advisory Committee on the Safe Transport of Radioactive Materials.

ACTS Action of Churches Together in Scotland; African Centre for Technology Studies; Australian Catholic Truth Society.

ACTSS Association of Clerical, Technical and Supervisory Staffs.

ACTT Association of Cinematograph Television and Allied Technicians.

ACU Association of Commonwealth Universities.

ACV actual cash value; air cushion vehicle.

ACW Aircraftwoman; alternating continuous waves.

ACWW Associated Countrywomen of the World.

ACY average crop yield.

ACYC Association of Combined Youth Clubs.

ACYW Associate of the Community and Youth Work Association.

AD *Anno Domini*, Latin 'in the year of the Lord', used in the Christian calendar for dates; Alzheimer's disease; air defence; active duty.

ad accumulated dose (radiation); *ante diem*, Latin 'before the day'.

ADA Action for Dysphasic Adults; Aluminium Development Association; Anti-Dumping Authority; Antiquities Dealers' Association; Association of Drainage Authorities; Australian Dental Association.

ADAPT Access for Disabled People in Arts Premises Today.

ADAR Art and Design Admissions Registry.

ADAS Agricultural Development and Advisory Service.

ADB Apple desktop bus (in computing).

ADC Aboriginal Development Commission; Aide-de-Camp; Alternative Defence Commission; Arsenic Development Committee (France); Association of District Councils; analogue-to-digital converter.

ADCJ Association of District Council Treasurers.

ADCM Archbishop of Canterbury's Diploma in Church Music.

ADCO Andean Development Company.

ADD Action on Disability and Development; Action on Drinking and Driving.

adf automatic direction finder.

ad fin *ad finem*, Latin 'near the end'.

ad gr. gust *ad gratum gustum*, Latin 'to an agreeable taste'.

ADH antidiuretic hormone (medical).

ADHD attention deficit hyperactivity disorder.

ADHOC Association of Departmental Heads of Catering.

ADI Approved Driving Instructor; acceptable daily intake.

ad imt. *ad initium*, Latin 'at the beginning'.

ad inf. *ad infinitum*, Latin 'to infinity'.

ad init. *ad initium*, Latin 'near the beginning'.

ad int. *ad interim*, Latin 'for the moment'.

ad lib. *ad libitum*, Latin 'as you like'.

adj. adjective.

ADL activities of daily living (medical).

ad loc. *ad locum*, Latin 'at the place cited'.

ADMA American Drug Manufacturers Association; Association of Dance and Mime Artists.

ADMG Association of Deer Management Groups.

ADO Association of Dispensing Opticians.

ADP Anguilla Democratic Party; Association for Dental Prosthesis; Association of Database Producers; Association of Disabled Professionals; Australian Democrats Party; adenosine diphosphate (medical); automatic data processing.

ADPCM adaptive differential pulse code modulation (term used in computing).

ADRA Adventist Development and Relief Agency International (USA); Animal Diseases Research Association; Association for the Study of Reptiles and Amphibia.

ADSA Art Deco Societies of America; Automated Door Suppliers' Association.

ADSCLAT Associations of Distributors to the Self-Service and Coin-Operated Laundry and Allied Trades.

ADSL asynchronous digital subscriber loop (term in computing).

ADsPH Association of Directors of Public Health.

ADT Addictive Diseases Trust.

ADTA American Dance Therapy Association.

ADTS automatic data and telecommunications service.

adv. *adversus*, Latin 'against'.

ad val. *ad valorem*, Latin 'according to value'.

ADW Air Defence Warning.

ADX automatic data exchange; automatic digital exchange.

AE account executive, age exemption; atomic energy.

AEA Action on Elder Abuse; Agricultural Engineers' Association; Aluminium Extruders' Association; American Electrolysis Association; Anglican Evangelical Association; Association of Electoral Administrators; Association of Established Agents (Eire); Association of European Airlines; Atomic Energy Authority.

AE & P Ambassador Extraordinary and Plenipotentiary.

AEB American Egg Board; Associated Examining Board; Atomic Energy Bureau (Japan).

aec at earliest convenience.

AECB Association for Environment Conscious Building; Association for the Export of Canadian Books.

AECI Associate Member of the Institute of Employment Consultants; Association of Electrical Contractors of Ireland; Association of European Cooperative Insurers.

AEE Association for Experiential Education; Atomic Energy Establishment.

AEEU Amalgamated Engineering and Electrical Union.

AEF Airfields Environment Federation; Allied Expeditionary Force; Amalgamated Union of Engineering and Foundry; American Euthanasia Foundation Workers.

AEGIS Aid for the Elderly in Government Institutions; Australian Electronic Government Information Service.

AEI Associated Electrical Industries.

AELTC All England Lawn Tennis Club.

AEMSM Association of European Metal Sink Manufacturers.

AEMT Association of Electrical Machinery Trades; Association of Emergency Medical Technicians.

AEMTM Association of European Machine Tool Merchants.

AENA All England Netball Association.

AENOC Association of European National Olympic Committees.

AEOM Association of European Open Air Museums.

AEP Association of Educational Psychologists; Association of Embroiderers and Pleaters.

AEPA All-Ethiopia Peasants Association.

AERE Atomic Energy Research Establishment.

aet after extra time.

aet. *aetatis*, Latin 'of his/her age'.

AEU Amalgamated Engineering Union.

AEW airborne early warning.

AEWHA All England Women's Hockey Association.

AEWLA All England Women's Lacrosse Association.

AF Associate Fellow; Admiral of the Fleet; Air Force; Anglo-French.

Af. Africa/n.

a/f *or* **A/F** as found.

AFA Access Flooring Association; Advocates for Animals; African Farmers Association; Amateur Fencing Association; Amateur Football Alliance; Anorexic Family Aid; Associate of the Institute of Financial Accountants; Amateur Football Association; atrial fibrillation (medical).

AFAM Ancient Free and Accepted Masons.

AFAS Associate of the Faculty of Architects and Surveyors (Architects).

AFASIC Association for All Speech-Impaired Children.

AFB Action for Bosnia; Airforce Base (USA); American Foundation of the Blind.

AFBA Associate of the Faculty of Business Administrators.

AFBC Association of Football Badge Collectors.

AFBD Association of Futures Brokers and Dealers.

AFBPSS Associate Fellowship of the British Psychological Society.

AFC Air Force Cross; Association Football Club; Association of Fish Canners; Australian Forestry Council; Authors For Choice.

afc automatic flight control; automatic frequency control.

AFCA Associate of the Association of Financial Controllers and Administrators.

afce automatic flight control equipment.

AFCI Associate of the Faculty of Commerce and Industry Ltd.

AFCMA Aluminium Foil Container Manufacturers Association; Asian Federation of Catholic Medical Associations; Australian Fibreboard Containers Manufacturers Association.

afco automatic fuel cut-off.

AFCS Associate of the Faculty of Secretaries.

afcs automatic flight control system.

AFEI Americans for Energy Independence; Arab Federation of Engineering Industries; Association of Finnish Electric Industries; Association of Freelance Editors and Indexers (Eire).

AFEMS European Association of Sporting Ammunition Manufacturers.

AFETUK Anne Frank Educational Trust.

AFFD Association of Fashion Fabric Distributors.

AFFHC Australian Freedom from Hunger Campaign.

AFI Acupuncture Foundation of Ireland; Aid for India; Arthritis Foundation of Ireland; Association for Futures Investment; Association of Finnish Industries.

AFIA Apparel and Fashion Industry Association of Great Britain.

AffIP Affiliate of the Institute of Plumbing.

AffIRTE Affiliate of the Institute of Road Traffic Engineers.

AffIWHTE Affiliate of the Institution of Works and Highways Technician Engineers.

AFHQ Allied Forces Headquarters.

AFIMA Associate Fellow of the Institute of Mathematics and its Applications.

AFISLO Licence Aerodrome Flight Information Service Officer's Licence.

AFM Air Force Medal; audio-frequency modulation.

AFP alpha fetoprotein (medical).

AFPVA Advertising Film and Videotape Producers Association.

AFPRB Army Forces Pay Review Board.

AFRAeS Associate Fellow of the Royal Aeronautical Society.

AFRC Agricultural and Food Research Council; Aluminium Foil Recycling Campaign.

AFrI Action From Ireland.

AFS American Fern Society; Associate of the Faculty of Architects and Surveyors (Surveyors); Association for Stammerers; Association of Football Statisticians; Australian Fishing Service; Auxiliary Fire Service.

AFT Association for Family Therapy.

AFTA Atlantic Free Trade Area.

AFTCom Associate of the Faculty of Teachers in Commerce.

AFTO Association of Flight Training Officers.

AFV armoured fighting vehicle.

AG Adventurers' Guild; Adjutant General; *Aktiengesellschaft*, German 'limited company'; Andean Group; Association for Gnotobiotics; Attorney-General.

Ag *argentum*, Latin ' 'silver'.

Aga *Aktiebolaget Gasackumulator*, Swedish for Gasometer Company, makers of kitchen ranges.

AGA American Gas Association; Arab Geologists' Association; Architectural Granite Association; Asparagus Growers' Association; appropriate for gestational age (medical).

agb any good brand.

AGBI Artists' General Benevolent Institution.

AGBM Association of Grey Board Makers.

AGC Agricultural Genetics Company.

AGCA automatic ground-controlled approach.

AGCD Association of Green Crop Driers.

AGCL Associate Member of the Guild of Cleaners and Launderers; automatic ground-controlled landing.

AGCS Association of Golf Club Secretaries.

AGE automatic guidance electronics.

Agfa *Aktiengesellschaft für Anilinfabrikation*, German for Dye-Manufacture Company.

AGHS Australian Garden History Society.

AGHW Association of Gardening and Hardware Wholesalers.

AGI Associate of the Greek Institute.

Agip *Agenzia Generale Italia Petroli*, Italian General Petrol Agency.

AGL above ground level.

AGLMH Association for Great Lakes Maritime History.

AGLOW Association of Greater London Older Women.

AGM air-to-ground missile; annual general meeting.

AGO Association of Gypsy and Romany Organisations.

AGOD International Association on the Genesis of Ore Deposits.

AGOR Advisory Group on Ocean Research.

AGR advanced gas-cooled reactor.

AGRA Association of Genealogists and Record Agents.

AGS Aero-Geophysical Survey (China); Al-

pine Garden Society; American Goat Society; Association for Gravestone Studies; Association of Geotechnical Specialists.

AGSM Associate of the Guildhall School of Music and Drama.

AGT advanced gas turbine.

AGTO Association of Group Tour Operators.

AGUM Association of Genito-Urinary Medicine.

AGW Association of Garden Wholesalers; Association of Golf Writers.

agw actual gross weight.

ah ampere hour.

AH *anno Hegirae*, Latin 'in the year of the Hegira'.

AHA American Hominological Association; Arab Historians Association; Area Health Authority; Association of Housing Aid.

AHCIMA Associate of the Hotel, Catering and Institutional Management Association.

AHFS Associate of the Council of Health Fitness and Sports Therapists.

ahl *ad hunc locum*, Latin 'at this place'.

AHPP Association of Humanistic Psychology Practitioners.

AHPWJC Association of High Pressure Water Jetting Contractors.

AHQ Allied Headquarters; Army Headquarters.

ahr acceptable hazard rate.

AHRC Alister Hardy Research Centre.

AHS American Harp Society; Antiquarian Horological Society; Association for Humanist Sociology; Australian Herpitological Society; *anno humanae salutis*, Latin 'in the year of human salvation'.

AHSS Architectural Heritage Society for Scotland.

AHUA Association of Heads of University Administrations.

ahv *ad hanc vocem*, Latin 'at this word'.

AHWA Association of Hospital and Welfare Administrators.

AI Amnesty International; artificial intelligence; artificial insemination.

a.i. *ad interim*, Latin 'in the meantime'.

AIA Abrasives Industries Association; Academy of Irish Art; Acupuncture International

Association; Allergy-Induced Autism Support and Self-Help Group; Anglo-Indian Association; Artists International Association; Asbestos International Association; Associate of the Institute of Actuaries; Association of Automobile and Allied High Duty Ironfounders.

AIAB Associate of the International Association of Book-keepers.

AIAgrE Associate of the Institution of Agricultural Engineers.

AIAT Associate of the Institute of Asphalt Technology.

AIB African Immigrants Bureau; Allied Irish Banks; American Institute of Baking; Associate of the Institute of Bankers; Association of Independent Businesses; Association of Insurance Brokers.

AIBA Associate of the Institution of Business Agents.

AIBCM Associate of the Institute of British Carriage and Automobile Manufacturers; Association of Industrialized Building Component Manufacturers.

AIC Agricultural Improvement Council; American Institute of Chemists; Appraisal Institute of Canada; Asbestos Information Centre; Association Internationale de Cybernétique; Association of Independent Cinemas; Association of Indian Communists.

AICR Association for International Cancer Research.

AICS Associate of the Institute of Chartered Shipbrokers.

AID Alternative for India Development; Association for Improving the Downtrodden (India); Army Intelligence Department; acute infectious disease; artificial insemination by donor.

AIDPM Associate of the Institute of Data Processing Management.

AIDS *or* **Aids** acquired immune deficiency syndrome (sexually transmitted disease).

AIDTA Associate of the International Dance Teachers' Association.

AIEM Associate of the Institute of Executives and Managers.

AIEP Association of Independent Electricity Producers.

AIExpE Associate of the Institute of Explosives Engineers.

AIFA Associate of the Institute of Field Archaeologists.

AIFF Associate of the Institute of Freight Forwarders.

AIGD Associate of the Institute of Grocery Distribution.

AIH American Institute of Homoeopathy; Association of Independent Hospitals; Australian Institute of Horticulture; artificial insemination by husband.

AIIB Allied Irish Investment Bank.

AIIM Associate of the Institution of Industrial Managers; Association for Information and Image Management; Association of Independent Investment Managers; Association of International Industrial Irradiation.

AIIMR Associate of the Institute of Investment Management and Research.

AIIRSM Associate of the International Institute of Risk and Safety Management.

AIL Associate of the Institute of Linguists.

AILAM Associate of the Institute of Leisure and Amenity Management.

Ailas automatic instrument landing approach system.

AIM Action in International Medicine; American Indian Movement; Association of Independent Museums; Association of Industrial Machinery Merchants; Association of Information Managers for Financial Institutions; Association of Innovation Management; Association of Insulation Manufacturers; Association of International Marketing; Associazione Italiana di Metallurgia; Atlantic International Marketing Committee; Australasian Institute of Metals; alternative investment market.

AIMBM Associate of the Institute of Maintenance and Building Management.

AIMechE Associate of the Institution of Mechanical Engineers.

AIMgt Associate of the Institute of Management.

AIMinE Associate of the Institute of Mining Engineers.

AIMIT Associate of the Institute of Musical Instrument Technology.

AIMLS Associate of the Institute of Medical Laboratory Sciences.

AIMM Associate of the Institute of Massage and Movement.

AInstAM Associate Member of the Institute of Administrative Management.

AInstBA Associate of the Institute of Business Administration.

AInstBB Associate of the Institute of British Bakers.

AInstBCA Associate of the Institute of Burial and Cremation Administration.

AInstMC Associate of the International Management Centre.

AInstP Associate of the Institute of Physics.

AInstPM Associate of the Institute of Professional Managers.

AInstSMM Associate of the Institute of Sales and Marketing Management.

AInstTA Associate of the Institute of Transport Administration.

AIOC Associate of the Institute of Carpenters.

AIOFMS Associate of the Institute of Financial and Management Studies.

AIP Associate of the Institute of Plumbing; American Independent Party; Association of Independent Producers; Australian Institute of Packaging.

AIPM Associate of the Institute of Personnel Management.

AIQS Associate of the Institute of Quantity Surveyors.

AIR All-India Radio; Alliance of Independent Retailers; American Institutes for Research in the Behavioural Sciences; Australian Institute of Radiography.

AIRTE Associate of the Institute of Road Transport Engineers.

AIS Androgen Insensitivity Support Group; Anglo-Italian Society; Association for Information Systems; Association for Integrative Studies; Australian Institute of Sport; Islamic Salvation Army (Algeria).

AISA Associate of the Incorporated Secretaries Association.

AISOB Associate of the Incorporated Society of Organ Builders.

AISTD Associate of the Imperial Society of Teachers of Dancing.

AISTDDip Associate Diploma of the Imperial Society of Teachers of Dancing.

AIStructE Associate of the Institution of Structural Engineers.

AIT Association of Inspectors of Taxes; Association of Insurance Teachers.

AITC American Institute for Timber Construction; Association of Investment Trust Companies; Australian Industry and Technology Commission.

AITO Association of Independent Tour Operators.

AITSA Associate of the Institute of Trading Standards Administration.

AIWEM Associate of the Institution of Water and Environmental Management.

AIWSc Associate Member of the Institute of Wood Science.

AJA Amateur Judo Association of Great Britain; Anglo-Jewish Association; Australian Journalists Association.

AJAG Assistant Judge Advocate General.

AJR Association of Jewish Refugees in Great Britain.

AJSM Association of Jute Spinners and Manufacturers.

aka also known as.

AKC Associateship of King's College, University of London.

AL Arab League.

Al aluminium (chemical element).

al. *alii*, Latin 'others'.

ALA Agricultural Law Association; American Landrace Association; Associate of the Library Association; Association of London Authorities.

ALAC Artificial Limb and Appliance Centre.

ALAR Association of Light Alloy Refiners.

ALAWP all letters answered with photograph.

ALBM air-launched ballistic missile.

ALC Associate of the former Loughborough College of Technology.

ALCD Association of Law Costs Draftsmen Limited.

ALCM Associate of the London College of Music; air-launched cruise missile.

ALD adrenoleukodystrophy.

ALDU Association of Lawyers for the Defence of the Unborn.

ALE Association for Liberal Education.

ALEA Air Line Employees Association International; American Law and Economics Association.

A-level Advanced Level.

ALF Animal Liberation Front.

Alf automatic letter facer (mail sorting machine).

ALG Association for London Government.

Algol Algebraically Oriented Language (computer language).

ALI Alfa-Laval International (Sweden); American Law Institute; Associate of the Landscape Institute.

ALIA Association of Lecturers in Accountancy; Australian Library and Information Association.

ALL acute lymphoblastic leukaemia.

allo *allegro*, Italian 'lively' (music).

all'ott. *all' ottava*, Italian 'at the octave' (music).

ALP automated language processing.

ALPA Airline Pilots' Association.

Alpurcoms all-purpose communications system.

ALRA Abortion Law Reform Association; Adult Literacy Resource Agency.

ALS Academy of Leisure Sciences; Alliance of Literary Societies; Associate of the Linnean Society; approach lighting system.

al seg. *al segno*, Italian 'to the sign' or 'at the sign' (musical).

ALSPT Associateship of the London School of Polymer Technology.

alt. dieb. *alternis diebus*, Latin 'every other day'.

alt. hor. *alternis horis*, Latin 'every other hour'.

alt. noct. *alternis noctibus*, Latin 'every other night'.

ALTU Association of Liberal Trade Unionists.

ALU Aboriginal Liaison Unit; Aluminium Can Recycling Association; arithmetic logic unit (term in computing).

ALUT Associateship of Loughborough University of Technology.

AM Academy of Management; Action Monégasque; Air Marshal; Albert Medal; *anno mundi*, Latin 'in the year of the world'; *Artium Magister*, Latin 'Master of Arts'; Associate Member; amplitude modulation (used in physics when radio waves are altered to transmit broadcasting signals).

Am americium (chemical element).

aM *am Main*, German 'on the Main', for places near this river.

am *ante meridiem*, Latin 'before noon'.

AMA Abstaining Motorists Association; Accumulator Makers Association; Aerial Manufacturers Association; African Music Association; Agricultural Marketing Association; Amateur Martial Association; Amateur Music Association; American Maritime Association; Architectural Metalwork Association; Arts Marketing Association; Association of Manufacturers Allied to the Electrical and Electronic Industry; Association of Metropolitan Authorities; Australian Medical Association; Associate of the Museums Association; Association of Metropolitan Authorities; against medical advice.

AMABAC Associate Member of the Association of Business and Administrative Computing.

AMABE Associate Member of the Association of Business Executives.

AMASI Associate Member of the Architects and Surveyors Institute.

AMBA Associate Member of the British Arts.

AMBBA Associated Master Barbers and Beauticians of America.

AMBCS Associate Member of the British Computer Society.

AMBEI Associate Member of the Institution of Body Engineers.

AMBES Association of Metropolitan Borough Engineers and Surveyors.

AMBII Associate Member of the British Institute of Innkeeping.

AMC Agricultural Mortgage Corporation; American Mining Congress; Association of Magistrates Courts; Association of Manufacturing Chemists; Australian Maritime College.

AMCL Association of Metropolitan Chief Librarians.

AMCS Airborne Missile Control System.

am. cur. *amicus curiae*, Latin 'friend of the court'.

AMDG *ad majorem Dei gloriam*, Latin 'to the greater glory of God'.

AMF Allied Mobile Force (NATO).

AMI Association of Meat Inspectors; acute myocardial infarction.

AMIA Affiliated Member of the Association of International Accountants.

AMIAEA *see* AMInstAEA.

AMIAgrE Associate Member of the Institution of Agricultural Engineers.

AMIAP Associate of the Institution of Analysts and Programmers.

AMIAT Associate Member of the Institute of Asphalt Technology.

AMIBC Associate Member of the Institute of Building Control.

AMIBCM Associate Member of the Institute of British Carriage and Automobile Manufacturers.

AMIBCO Associate Member of the Institution of Building Control Officers.

AMICE Associate Member of the Institution of Civil Engineers.

AMICorrST Associate Member of the Institution of Corrosion Science and Technology.

AMIEE Associate Member of the Institution of Electrical Engineers.

AMIEIE Associate Member of the Institution of Electrical and Electronics Incorporated Engineers.

AMIEx Associate Member of the Institute of Export.

AMIGasE Associate Member of the Institution of Gas Engineers.

AMIHIE Associate Member of the Institute of Highway Incorporated Engineers.

AMIHT Associate Member of the Institution of Highways and Transportation.

AMIIEXE Associate Member of the Institution of Incorporated Executive Engineers.

AMIISE Associate Member of the International Institute of Social Economics.

AMIM Associate Member of the Institute of Materials.

AMIManf Associate Member of the Institute of Manufacturing.

AMIMarE Associate Member of the Institute of Marine Engineers.

AMIMatM Associate Member of the Institute of Materials Management.

AMIMechE Associate Member of the Institution of Mechanical Engineers.

AMIMechIE Associate Member of the Institution of Mechanical Incorporated Engineers.

AMIMI Associate Member of the Institute of the Motor Industry.

AMIMS Associate Member of the Institute of Management Specialists.

AMIMinE Associate Member of the Institute of Mining Engineers.

AMInstAEA Associate Member of the Institute of Automotive Engineers Assessors.

AMInstBE Associate Member of the Institute of British Engineers.

AMInstE Associate Member of the Institute of Energy.

AMInstME *or* **AMInstME(Dip)** Associate Member of the International Institute of Management Executives.

AMInstR Associate Member of the Institute of Refrigeration.

AMInstTA Associate Member of the Institute of Transport Administration.

AMIPA Associate Member of the Institute of Practitioners in Advertising.

AMIPC Associate Member of the Institute of Production Control.

AMIPlantE Associate Member of the Institution of Plant Engineers.

AMIPM Associate Member of the Institute of Personnel Management.

AMIPR Associate Member of the Institute of Public Relations.

AMIQ Associate Member of the Institute of Quarrying.

AMIQA Associate Member of the Institute of Quality Assurance.

AMIRSO Associate Member of the Institute of Road Safety Officers.

AMIRT Associate Member of the Institute of Reprographic Technology.

AMIRTE Associate Member of the Institute of Road Transport Engineers.

AMISM Associate Member of the Institute of Supervisory Management.

AMIStructE Associate Member of the Institution of Structural Engineers.

AMITD Associate Member of the Institute of Training and Development.

AMIWPC Associate Member of the Institute of Water Pollution Control.

AML acute myelogenous leukaemia.

AMM anti-missile missile.

AMMA Assistant Masters' and Mistresses' Association.

AMMI Affiliate of the Institute of the Motor Industry.

AMNI Associate Member of the Nautical Institute.

AMP adenosine monophosphate (medical).

amp ampere (term used in physics for a unit of electric current).

AMPA Associate Member of the Master Photographers Association.

AMPDE Associated Master Plumbers & Domestic Engineers.

AMPRI Association Member of the Plastics and Rubber Institute.

AMProfBTM Associate Member of Professional Business and Technical Management.

AMPS Association of Management and Professional Staffs; Association of Motorists Protection Service; automated message-processing system.

AMPW Association of Makers of Printings and Writings.

AMR Associate of the Association of Health Care Information and Medical Record Officers; Association of Minor Railway Companies; automatic message routing.

AMRA Ancient Mediterranean Research Association; Automotive Manufacturers Racing Association.

AMRAAM advanced medium-range air-to-air missile.

AMRSH Associate Member of the Royal Society of Health.

AMS Agricultural Manpower Association; Agricultural Marketing Service; American Magnolia Society; Ancient Monuments Society; Associate of the Institute of Management Services Association of Metal Sprayers; Association of Missionary Societies; Assurance Medical Society; Australian Musicology Society.

AMS(Aff) Affiliate, Association of Medical Secretaries, Practice Administrators and Receptionists.

AMSE Associate Member of the Society of Engineers (Incorporated).

AMSL above mean sea level.

AMTDA Agricultural Machinery and Tractor Dealers' Association; American Machine Tool Distributors Association.

AMTE Admiralty Marine Technology Establishment.

AMTRA Animal Medicine Training Regulatory Authority.

AMTRI Advanced Manufacturing Technology Research Association.

AMU American Malacological Union; Associated Metalworkers Union; Association of Master Upholsterers; Association of Minicomputer Users (USA).

amu atomic mass unit.

AMusLCM Associate in Music of the London College of Music.

AMusTCL Associate in Music of Trinity College of Music, London.

AMWES Associate Member of the Women's Engineering Society.

AN Anglo-Norman.

an above named.

an. *anno*, Latin 'in the year'.

a/n advice note.

ANA American Naprapathic Association; Anguilla National Alliance; Article Number Association; Association of Nordic Aeroclubs; Association of Nurse Administrators; Australian National Airways.

ANAEA Associate of the National Association of Estate Agents.

ANC African National Congress.

ANCA Advanced National Certificate in Agriculture.

and. *andante*, Italian 'flowing' (term used to indicate speed in music).

Anfo ammonium nitrate and fuel oil.

ANIC Australian National Insect Collection.

anim. *animato*, Italian 'animated' (music).

ANIN Associated Northern Ireland Newspapers.

ANL Anti-Nazi League; Australian National Line.

ANN Anti-Nuclear Network; Asian-Pacific News Network.

ann. *anno*, Latin 'in the year'.

anon. anonymous.

ANS American Name Society; Army Nursing Service; Australian Numismatic Society; autonomic nervous system.

ANSA Abbey National Staff Association.

ANSI American National Standards Institute.

ANSM Former award of Associate of the Northern School of Music, *see* GNSM.

ANZA Association of New Zealand Advertisers.

ANZAC Australian and New Zealand Army Corps.

ANZUS Australia, New Zealand, United States Security Treaty.

AO Aide Olympique; Association of Optometrists; Army Order.

aO *an der Oder*, German 'on the Oder', for places in Germany near this river.

a/o account of.

AOA Ambulance Officers' Association; American Ontoanalytic Association; Association of Official Architects.

AOB Association of Ballrooms; Association Ornithologique de Belgique; any other business.

AOC Air Officer Commanding; Associated Overseas Countries (EU); Association of Old Crows (USA); *appellation d'origine contrôlée*, French 'regulated naming', used in the origin of wines.

AOCB any other competent business.

AOCI Airport Operators Council International.

AOC-in-C Air Officer Commander-in-Chief.

AOCP Associated Owners of City Properties.

AOD Ancient Order of Druids; Army Ordnance Department.

AOF Ancient Order of Foresters; Australian Orchid Foundation.

AOH Ancient Order of Hibernians.

AOK all items satisfactory.

AONB Area of Outstanding Natural Beauty.

AOPA Aircraft Owners and Pilots Association.

AP Associated Press; anti-personnel; armour-piercing.

ap additional premium; *ante prandium*, Latin 'before meals'; author's proof.

ap. *apud*, Latin 'in the works of'.

APA Airhawk Pilots Association; Aluminium Prefabs Association; American Poultry Association; Army Parachute Association; Association for the Prevention of Addiction; Association of Paediatric Anaesthetists; Association of Piping Adjudicators; Association of Preventive Medicine; Association of Professional Astrologers; Association of Public Analysts; Association of Publishing Agencies; Australian Physiotherapy Association.

APACS Association for Payment Clearing Services.

APC armoured personnel carrier (military vehicle); aspirin, phenacetin and caffeine; automatic public convenience; automatic phase control.

APCC Animal Population Control Clinic.

APCT Association of Polytechnic and College Teachers.

APD Airport Passenger Duty.

APEC Asia Pacific Economic Cooperation.

Apex Apex Trust for the Advancement of the Employment Prospects of Ex-Offenders; Association of Professional, Executive, Clerical and Computer Staff; advance purchase excursion (travel tickets).

APH antepartum haemorrhage.

APInstCF Approved Fitter of the National Institute of Carpet Fitters.

APL A Programming Language.

APPA Aluminium Powder and Paste Association; Aluminium Primary Producers' Association; Antigua Planned Parenthood Association.

APR annual percentage rate.

APRC *anno post Romam conditam*, Latin 'in the year from the founding of' Rome.

APS Aborigines Protection Society; Associate of the Pharmaceutical Society; Association of Planning Supervisors; Association of Plastics Societies; Association of Police Surgeons; Association of Productivity Specialists.

APT advanced passenger train; automatic picture transmission.

APWR advanced pressurised water reactor.

APWU Amalgamated Postal Workers' Union.

AQ achievement quotient.

AQPS *autre que pur sang*, French 'other than pure blood' (term used in horse breeding).

AR Accommodation for Recovery from Addiction; Aerial Ropeways Association; Aircraft Research Association; Amateur Riders' Association of Great Britain; Amateur Rowing Association; Anti-Racist Alliance; Asian Recycling Association; Association of Relocation Agents; Association of River Authorities; Australian Robot Association; *anno regni*, Latin 'in the year of the reign of'; artificial respiration; assisted respiration (medical).

Ar argon (chemical element).

aR *am Rhein*, German 'on the Rhine', used for places near the river.

a/r all risks.

ARA Aircraft Research Association; Amateur Rowing Association; Associate of the Royal Academy; Association of the River Authorities.

ARAA Associate of the Royal Academy of Arts.

ARAD Associate of the Royal Academy of Dancing.

ARAM Associate of the Royal Academy of Music.

ARAS Association of the Royal Astronomical Society.

ARBS Association for the Recognition of Business Schools.

ARC Aeronautical Research Council; Agricultural Research Council; Aids-related Complex; Animal Resources Centre; Animal Rights Coalition; Anthropological Research Council; Architects Registration Council; Arthritis and Rheumatism Council for Research; Association of Registered Childminders; Association of Rover Clubs; Asthma Research Council; Asylum Rights Campaign; Atlantic Research Centre.

ARCA Associate of the Royal College of Art.

ARCIC Anglican-Roman Catholic International Commission.

ARCM Associate of the Royal College of Music.

ARCnet attached resource computer network.

ARCO Associate of the Royal College of Organists.

ARCO(CHM) Associate of the Royal College of Organists (Choir-training Diploma).

ARCS Associateship of the Royal College of Science, Imperial College, University of London.

ARCUK Architects' Registration Council of the United Kingdom.

ARCVS Associate of the Royal College of Veterinary Surgeons.

ARD acute respiratory disease.

ARDS acute respiratory distress syndrome; adult respiratory distress syndrome.

ARE Admiralty Research Establishment.

ARELS-FELCO Association for Recognised English Language Teaching Establishments in Britain.

ARF acute renal failure; acute respiratory failure.

arg. *argentum*, Latin 'silver'.

ARI acute respiratory infection.

ARIA Accounting Researchers International Association; automated radio-immuno-assay.

ARIBA Associate of the Royal Institute of British Architects.

ARIC Associateship of the Royal Institute of Chemistry.

ARICS Professional Associate of the Royal Institution of Chartered Surveyors.

ARIPHH Associate of the Royal Institute of Public Health and Hygiene.

ARLL advanced run-length limited (term in computing).

ARM artificial rupture of the membranes; anti-radar missile.

ARMS Action for Research into Multiple Sclerosis.

arp. *arpeggio*, Italian 'harped' (i.e. notes in music played as a broken chord).

ARP air raid precautions.

Arpanet Advanced Research Projects Agency Network (early Internet).

ARPMA Aluminium Rolled Products Manufacturers Association.

ARPS Associate of the Royal Photographic Society.

ARR Association for Radiation Research; *anno regni reginae*, Latin 'in the year of the queen's reign'; *anno regni regis*, Latin 'in the year of the king's reign'.

ARRA Amateur Radio Retailers Association.

ARRI Aboriginal Rural Resource Initiative.

ARROW Active Resistance to the Roots of War; Asian-Pacific Research Centre for Women.

ARRRI Alligator Rivers Region Research Institute.

ARSA Associate of the Royal Society of Arts.

ARSCM Associate Member of the Royal School of Church Music.

ARSR air route surveillance radar.

ARTC air route traffic control.

ARV Aids-associated retrovirus.

AS Aetherius Society; Aristotelian Society; Association of Secretaries; Association of Stammerers; Association of Surgeons of Great Britain and Ireland; Assistant Secretary; Avicultural Society; air speed; *al segno*, Italian 'to the sign' (music); *anno salutis*, Latin ' in the year of salvation '.

As arsenic (chemical element).

A/S *Aktieselskab*, Danish 'joint-stock company'; *Aksjeselskap*, Norwegian 'limited company'.

ASA Advertising Standards Authority; Ad-

vice Services Alliance; Aluminium Stockholders Association; Amateur Swimming Association; Anglican Stewardship Association; Asian Students Association; Association of Sealant Applicators; Atomic Scientists Association; Australian Society of Archivists; Austrian Space Agency.

asap as soon as possible.

ASAPHA Association of Sea and Air Port Health Authorities.

ASAT anti-satellite.

ASB Accounting Standards Board; Alternative Service Book; Association of Shell Boilermakers; anencephaly and spina bifida.

ASBM air-to-surface ballistic missile.

ASBTH Associate of the Society of Health and Beauty Therapists.

ASCA Airline Sports and Cultural Association; Arab Society of Certified Accountants; Asian Crystallographic Association (Taiwan); Associate of the Institute of Company Accountants.

ASCC Association of Scottish Chambers of Commerce; Australian Society of Cosmetic Chemists.

ASCII American Standard Code for Information Interchange (in computing).

ASCT Associate of the Society of Cardiological Technicians.

ASD atrial septal defect.

Asda Associated Dairies.

ASDC Associate of the Society of Dyers and Colourists.

ASDIC Anti-Submarine Detection Investigation Committee (a name for sonar equipment).

ASDSFB Association of Scottish District Salmon Fishery Boards.

ASE American Society of Enologists; Association for Science Education; Associate of the Society of Engineering; Association for Science Engineering; Astronomical Society of Edinburgh; Athens Stock Exchange; Australian Society of Endodontology.

a.s.e. *or* **ase** air standard efficiency.

ASH Action on Smoking and Health; Association Suisse des Horticulteurs.

ASI Adam Smith Institute; Ambulance Service Institute; Anti-Slavery International; Architects' and Surveyors' Institute (Eire); Astronomy Society of India; Aviation Society of Ireland; air speed indicator.

ASIAD Associate of the Society of Industrial Artists and Designers.

ASIC application specific integrated circuit.

ASIF Amateur Swimming International Federation.

ASL above sea level.

ASLC Advanced Secretarial Language Certificate; Association of Street Lighting Contractors.

ASLDC Association of Social and Liberal Democrat Councillors.

ASLEF Associated Society of Locomotive Engineers and Firemen.

ASLIB Association for Information Management (formerly Association of Special Libraries and Information Bureaux).

ASLO Associated Scottish Life Officers; Australian Scientific Liaison Office.

ASM air-to-surface missile; assistant stage manager.

ASMA Associate of the Society of Sales Management Administrators Ltd.

ASN Army service number.

ASP American Society of Papyrologists; Association of Service Providers; Australian Society of Prosthodontists.

ASPS Association of Scottish Police Superintendents.

ASR airport surveillance radar; answer, send and receive; air-sea rescue; automatic send and receive.

ASRA Association for the Study of Reptilia and Amphibia.

A/SRS air-sea rescue service.

ASS Anti-Slavery Society.

Ass. Associated; Associate; Association.

Asset Association of Supervisory Staffs, Executives and Technicians.

ASSG Acne Sufferers Support Group; Association of Scottish Shellfish Growers.

ASSGB Association of Ski Schools in Great Britain.

AST Atlantic Standard Time; advanced supersonic transport; automatic station tuning.

ASTMS Association of Scientific, Technical and Managerial Staffs.

ASNNA Associate of the Society of Nursery Nursing Administrators.

AssociateIEIE Associate of the Institution of Electrical and Electronics Incorporated Engineers.

AssocInstAEA Associate of the Institute of Automotive Engineer Assessors.

AssocInstAEA Associate (Body Division) of the Institute (Body Dvn) of Automotive Engineer Assessors.

AssocIPHE Associate of the Institution of Public Health Engineers.

AST Association of Stress Therapists; Association of Swimming Therapy; Astronomical Society of Tasmania; Atlantic Salmon Trust.

ASTA American Seed Trade Association; Association of Shippers to Africa; Association of Short-Circuit Testing Authorities; Associate of the Swimming Teachers' Association; Auckland Science Teachers Association.

ASTRA Association in Scotland to Research into Astronautics.

ASVA Associate of the Incorporated Society of Valuers and Auctioneers.

ASW Amalgamated Society of Woodworkers; anti-submarine warfare.

AT alternative technology; anti-tank; appropriate technology; automatic transmission.

At astatine (chemical element).

ATA Africa Travel Association; Air Transport Auxiliary; American Trucking Association; Angling Trade Association; Animal Technicians Association; Atlantic Treaty Association.

AT & T American Telephone and Telegraph Company.

ATB Agricultural Training Board; advanced technology bomber.

ATC Air Traffic Control; Air Training Corps; Art Teacher's Certificate; automated train control.

ATC Licence Air Traffic Controller's Licence.

ATCC air traffic control centre.

ATCL Associate Diploma in Speech and Drama, Trinity College, London; Associate of Trinity College, London.

ATCRBS air traffic control radar beacon system.

ATD Art Teacher's Diploma; actual time of departure.

ATE Automatic Telephone and Electric Company; Association of Tanzania Employers; Association of Teachers of English; Association of Therapeutic Education; automatic test equipment.

ATG Appropriate Technology Group; Association of Teachers of Geology.

ATI Associate of the Textile Institute; Association of Teachers of Italian; Australian Textile Institute.

ATIG Alternative Technology Information Group.

ATL Association of Teachers and Lecturers.

Atlas automated telephone line address system; automatic tabulating, listing and sorting package.

ATLB Air Transport Licensing Boards.

ATM Adobe Type Manager (in computing); Association of Teachers of Mathematics; Association of Trailer Manufacturers; anti-tank missile; automated/automatic teller machine.

at. no. atomic number.

ATOM Against Tests on Muroroa.

ATP Association for Teaching Psychology; Association of Tennis Professionals (USA); Automatic Train Protection; adenosine triphosphate (biochemical/medical); advanced turboprop.

ATPL Airline Transport Pilot's Licence.

ATR Association of Teachers of Russian; advanced test reactor.

ATS American Tolkien Society; American Thyroid Society; Auxiliary Territorial Service (now WRAC); administrative terminal system (computing); anti-tetanus serum.

a.t.s. *or* **ats** at the suit of (legal).

ATSC Associate in the Technology of Surface Coatings.

ATSP Association of Teachers of Spanish and Portuguese.

ATSS Association for Teaching of the Social Sciences.

ATT Association of Taxation Technicians.

ATTC Association of Travel Trades Clubs.

ATTITB Air Transport and Travel Industry Training Board.

ATV Associated Television; all-terrain vehicle.

at. wt. atomic weight.

AU Angstrom unit; Artists' Union (Afghanistan).

Au *aurum*, Latin 'gold' (chemical element).

AUBTW Amalgamated Union of Building Trade Workers.

AUC Air Transport Users Committee; American University in Cairo; Association of Underwater Contractors; *ab urde condita*, Latin 'from the building of the city'; *anno urbis conditae*, Latin 'in the year from the building of the city'.

AUCET Association of University Chemical Education Tutors.

AUCL Association of University and College Lecturers.

AUEW Amalgamated Union of Engineering Workers.

AUEW-TASS Amalgamated Union of Engineering Workers, Technical, Administrative and Supervisory Section.

AUKOI Association of United Kingdom Oil Independents.

AUKWPP Association of UK Wood Pulp Producers.

AUM air-to-underwater missile.

AURPO Association of University Radiation Protection Officers.

AUT Association of University Teachers.

AUTM Association of Unit Trust Managers; Association of Used Tyre Manufacturers.

AV Authorized Version; alternative vote; arteriovenous; atrioventricular; auriculoventricular (medical); audiovisual.

av *annos vixit*, Latin 'lived (so many) years'.

av. average; avoirdupois.

a/v *or* **A/V** *ad valorem*, Latin 'according to value' (a tax system).

A-V *or* **a-v** audiovisual.

AVA Academy of Visual Arts; American Ventilation Association; Association of Veterinary Anaesthetists; Atlantic Visitors Association (Belgium); Audio Visual Association.

AVAMA Audio Visual Aids and Allied Manufacturers Association.

AVASS Association of Voluntary Aided Secondary Schools.

AVB atrioventricular block.

AVC additional voluntary contribution; automatic volume control.

AVCA Agriculture and Veterinary Chemicals Association.

AVCI Association of Vocational Colleges International.

AVCPT Association of Veterinary Clinical Pharmacology and Therapeutics.

AVCU Agriculture and Veterinary Chemicals Unit.

AVI Automatic Vehicle Identification.

AVLP Association of Valuers of Licensed Property.

AVM Air Vice-Marshal; automatic vending machine.

AVPC Association of Vice-Principals of Colleges.

AVR Army Volunteer Reserve.

AVRC Applied Vision Research Centre.

AVRDC Asian Vegetable Research and Development Centre.

AVRO Animal Virus Research Organisation; Association of Vehicle Recovery Operators.

AVS American Vacuum Society; Anti-Vivisection Society.

AVTRW Association of Veterinary Teachers and Research Workers.

a/w actual weight; artwork.

AWACS Airborne Warning and Control System (surveillance system used in 1991 Gulf War).

AWAP All-Wales Advisory Panel on the Development of Services with Mental Handicaps.

AWB Agricultural Wages Board; Asian Wetland Bureau; Australian Wool Board.

AWC Assembly of Welsh Counties; Association for Women in Computing; Australian Wool Corporation.

AWCF Associate of the Worshipful Company of Farriers.

AWCH Association for the Welfare of Children in Hospital (Eire).

AWCVIE Ancient and Worshipful Company of Village Idiots.

AWD Association of Welding Distributors.

AWE Afghan Wool Enterprises.

AWEBB Association of Wholesale Electrical Bulk Buyers.

AWeldI Associate of the Welding Institute.

AWES Association of West Europe Shipbuilders.

AWF Animal Welfare Foundation.

AWG Art Workers Guild.

AWID Association of Women Industrial Designers.

AWISE Association for Women in Science and Engineering.

AWLA Association of Welsh Local Authorities.

AWLLA All Wales Ladies Lacrosse Association.

AWLREM Association of Webbing Load Restraint Equipment Manufacturers.

AWMC Association of Wardens of Mountain Centres.

AWOL absent without official leave.

AWPR Association of Women in Public Relations.

AWRE Atomic Weapons Research Establishment.

AWS Agricultural Wholesale Society; Association of Women Solicitors.

AWT Animal Welfare Trust; Association of Woodwind Teachers.

AWTA Australian Wool Testing Authority.

awu atomic weight unit.

AXrEM Association of X-ray Equipment Manufacturers.

AYF Asian Yachting Federation.

AYRO Action on Youth Rights and Opportunities.

AYRS Amateur Yacht Research Society.

AYSA American Yarn Spinners Association.

az. azimuth.

AZF American Zionist Federation.

AZRC Arid Zone Research Centre (Australia).

AZT azidothymidine.

B

B Bachelor; Baron; Bible; boron (chemical element); Britain; British; bass (music); bishop (chess).

b billion; born; bowled; breadth; bye (cricket).

BA *Baccalaureus Artium*, Latin 'Bachelor of Arts' (a degree in education); Benefits Agency; Booksellers' Association; British Academy; British Airways; British Association for the Advancement of Science.

Ba barium (chemical element).

BAA Bahamas Association of Architects; Biodynamic Agricultural Association; Booking Agents Association of Great Britain; British Acupuncture Association; British Aikido Association; Business Administrative Assistant, Faculty of Business Administrators; British Anodising Association; British Archaeological Association; British Airports Authority; British Astronomical Association; Burlington Arcade Association.

BAAB British Amateur Athletic Board.

BAAC British Association of Aviation Consultants; British Aviation Archaeological Council.

BAACI British Association of Allergy and Clinical Immunology.

BAAF British Agencies for Adoption and Fostering.

BAAG British Aerospace Aircraft Group.

BAAL British Association of Applied Linguistics.

BAALPE British Association of Advisers and Lecturers in Physical Education.

BAAO British Association of Abattoir Owners.

BAAP British Association of Academic Phoneticians; British Association of Audiological Physicians.

BAAPS British Association of Aesthetic Plastic Surgeons.

BAAR British Acupuncture Association and Register.

BAARC British Association of Automation and Robotics in Construction.

BAAS British Academy for the Advancement of Science.

BAB British Aerospace Board.

BABA British Air Boat Association; British Anaerobic and Biomass Association; British Artists Blacksmiths Association.

BABIE British Association for Betterment of Infertility and Education.

Babs blind approach beacon system.

BABS British Aluminium Building Service; British Association for Brazing and Soldering; British Association of Barbershop Singers.

BABT British Approval Board for Telecommunications.

BABTAC British Association of Beauty Therapy and Cosmetology.

BAc Bachelor of Acupuncture.

BAC British Accreditation Council for Independent Further and Higher Education; British Aerospace Campaign; British Aircraft Corporation; British Archives Council; British Association of Chemists; British Atlantic Committee; Burma Airways Corporation; blood alcohol concentration.

BACA Baltic Air Charter Association; British Advisory Committee for Aeronautics; British Association of Clinical Anatomists; British Association of Concert Agents.

BACAN British Association for the Control of Aircraft Noise.

BACCHUS British Aircraft Corporation Commercial Habitat under the Sea.

BACE British Association of Corrosion Engineers.

BAce Bachelor of Accountancy.

BACG British Association of Crystal Growth.

BACI British Association of Caving Instructors.

BACM British Association of Colliery Management.

BACMA British Artists Colour Manufacturers Association.

BACO British Aluminium Company.

BACS Bankers' Automated Clearing Service; British Association for Canadian Studies; British Association for Chemical Specialists; British Association for Chinese Studies; British Association of Cosmetic Surgeons.

BACSA British Association for Cemeteries in South Asia.

BACT British Association of Canoe Trades; British Association of Conference Towns; British Association of Creative Therapists.

BAD British Association of Dermatologists.

BADA British Antique Dealers' Association; British Audio Dealers Association.

BAdmin Bachelor of Administration.

BADS British Association for Day Surgery.

BAECE British Association of Early Childhood Education.

BAE Badminton Association of England; British Academy of Experts; British Association of Electrolysists.

BAe British Aerospace.

BAEA British Actors' Equity Association.

BAEC Bangladesh Atomic Energy Commission.

BA(Econ) Bachelor of Arts in Economics and Social Studies.

BA(Ed) Bachelor of Arts (Education).

BAF British Abrasive Federation; British Aerophilatelic Federation; British Allergy Foundation; British Athletics Federation.

BAFM British Association of Forensic Medicine; British Association of Friends of Museums.

BAFMA British and Foreign Maritime Agencies.

BAFO British Army Forces Overseas.

BAFTA British Academy of Film and Television Arts.

BAG Bank Action Group; British Artists in Glass; Burma Action Group.

BAGA British Amateur Gymnastics Association.

BAGB Baltic Association of Great Britain; Bates Association of Great Britain; Bingo Association of Great Britain; Bicycle Association of Great Britain.

BAGCC British Association of Golf Course Constructors.

BAGCD British Association of Green Crop Driers.

BAgr Bachelor of Agriculture.

BAgric Bachelor of Agriculture.

BAgrSc Bachelor of Agricultural Science.

BAHA British Activity Holiday Association; British Association of Hotel Accountants.

BAHO British Association of Helicopter Operators.

BAHOH British Association of the Hard of Hearing.

BAHVS British Association of Homoeopathic Veterinary Surgeons.

BAIE British Association of Industrial Errors.

BAIR British Airports Information Retrieval.

BAIS British Association for Irish Studies.

BAKDA Bathroom and Kitchen Distributors' Association.

BAJ Bachelor of Arts, Journalism; British Association of Journalists.

BAL basic assembly language (computing); blood alcohol level.

BALD British Association of Laser Dentistry.

BA(Lan) Bachelor of Languages.

BA(Law) Bachelor of Arts in Law.

BALH British Association for Local History.

BALPA British Air Line Pilots' Association.

BALPPA British Association of Leisure Parks, Piers and Attractions.

BALT British Association for Language Teaching.

BAM Brothers to All Men International.

BAMA British Aerosol Manufacturers Association; British Amsterdam Maritime Association; British Army Motoring Association.

BAMW British Association of Meat Wholesalers.

BAN British Association of Neurologists.

BANC British Association of Nature Conservationists; British Association of National Coaches.

B & B *or* **b. and b.** bed and breakfast.

B & FBS British and Foreign Bible Society.

b & w black and white.

BANPR British Association of Nursery and Pram Retailers.

BANS British Association of Numismatic Societies.

BAO Bachelor of Obstetrics; Bankruptcy Annulment Order; Beijing Astronomical Society; British Association of Orthodontists.

BAODA British Association of Operating Department Assistants.

BAOMS British Association of Oral and Maxillofacial Surgeons.

BAOR British Army of the Rhine.

BAOT British Association of Occupational Therapists.

BAPA British Airline Pilots Association; British Amateur Press Association.

BAPC British Aircraft Preservation Council; British Association of Paperback Collectors; British Association of Print and Copyshops.

BAPE Barbados Association of Professional Engineers.

BAPH British Association of Paper Historians.

BAPP British Association of Pig Producers.

BAppArts Bachelor in Applied Arts.

BAppSc Bachelor in Applied Science.

BAPS British Association of Paediatric Surgeons; British Association of Plastic Surgeons; British Astrological and Psychic Society.

BApS British Appaloosa Society.

BAPSH British Association for the Purebred Spanish Horse.

BAPTO British Association of Pool Table Operators.

BAR British Association of Removers.

BARB British Association Representing Breeders; Broadcasters' Audience Research Board.

BArch Bachelor of Architecture.

BArchE Bachelor of Architectural Engineering.

BARD Bangladesh Academy for Rural Development; British Association of Rally Doctors; British Association of Record Dealers.

BARLA British Amateur Rugby League Association.

BARMA Boiler and Radiator Manufacturers Association.

Bart Baronet.

BAS Bachelor of Applied Science; Bachelor of Agricultural Science; Brewers' Association of Scotland; British Alpine Society; British Ambulance Society; British Antarctic Survey; British Association of Stammerers; Bulgarian Academy of Sciences; Bureau of Analysed Samples.

BASA Bahamas Association of Shipping Agents; British Adhesives and Sealants Association; British Air Survey Association; British Amputee and Les Autres Sports Association; British Architectural Students' Association; British Association of Seed Analysts; British Australian Studies Association; British Automatic Sprinkler Association.

BASc Bachelor of Agricultural Science; Bachelor of Applied Science.

BASELT British Association for State English Language Teaching.

BASIC Beginners' All-Purpose Symbolic Instruction Code (computer language); British American Security Information Centre.

BASICS British Association for Immediate Care Schemes.

BASMA Boot and Shoe Manufacturers Association and Leather Trades Protection Society; British Adhesives & Sealants Manufacturers' Association.

BASRA British Amateur Scientific Research Association.

BASS Belgian Archives for the Social Sciences; British Association of Ship Suppliers; British Association of Sports Sciences.

BASSA British Airline Stewards and Stewardesses Association.

BASW British Association of Social Workers.

BAT British-American Tobacco Company.

BATA Bakery Allied Traders Association; British Air Transport Association.

BATHC British Amateur Treasure Hunting Clubs.

BATS British Association of Tennis Supporters; British Association of Trauma in Sport; Brotherhood of Asian Trade Unionists; Building and Allied Trades Union (Eire).

BAU Bangladesh Agricultural University; British Association Unit; business as usual.

BAW Basketball Association of Wales.

BAWA British Amateur Wrestling Association.

BB Boys' Brigade; double black (pencils).

BBA Bachelor of Business Administration; Barbados Builders' Association; British Backgammon Association; British Bingo Association; British Bison Association; British Board of Agrément; British Bobsleigh Association; British Bonsai Association; British Buddhist Association; British Burn Association.

BBAC British Balloon and Airship Club.

BBB Bulletin Board Service (Internet); triple black (pencils).

BBBA British Bird Breeders' Association; British Boat Builders Association.

BBBC British Boxing Board of Control.

BBBIMA British Bronze & Brass Ingot Manufacturers' Association.

BBC British Bathroom Council; British Broadcasting Corporation.

BBCC British Bottle Collectors' Club.

BBCCS British Beer Can Collectors Society.

BBCF British Bacon Curers Federation.

BBCFMA British Baby Carriage and Furniture Manufacturers Association.

BBCPF British Ball Clay Producers' Federation.

BBCS British Butterfly Conservation Society; British Beer Mat Collectors Society.

BBEM bed, breakfast and evening meal.

BBF British Baseball Federation; Brother's Brother Foundation (USA).

BBFC British Board of Film Classification; British Board of Film Censors.

BBIP British Books in Print.

BBKA British Beekeepers Association.

BBL British Bridge League.

BBMC British Board of Marbles Control.

BBNA Black Bolt and Nut Association of Great Britain.

BBO British Ballet Organisation.

BBQC British Board of Quality Control.

BBPA British Bedding Plant Association.

BBPC Basil Bunting Poetry Centre & Archive.

BBS Bachelor of Business Science; Bachelor of Business Studies; Barbados Broadcasting Society; British Blind Sport; British Boomerang Society; British Brick Society; British Bromeliad Society; British Button Society; Brittle Bone Society; Burma Broadcasting Service.

BC *Baccalaureus Chirurgiae*, Latin 'Bachelor of Surgery'; Bachelor of Chemistry; Bachelor of Commerce; Backpackers Club; Badminton Club; Board of Control; Boat Club; Bomber Command; Borough Council; Bowls Club; Boxing Club; British Coal; British Council; Builders Conference; before Christ (for dates in Christian calendar).

bc *basso continuo*, Italian 'continuous bass', in music an underlying bass part.

BCA Bliss Classification Association; Bomber Command Association; Box Culvert Association; British Carton Association; British Casino Association; British Chicken Association; British Chiropractic Association; British Colostomy Association; British Crystallographic Association; Business Council of Australia.

BCAB British Computer Association for the Blind.

BCAC British Conference on Automation and Computation.

BCAP British Code of Advertising Practice.

BCAR British Council for Aid to Refugees; British Civil Airworthiness Requirements.

BCBC British Cattle Breeders Club; British Citizens Band Council.

BCC Birth Control Campaign; Breast Cancer Care; British Caravanners Club; British Cleaning Council; British Colour Council; British Copyright Council; British Council of Churches; British Crafts Centre; Broadcasting Complaints Commission; Burundi Coffee Company; Bus and Coach Council; Bypost Collectors' Club; basal-cell carcinoma.

BCCA Beer Can Collectors of America; British Columbia Cattlemen's Association; British Correspondence Chess Association; British Cycle-Cross Association.

BCCF British Calcium Carbonates Federation; British Cast Concrete Federation.

BCCG Bean Curd Canners' Group; British Chamber of Commerce in Germany; British Cooperative Clinical Group.

BCCI Bank of Credit and Commerce International.

BCCS British Cheque Collectors' Society; British Correspondence Chess Society.

BCD Benevolent Confraternity of Dissectologists; British Crop Driers; binary coded decimal notation (computing).

BCDA Barge and Canal Development Association; British Chemical Dampcourse Association.

BCDP balloon catheter dilatation of the prostate.

BCE Bachelor of Chemical Engineering; Bachelor of Civil Engineering; before Christian era.

BCF Bacon Curers Federation; British Ceramic Confederation; British Chess Federation; British Cycling Federation.

BCFS British Columbia Forestry Society.

BCFSSA Brake Cable and Fine Steel Strand Association.

BCG Biology Curators' Group; British Chelonia Group; bacillus of Calmette and Guérin (vaccine that gives immunity to tuberculosis).

BCGA British Carrot Growers Association; British Compressed Gases Association.

BCGBA British Crown Green Bowling Association.

BCGTMA British Ceramic Gift and Tableware Manufacturers Association.

BCh *Baccalaureus Chirurgiae*, Latin 'Bachelor of Surgery'.

BChD *Baccalaureus Chirurgiae Dentalis*, Latin 'Bachelor of Dental Surgery'.

BChE *or* **BChemEng** Bachelor of Chemical Engineering.

BChir *Baccalaureus Chirurgiae*, Latin 'Bachelor of Surgery'.

BCIS Building Cost Information Service.

BCL Bachelor of Civil Law; Bachelor of Canon Law.

BCLA British Contact Lens Association.

BCLDI British Clayware Land Drain Industry.

BCMA Breast Care and Mastectomy Association; British Canoe Manufacturers Association; British Caramel Manufacturers Association; British Carpet Manufacturers Association; British Complementary Medicine Association; British Cookware Manufacturers Association; British Country Music Association; British Crayfish Marketing Association.

BCO British College of Optometrists.

BCOG British College of Obstetricians and Gynaecologists.

BCom Bachelor of Commerce.

BCombStuds Bachelor of Combined Studies.

BComm Bachelor of Commerce.

BCommunications Bachelor of Communications.

BComSc Bachelor of Commercial Science.

BCP Book of Common Prayer.

BCPL Basic Computer Programming Language.

BCRA British Ceramic Research Association; British Coke Research Association; British Commercial Rabbit Association.

BCRC British Cave Rescue Council; British Columbia Research Council.

BCRU British Committee on Radiological Units.

BCRUM British Committee on Radiation Units and Measurements.

BCS Bachelor of Combined Studies; Bachelor of Chemical Science; Bachelor of Commercial Science; Biblical Creation Society; Bishops' Conference of Scotland; Black Country Society; British Cardiac Society; British Clematis Society; British Computer Society; British Crossbow Society.

BCSI British Campaign to Stop Immigration.

BCT Bat Conservation Trust; British Caspian Trust; Building Conservation Trust.

BCTA British Canadian Trade Association; British Children's Theatre Association;

BCU British Canoe Union.

BD Bachelor of Divinity.

bd *bis die*, Latin 'twice a day'.

BDA British Darts Association; British Deaf Association, British Decorators Association; British Dental Association;British Diabetic Association; British Dragon Boat Racing Association; British Drilling Association; British Dyslexia Association; Bulb Distributors' Association.

BDAMA British Distributors of Animal Medicines Association.

BDBJ Board of Deputies of British Jews.

BDC Bentley Drivers Club; Book Development Council.

BDDA British Deaf and Dumb Association.

BDentSc Bachelor of Dental Science.

BDF Ballroom Dancers Federation; Barbados Defence Force; British Digestive Foundation.

BDFA British Dairy Farmers' Association.

BDH British Drug Houses Limited.

BDI British Dyslexia Institute.

BDL below detectable limits.

BDM branch delegates' meeting.

BDO British Darts Organization.

BDRA British Drag Racing Association.

BDS Bachelor of Dental Surgery; British Dam Society; British Deer Society; British Dragonfly Society; British Driving Society.

BDSc Bachelor of Dental Science.

BDST British Double Summer Time.

BDWCA British Decoy Wildfowl Carvers' Association.

BDU Bomb Disposal Unit.

BE Bachelor of Economics; Bachelor of Engineering; Board of Education.

Be beryllium (chemical element).

BEA British Egg Association; British Entertainment Agencies; British Epilepsy Association; British Esperanto Association; British Euchre Association.

BEAB British Electrotechnical Approvals Board.

BEACON British Electronic Auction Comparing Network.

BEADA British Export Accessory and Design Association.

BEAG British Egg Art Guild.

BEAMA British Electrical and Allied Manufacturers' Association.

BEC Bermuda Employer's Council; British Evangelical Council; Building Employers' Confederation.

BEc Bachelor of Economics.

BECC British Empire Cancer Campaign.

BEcon Bachelor of Economics.

BECTA British Engineers' Cutting Tools Association.

BECTO British Electric Cable Testing Organisation.

BECTU Broadcasting, Entertainment, Cinematograph and Theatre Union.

BEd Bachelor of Education.

BEE Bachelor of Electrical Engineering.

BEF British Employers Federation; British Equestrian Federation; British Expeditionary Force.

BEFA British Emigrant Families Association.

BEIC British Egg Industry Council.

BEM British Empire Medal.

BEN Black Empire Network.

Benelux Belgium, Netherlands, Luxembourg (Benelux Economic Union).

BEng Bachelor of Engineering.

BEng and Man Bachelor of Mechanical Engineering, Manufacture and Management.

BENS British Electroless Nickel Society.

BEPA British Edible Pulses Association; British Egg Products Association; British European Potato Association.

BER Board for Engineers' Registration.

BERSA British Elastic Rope Sports Association.

BES Bachelor of Engineering Science; Business Expansion Scheme.

BESI bus electronic scanning indicator.

BESS Bank of England Statistical Summary.

BeV billion electron-volts.

b.f. *bona fide*, Latin 'genuine', 'genuinely'.

BFA Bachelor of Fine Arts; Battle of the Flowers Association (Jersey); British Fabric Association; British Fragrance Association; British Franchise Association.

BFBB British Federation of Brass Bands.

BFBS British Forces Broadcasting Service.

BFF Born Free Foundation; British Fishing Federation; Bureau of Flora and Fauna.

BFFC British Federation of Folk Clubs.

BFFF British Frozen Food Federation.

BFFS British Federation of Film Societies.

BFI British Film Institute; Benefit Fraud Inspectorate.

BFMP British Federation of Master Printers.

BFN British Forces' Network (radio).

BFO beat frequency oscillator.

BFor Bachelor of Forestry.

BForSc Bachelor of Forestry Science.

BFP Bureau of Freelance Photographers.

BFPA Barbados Family Planning Association; British Fibreboard Packaging Association; British Fluid Power Association.

BFPO British Forces Post Office.

BFS Branded Furniture Society; British Fantasy Society; British Fluoridation Society; British Flute Society; British Fuchsia Society.

BFSS British Field Sports Society.

BG Brigadier General; blood group.

BGA Behaviour Genetics Association; British Gaming Association; British Gliding Association; British Go Association; British Grit Association.

BGC bank giro credit.

BGH bovine growth hormone.

BGM Bethnal Green Museum.

BGRB British Greyhound Racing Board.

BGS Brigadier, General Staff; British Geological Survey, British Geriatrics Society; British Gladiolus Society; British Goat Society; British Grassland Society.

Bh bohrium (chemical element).

b/h bill of health.

BHA Black History for Action; British Hamster Association; British Handball Association; British Homoeopathic Association; British Humanist Association; British Hypnotherapy Association.

BHAC British Horn of Africa Council.

BHAFRA British Hat and Allied Feltmakers Research Association.

BHB British Hockey Board.

BHBA British Hacksaw and Bandsaw Manufacturers Association.

BHC British High Commissioner.

BHE Bachelor of Home Economics.

BHF British Heart Foundation.

BHGA British Hang Gliding Association.

BHHS British Hosta and Hemerocallis Society.

BHI British Horological Institute.

BHIF British Headware Industries Federation.

BHIPA British Honey Importers' and Packers' Association.

BHKA British Hand Knitting Association.

BHL biological half-life.

BHort Bachelor of Horticulture.

BHortSc Bachelor of Horticultural Science.

bhp brake horsepower.

BHQ Brigade Headquarters.

BHS Barbados Horticultural Society; British Horse Society; British Home Stores; British Hypertension Society.

BHSI British Horse Society's Instructor's Certificate.

BHSMA British Hay and Straw Merchants Association.

BHT Brogdale Horticultural Trust.

BHTA British Herb Trade Association.

BI Agricultural Society of Iceland; Befrienders International.

Bi bismuth (chemical element).

BIBBA British Isles Bee Breeders' Association.

BIBRA British Industrial Biological Research Association.

BIC Butter Information Council.

BICC British Insulated Callender's Cables Limited.

BID Bachelor of Industrial Design.

bid *bis in die*, Latin 'twice daily'.

BIE Bachelor of Industrial Engineering.

BIET British Institute of Engineering Technology.

BIFD British Institute of Funeral Directors.

BIFF British Industrial Fasteners Federation.

BIFU Banking, Insurance and Finance Union.

BIHA British Ice Hockey Association.

BII British Institute of Innkeeping.

BIIBA British Insurance and Investment Brokers' Association.

BIJS British Institute of Jazz Studies.

BIM British Institute of Management; British Insulin Manufacturers.

BIOS Basic Input-Output System.

BIR British Institute of Radiology.

BIRC British Industry Roads Campaign.

BIRE British Institute of Radio Engineers.

BIRS British Institute of Recorded Sound.

BIS Bank for International Settlements; Bird Information Service; British Ichthyological Society; British Interplanetary Society; British Iris Society; British Ivy Society; Bureau of Indian Standards.

BISF British Iron and Steel Federation.

BISP British Institute of Sewage Purification.

BISPA British Independent Steel Producers' Association.

BISYNC binary synchronous communications.

bit binary digit.

BIWS Bureau of International Whaling Statistics.

BJ Bachelor of Journalism.

BJA British Judo Association.

BJJA British Ju Jitsu Association.

BJPL British Jigsaw Puzzle Library.

BJuris Bachelor of Jurisprudence.

Bk berkelium (chemical element).

BKA British Karate Association; British Korfball Association.

BKBA British Kick Boxing Association.

BKCA British Knitting and Clothing Association.

BL Bachelor of Law; Bachelor of Letters; British Legion (now RBL); British Leyland; British Library; Broad Left.

bl bill of lading.

BLA British Legal Association; British Lift Association; British Lime Association.

BLAISE British Library Automated Information Service.

BLAVA British Laboratory Animals Veterinary Association.

BLBEG British Lawn Bowls Export Group.

BLBSD British Library, Bibliographic Services Division.

BLD Bachelor of Landscape Design.

BLDSC British Library, Document Supply Centre.

BLE Bachelor of Land Economy.

BLESMA British Limbless Ex-Servicemen's Association.

BLHSS British Library, Humanities and Social Sciences.

BLib Bachelor of Librarianship.

BLibSc Bachelor of Library Science.

BLing Bachelor of Linguistics.

BLitt *Baccalaureus Litterarum*, Latin 'Bachelor of Letters'.

BLL Bachelor of Laws.

BLLD British Library, Lending Division.

BLNL British Library Newspaper Library.

BLRD British Library, Reference Division.

BLS Bachelor of Library Studies; Bachelor of Library Science.

BM Bachelor of Medicine; Bachelor of Music; *Beatae Memoriae*, Latin 'of blessed memory'; British Museum; bench mark.

BMA Baby Milk Action; Blanket Manufacturers' Association; British Medical Association; British Midland Airways.

BMAA British Marine Aquarists Association; British Microlight Aircraft Association.

BMath Bachelor of Mathematics.

BMATT British Military Advisory and Training Team.

BM, BCh conjoint degree of Bachelor of Medicine, Bachelor of Surgery.

BMBF British Mountain Bike Federation.

BM, BS conjoint degree of Bachelor of Medicine, Bachelor of Surgery.

BMC British Match Corporation; British Medical Council; British Metal Corporation; British Motor Corporation; British Mountaineering Council.

BME Bachelor of Mechanical Engineering; Bachelor of Mining Engineering.

BmedBiol Bachelor of Medical Biology.

BMedSci Bachelor of Medical Science.

BMedSci(Speech) Bachelor of Medical Sciences (Speech).

BMEP brake mean effective pressure.

BMet Bachelor of Metallurgy.

BMetE Bachelor of Metallurgical Engineering.

BMEWS ballistic missile early warning system.

BMG British Measures Guild; British Menswear Guild.

BMGA British Mountain Guides Association.

BMHS British Morgan Horse Society; British Music Hall Society.

BMI ballistic missile interceptor.

BMJ *British Medical Journal*.

BML British Museum Library.

BMLBS British Matchbox Label and Booklet Society.

bmp brake mean power.

BMR basal metabolic rate.

BMRB British Market Research Bureau.

BMS Baptist Missionary Society; Birmingham Metallurgical Society; British Magical Society; British Menopause Society; British Mexican Society; British Mule Society; British Mycological Society.

BMSc Bachelor of Medical Science.

BMTA British Measurement and Testing Association; British Mining Tools Association; British Motor Trade Association.

BMus Bachelor of Music.

BMW *Bayerische Motoren Werke*, German 'Bavarian Motor Works'.

BMWS ballistic missile weapon system.

BMX bicycle motocross.

BN Bachelor of Nursing.

BNA British Naturopathic Association; British Nursing Association.

BNB Barbados National Bank; British National Bibliography.

BNC British National Corpus; British Needlecraft Council.

BNCAR British National Committee for Antarctic Research.

BNCC British National Committee for Chemistry.

BNCOLD British National Committee on Large Dams.

BNCS British National Carnation Society.

BNCSR British National Committee on Space Research.

BNEC British Nuclear Energy Council; British National Export Council.

BNF British Nutrition Foundation; Backus-Naur Form (computing).

BNFL British Nuclear Fuels plc.

BNHQ battalion headquarters.

BN Nursing Bachelor of Nursing, Nursing Studies.

BNOC British National Opera Company; British National Oil Corporation.

BNP British National Party.

BNRS British National Radio School.

BNS British Neuropathological Society; British Numismatic Society.

BNSc Bachelor of Nursing Science.

BNTVA British Nuclear Test Veterans' Association.

BNurs Bachelor of Nursing.

BO body odour; bowels opened; box office; broker's order; buyer's option.

BOA British Octopus Association; British Olympic Association; British Oncological Association; British Optical Association; British Oncological Association; British Orthopaedic Association.

BOAC Bank of the Arab Coast (Dubai); British Overseas Airways Corporation.

BOBMA British Oat and Barley Millers Association; British Oil-Burners Manufacturers Association.

BOBS Board of Banking Supervision.

BOC British Orchid Council; British Ornithologists' Club; British Oxygen Corporation.

BOCM British Oil and Cake Mills Limited.

BOD biological oxygen demand.

BODY British Organ Donor Society.

BoE Bank of England.

BOF British Organic Farmers; British Orienteering Federation; British Othello Federation; British Overseas Fairs Limited.

BOLTOP better on lips than on paper.

BON British Organization of Non-Parents.

BOOBA British Olive Oil Buyers' Association.

BOP Boys' Own Paper.

BOPA British Outdoor Professionals Association.

BOptom Bachelor of Optometry.

BOS British Origami Society; British Orthoptic Society.

BOSCA British Oil Spill Control Association.

BoT Board of Trade.

BOTB British Overseas Trade Board.

BP Bachelor of Pharmacy; Bachelor of Philosophy; British Petroleum; British Pharmacopoeia; before present (with radiocarbon dates).

bp boiling point; blood pressure; birthplace.

BPAS British Pregnancy Advisory Service.

BPC British Pharmaceutical Codex; British Pharmacopoeia Commission; British Printing Company Limited.

BPCRA British Professional Cycle Racing Association.

BPE Bachelor of Physical Education.

BPF British Philatelic Federation; British Polio Fellowship; British Property Federation; Buddhist Peace Fellowship.

BPGA British Potplant Growers' Association.

BPGMA British Pressure Gauge Manufacturers Association.

BPGS British Pelargonium and Geranium Society.

BPH benign prostatic hypertrophy.

BPh Bachelor of Philosophy.

BPharm Bachelor of Pharmacy.

BPhil Bachelor of Philosophy.

BPhil(Ed) Bachelor of Philosophy (Education).

BPHS British Percheron Horse Society; British Polled Hereford Society.

bpi bytes per inch; bits per inch.

BPIF British Printing Industries Federation.

BPL Bachelor of Planning.

BPMA British Payroll Managers Association; British Pottery Managers Association; British Promotional Merchandise Association; British Pump Manufacturers' Association.

bps bit per second; bytes per second.

BP British Petroleum; British Pharmacopoeia.

BPO Berlin Philharmonic Orchestra.

BPsych Bachelor of Psychology.

BR British Rail.

Br bromine (chemical element).

BRA Bee Research Association; Brain Research Association; British Rheumatism and Arthritis Association; British Rivet Association; British Robot Association.

BRC British Rabbit Council; British Record Centre; British Refugee Council; British Retail Consortium.

BRCA British Roller-Canary Association.

BRCS British Red Cross Society; British Romagnola Cattle Society.

BRDB British Rubber Development Board.

BRDC British Racing Drivers' Club; British Research and Development Corporation.

BRE Bachelor of Religious Education; Building Research Establishment.

BREA Bahamas Real Estate Association.

BREL British Rail Engineering Limited.

BRF Bible Reading Fellowship; British Road Federation.

brill. *brillante*, Italian 'brilliant' (music).

BRM British Racing Motors.

BRMA Board of Registration of Medical Auxiliaries; Boiler and Radiator Manufacturers Association; British Reinforcement Manufacturers Association; British Rubber Manufacturers' Association.

BRNC Britannia Royal Naval College.

BROA British Rig Owners' Association.

BRPB British Rail Properties Board.

BRPF Bertrand Russell Peace Foundation.

BRPFA British Retail and Professional Florists Association.

BRPS British Retinitis Pigmentosa Society.

BRR Bureau of Rural Resources.

BRRA Bangladesh Rice Research Association; British Rayon Research Association; British Refractories Research Association.

BRS British Record Society; British Road Services; Burma Research Society.

BRSCC British Racing and Sports Car Club.

BS Bachelor of Science; Bachelor of Surgery; Beaumont Society; Biochemical Society; Blessed Sacrament; Bookplate Society; British Shipbuilders; British Standard; Budgerigar Society; Building Society.

BSA Bachelor of Agricultural Science; Birmingham Small Arms Company; Boarding Schools Association; British Sandwich Association; British Surfing Association; Building Societies Association; Business Spouses Association (Eire); Byzantine Studies Association; body surface area.

BSAA British School of Archaeology at Athens.

BSAC British Screen Advisory Council; British Society of Antimicrobial Chemotherapy; British Sub-Aqua Club.

BSAF British Sulphate of Ammonia Federation.

BSAgr Bachelor of Science in Agriculture.

BSArch Bachelor of Science in Architecture.

BSAP British Society of Animal Production.

BSAS British Sausage Appreciation Society.

BSATA Ballast, Sand and Allied Trades Association.

BSAVA British Small Animal Veterinary Association.

BSB British Satellite Broadcasting; British Society of Baking.

BSBA Bachelor of Science in Business Administration; British Starter Battery Association.

BSBSW Boilermakers, Shipwrights, Blacksmiths and Structural Workers.

BSBus Bachelor of Science in Business.

BSC Bachelor of Science in Commerce; Bicycle Stamps Club; Botanical Society of China; British Safety Council; British Seeds Council; British Shoe Corporation; British Steel Corporation; British Sugar Corporation; British Sulphur Corporation; Broadcasting Standards Council; Building Societies Commission.

BSc *Baccalaureus Scientiae*, Latin 'Bachelor of Science'.

bsc binary synchronous communications.

BScAg *or* **BScAgr** Bachelor of Science in Agriculture.

BSc(Architecture) Bachelor of Science (Architecture).

BSCC British Shell Collectors Club; British Society for Clinical Cytology; British Steelmakers Creep Committee; British Sweden Chamber of Commerce in Sweden; British Synchronous Clock Conference.

BScChemE Bachelor of Science in Chemical Engineering.

BSCD British Ski Club for the Disabled.

BScD Bachelor of Dental Science.

BSCDA British Stock Car Drivers Association.

BSc(DentSci) Bachelor of Science in Dental Science.

BSCE Bachelor of Science in Civil Engineering; Bird Strike Committee Europe.

BSc(Econ) Bachelor of Science in Economics.

BScEng Bachelor of Science in Engineering.

BScFor Bachelor of Science in Forestry.

BScMed Bachelor of Medical Science.

BSc(MedSci) Bachelor of Science (Medical Sciences).

BSCP British Standard Code of Practice.

BScSoc Bachelor of Social Sciences.

BSc(Social Science) Bachelor of Science (Social Science).

BScTech Bachelor of Technical Science.

BSc(Town & Regional Planning) Bachelor of Science (Town & Regional Planning).

BSD British Society of Dowsers; bound stock date.

BSDA British Sheep Dairying Association; British Soft Drinks Association; British Spinners and Doublers Association.

BSDH British Society of Dentistry for the Handicapped.

BSE Bachelor of Science in Education; bovine spongiform encephalopathy.

BSF Bachelor of Science in Forestry; British Scrap Federation; British Screen Finance; British Shogi Federation; British Society of Flavourists; British Spas Federation; British Stone Federation.

BSFA British Sanitary Fireclay Association; British Science Fiction Association; British Snail Farmers Association; British Steel Founders Association.

BSG British Society of Gastroenterology; British Standard Gauge; British Stickmakers Guild.

BSGB Bread Society of Great Britain.

BSH British Society for Haematology; British Society of Hypnotherapists.

BSHA Bachelor of Science in Hospital Administration; British Skater Hockey Association.

BSI Bloody Sunday Initiative; British Society for Immunology; British Standards Institution; Building Societies' Institute.

BSIDA British Starch Importer & Dealers Association.

BSIE Bachelor of Science in Industrial Engineering.

BSJA British Show Jumping Association.

BSkyB British Sky Broadcasting.

BSL Botanical Society of London; British Sign Language.

BSM British School of Motoring; British Society of Mycopathology.

BSMA British Secondary Metals Association; British Skate Makers Association; British Strapping Merchants Association.

BSMALTPS Boot and Shoe Manufacturers' Association and Leather Trades' Protection Society.

BSMGP British Society of Master Glass Painters.

BSMMA British Sugar Machinery Manufacturers Association.

BSN Bachelor of Science in Nursing.

BSocSc Bachelor of Social Science.

BSOUP British Society of Underwater Photographers.

BSP British Society for Parasitology; British Society for Phenomenology; British Society of Perfumers; British Society of Periodontology.

BSPA Basic Slag Producers Association; British Speedway Promoters Association; British Sports Photographers Association.

BSPGR British Society for Plant Growth Regulation.

BSPP British Society of Plant Pathology.

BSpPS British Spotted Pony Society.

BSR Board for Social Responsibility (Church of England); British Society for Rheumatology; British Society of Rheology.

BSRA British Shoe Repair Association; British Society for Research on Ageing; British Sound Recording Association.

BSS Bachelor of Social Science; Bird Stamp Society; Botanical Society of Scotland; British Sailors Society; British Sheep Society; British Standards Specification; British Steam Specialities Limited; Broadcasting Support Services.

BSSAA British Snoring and Sleep Apnoea Association.

BSSC Bachelor of Social Science; British Shooting Sports Council.

BSSEA British Special Ships Equipment Association.

BSSG British Society of Scientific Glassblowers.

BSSH British Society for Surgery of the Hand; British Society of Sports History.

BST British Sports Trust; British Standard Time; British Steel Technical; British Summer Time; bovine somatotrophin.

BT Book Trust; British Telecom.

BTA British Theatre Association; British Throwsters Association; British Tinnitus Association; British Triathlon Association; British Tourist Authority; British Travel Association; British Trout Association; British Tugowners Association; Bulgarian Telegraph Agency.

BTCV British Trust for Conservation Volunteers.

BTEC Business and Technician Education Council.

BTech Bachelor of Technology.

BTEC HC Business and Technology Education Council Higher Certificate.

BTEC HD Business and Technology Education Council Higher Diploma.

BTEC HNC Business and Technology Education Council Higher National Certificate.

BTEC HND Business and Technology Education Council Higher National Diploma.

BTEC NC Business and Technology Education Council National Certificate.

BTEC ND Business and Technology Education Council National Diploma.

BTFHA British Touch for Health Association.

BTG British Technology Group; British Toymakers' Guild.

BTh Bachelor of Theology.

BThU British Thermal Unit.

BTIA British Tape Industry Association; British Turf Irrigation Association.

BTO British Trust for Ornithology.

BTP Bachelor of Town and Country Planning.

BTS Blood Transfusion Service; Book Trust Scotland; British Tarantula Society; British Temperance Society; British Titanic Society; British Transplantation Society; British Trolleybus Society; British Trombone Society; British Tunnelling Society; Burma Translation Society.

BTTMC British Truck Trailer Manufacturers Association.

BTU Board of Trade Unit.

Btu British thermal unit.

BU Bakers, Food and Allied Workers Union; Baptist Union of Great Britain and Ireland.

bu base unit.

BUAV British Union for the Abolition of Vivisection.

BUC Bangor University College.

BUCOP British Union Catalogue of Periodicals.

BUF British Union of Fascists.

BUFORA British Unidentified Flying Object Research Association.

BUI Badminton Union of Ireland.

BUJ *Baccalaureus Utriusque Juris*, Latin 'Bachelor of Both Laws' (civil and canon).

BUN Biomass Users' Network.

BUP British United Press.

BUPA British United Provident Association.

BUSF British Universities Sports Federation.

BUSTA British Universities Student Travel Association.

BUTEC British Underwear Testing Evaluation Centre.

BV *Beata Virgo*, Latin 'Blessed Virgi; *Besloten Vennootschap*, Dutch 'Company Limited'; *bene vale*, Latin ' farewell'; blood vessel; blood volume.

BVA Britain-Vietnam Association; British Veterinary Association; British Videogram Association; British Vigilance Association; British Voice Association.

BVC British Vacuum Council.

BVetMed Bachelor of Veterinary Medicine.

BVetSc Bachelor of Veterinary Science.

BVIFLA British Virgin Islands Family Life Association.

BVM *Beata Virgo Maria*, Latin 'Blessed Virgin Mary'; Bachelor of Veterinary Medicine.

BVM&S Bachelor of Veterinary Medicine and Surgery.

BVMS Bachelor of Veterinary Medicine and Surgery.

BVP British Visitors' Passport.

BVS Bachelor of Veterinary Surgery.

BVSc Bachelor of Veterinary Science.

BW British Waterways; biological warfare; body weight; body water.

BWA Baptist World Alliance; Black Watch Association; Bridge Deck Waterproofing Association; British Waterfowl Association; British Westerners Association.

BWAHDA British Warm Air Hand Drier Association.

BWB British Waterways Board.

BWBA British Wild Boar Association.

BWBF British Wireless for the Blind Fund.

BWBW British Warm-Blooded Society.

BWC Beauty Without Cruelty International.

BWCC British Weed Control Council.

BWCMA British Wood Chipboard Manufacturers Association.

BWCMG British Watch and Clock Makers Guild.

BWCS British White Cattle Society.

BWDA British Western Dance Association.

BWEA British Wind Energy Association.

BWF British Woodworking Federation; British Wool Federation.

BWI Boating Writers International.

BWOY British Wheel of Yoga.

BWPA British Waste Paper Association; British Women Pilots' Association; British Wood Preserving Association.

BWR boiling-water reactor.

BWRRA British Wire Rod Rollers Association.

BWS British Water Colour Society.

BWSF British Water Ski Federation.

BWTA British Women's Temperance Association; British Wood Turners Association.

BWV *Bach Werke Verzeichnis*, German 'catalogue of Bach's works'.

BWW Buses Worldwide.

BWWA British Waterworks Association.

BWWEA British Woven Wire Export Association.

BWWFH Black Women for Wages for Housework.

BYBA British Youth Band Association.

BYC British Youth Council.

BYNA British Young Naturalists Association.

BYO bring your own.

BYPC Beijing Youth Politics College.

Bz benzene (organic chemical compound).

BZS Britain-Zimbabwe Society.

C

C Canon; Captain; carbon (chemical element); Catholic; Celsius, Chancellor; Conservative; Constable; Congress Corps; Council; County; centigrade; century; 100 (Roman numeral).

°C represents degrees Celsius.

c capacity; *caput*, Latin 'chapter'; carat; century.

c. candle; carat; cathode; *circa*, Latin 'about' (used with dates that are not certain); constant (maths); copyright; specific heat capacity (physics).

C4 Channel Four (commercial television channel).

C18 Combat 18.

CA Member of the Institute of Chartered Accountants of Scotland; Cadmium Association; Cat Association of Britain; Champagne Association; Church Army; Classical Association; Cockburn Association; Coir Association; College of Arms; Consumers' Association; Contributions Agency; Court of Appeal; Cromwell Association; Crown Agent; Cruising Association; Cultists Anonymous.

Ca calcium (chemical element).

ca *coll' arco*, Italian 'with the bow' (music); *circa*, Latin 'about'.

c/a capital account; credit account; current account.

CAA Cathedral Architects' Association; Campaign for the Abolition of Angling; Cement Admixtures Association; Chinese Aeromedical Association; Christian Adventure Association; Cigar Association of America; Cinema Advertising Association; Civil Aviation Authority; Commonwealth Association of Architects; Cost Accountants' Association.

CAADRP civil aircraft airworthiness data recording program.

CAAIS computer-assisted action information system.

CAAT Campaign Against Arms Trade.

CAB Citizens' Advice Bureau; Condensation Advisory Bureau; Corrosion Advice Bureau.

CABAS City and Borough Architects Society.

CABFAA Coach and Bus First Aid Association.

CABG coronary artery bypass graft.

CABS Conservation Association of Botanical Societies; coronary artery bypass surgery.

CABE Companion of the Association of Business Executives.

CAC Campaign Against Censorship; Central Advisory Committee; Central Arbitration Committee; Colonial Advisory Council; Commonwealth Association of Architects; Council for Arms Control.

CACA Canadian Agricultural Chemicals Association; Cement and Concrete Association; Chinese Arts and Crafts Association.

CACAC Civil Aircraft Control Advisory Committee.

CACC Civil Aviation Communications Centre; Council for the Accreditation of Correspondence Colleges.

CACE Central Advisory Council for Education.

CACLB Churches' Advisory Committee on Local Broadcasting.

CACTM Central Advisory Council for the Ministry.

CAD Chinese Association for the Disabled; Commonwealth Association for Development; compact audio disc; computer-aided design; computer-aided draughting.

cad. *cadenza*, Italian 'final flourish' (music).

CADA Campaign Against Drug Addiction;

Confederation of Art and Design Associations.

CADCAM computer-aided design and manufacture.

CADD computer-aided draughting and design.

CADE Coalition Against Dangerous Exports; computer-aided design evaluation.

CADMAT computer-aided design, manufacture and testing.

CADPOS Communications and Data Processing Operations System.

CADV Campaign Against Domestic Violence.

CADW Welsh Historic Monuments.

CAE computer-aided engineering.

CAES compressed air energy storage.

CAF Charities Aid Foundation; Chinese Academy of Forestry; Club Alpin Français.

caf cost and freight.

CAFE Campaign Against Fascism in Europe; Council of American Forensic Entomologists; Creative Activity For Everyone (Eire).

cafm commercial air freight movement.

CAFOD Catholic Fund for Overseas Development.

CAFU Civil Aviation Flying Unit.

CAI Cereals Association of Ireland; Concrete Association of India; Consumers Association of Ireland; Container Aid International (Belgium); Crochet Association International; computer-aided instruction.

CAIAD Campaign Against Immigration Act Detentions.

CAIB Certified Associate of the Institute of Bankers.

CAIC Children's and Adolescents' International Cooperation; Chinese Academy of International Culture.

CAILS Chinese Association of Indian Literature Studies.

cal calorie.

cal. *calando*, Italian 'decreasing' (music).

Cal computer-aided learning.

CAL China Association of Land; Cocoa Association of London; Conversational Algebraic Language (computing).

CALF Campaign Against Leather and Fur.

calo. *calando*, Italian 'decreasing' (music).

CALPOM Committee for the Liberation of Prisoners of Opinion in Morocco.

CAM Campaign Against Militarism; Chinese Association of Musicians; Commonwealth Association of Musicians; computer-aided manufacture.

CAMDA Car and Motorcycle Drivers Association.

CAMRA Campaign for Real Ale.

CAN Climate Action Network; Committee on Aircraft Noise.

CANA Centre for Advice on Natural Alternatives; Clergy Against Nuclear Arms.

CANCIRCO Cancer International Research Co-operative.

CAND Campaign Against Nuclear Dumping.

C & A Clemens and Auguste (Christian names of Dutch brothers who founded the chain store).

c & b caught and bowled by (cricket).

c & d collection and delivery.

C & E Customs and Excise.

c & f cost and freight.

C & G Cheltenham and Gloucester Building Society; City and Guilds of London Institute.

c & i cost and insurance.

c & lc capital and lower case (printing).

c & p carriage and packing.

C&PC Corrosion & Protection Centre.

c & r convalescence and rehabilitation.

c & sc capital and small capitals (printing).

C & W country and western (music).

CANE Consumers Against Nuclear Energy.

CANSAD Caribbean Network of Cooperation in Small Animal Development (Chile).

CANSG Civil Aviation Navigational Services Group.

CANSTAT Canadian Society of Teachers of the Alexander Technique.

Cantab. *Cantabrigiensis*, Latin 'of Cambridge'.

Cantuar. *Cantuariensis*, Latin 'of Canterbury'.

CAO Chief Administrative Officer.

CAP Campaign Against Pornography; Canadian Association of Palynologists; Church

cap. Action on Poverty; Code of Advertising Practice; Common Agricultural Policy; Commonwealth Association of Museums; Community Action Projects; computer-aided production.

cap. *capiat*, Latin 'let him take'; *caput*, Latin 'chapter'.

CAPD continuous ambulatory peritoneal dialysis.

CAPE Children's Alliance for Protection of the Environment; Council for American Private Education.

CAPITB Clothing and Allied Products Industry Training Board.

CAPS Captive Animals' Protection Society.

CAPT Child Accident Prevention Trust; Citizens Against the Poll Tax.

CAR compounded annual rate.

CARA combat air rescue aircraft.

CARAF Christians Against Racism and Fascism.

CARD compact automatic retrieval device; Campaign Against Racial Discrimination.

CARE Christian Action for Research and Education; Community Action in the Rural Environment; Cottage and Rural Enterprises Limited.

CARJ Catholic Association for Racial Justice.

Carliol. *Carliolensis*, Latin 'of Carlisle'.

CART Community Alliance for Responsible Transport; collision avoidance radar trainer.

CAS Canadian Astronomical Society; Caribbean Air Services; Catgut Acoustical Society; Centre for Agricultural Strategy; Certification of Accountancy Studies; Chief of Air Staff; Church Adoption Society; Committee on Atlantic Studies; Collision Avoidance System; Contemporary Art Society.

CASD Campaign Against Sea Dumping.

CASE Caithness and Sutherland Enterprise; Campaign Against the Sale of Estates; Campaign for the Advancement of State Education; Committee on the Atlantic Salmon Emergency; computer-aided software engineering; computer-aided systems engineering.

CASS Certificate of Applied Social Studies.

CAT Centre for Alternative Technology; Certificate for Accounting Technicians; College of Advanced Technology; computer-aided typesetting; computerised axial tomography.

CATE Committee for the Accreditation of Teacher Education.

CATU Ceramic and Allied Trades Union.

CATV cable television; community antenna television.

CAVIAR Cinema and Video Industry Audience Research.

CAW Campaign Against the Witchhunt; Co-ordinating Animal Welfare.

CAWTU Church Action With The Unemployed.

CAYA Catholic Association of Young Adults.

CAZS Centre for Arid Zone Studies.

CB Companion of the Order of the Bath; County Borough; citizens' band (radio); *contrabasso*, Italian 'double bass'.

Cb columbium (chemical element).

cb circuit breaker.

c/b caught and bowled (cricket).

CBA Certified Bailiffs Association of England and Wales; Chinese Buddhist Association; Christian Booksellers Association; Citizens Band Association; Community Boats Association; Council for British Archaeology; Criminal Bar Association.

CBC Confederation of Building Contractors; Cyprus Broadcasting Corporation; complete blood count.

cbd cash before delivery.

CBE Commander of the Order of the British Empire.

CBEL Cambridge Bibliography of English Literature.

CBF cerebral blood flow.

CBI Confederation of British Industry; Convention Bureau of Ireland; Cooperative Business International.

cbi computer-based information.

CBIS computer-based information system.

CBIM Companion of the British Institute of Management.

CBMIS computer-based management information system.

CBiol Chartered Biologist.

C-bomb cobalt bomb.

CBR complete bed rest.

CBRD cattle birth record document.

CBRW chemical, biological and radiological warfare; chemical, biological and radiological weapons.

CBS Community Business Scotland.

CBSI Chartered Building Societies' Institute.

CBSO City of Birmingham Symphony Orchestra.

CBSSG Craft Member of the British Society of Scientific Glassblowers.

CBT computer-based training.

CBU Clearing Banks Union.

CBW chemical and biological warfare.

CC Central Committee; Chamber of Commerce; Charity Commission; Chess Club; Chief Clerk; City Council; Countryside Commission; County Council; County Councillor; Craft Council; Cricket Club; Croquet Club; Cycling Club.

cc carbon copy; cubic centimetre.

CCA Canadian Centre for Architecture; Caribbean Conservation Association; Carpet Cleaners Association; China Clay Association; Christian Colportage Association; Coastal Cruising Association; Commission on Crystallographic Apparatus; Commonwealth Chess Association; Company Chemists Association; Copper Conductors Association; County Councils Association.

CCAT Central Council for the Amateur Theatre.

CCBN Central Council for British Naturism.

CCBW Committee on Chemical and Biological Warfare.

CCC Camping and Caravanning Club of Great Britain and Ireland; Campus Crusade for Christ; Capricorn Conservation Council; Caribbean Council of Churches; Catholic Communications Centre; Central Criminal Court; Chinese Cultural Centre; Club Cricket Conference; Club des Chefs des Chefs; Coalfield Communities Campaign; Corporate Conservation Council; Council for the Care of Churches; County Cricket Club.

ccc *cwmni cyfyngedig cyhoeddus*, Welsh 'public limited company'.

CCCBR Central Council of Church Bell Ringers.

CCCC Charity Christmas Card Council.

CCCM Central Committee for Community Medicine.

CCCO Committee on Climatic Changes and the Ocean.

CCCR Co-odinating Committee for Cancer Research.

CCCWA Christian Consultative Council for the Welfare of Animals.

CCD charge coupled device; cattle control document.

CCE Counsel and Care for the Elderly.

CCETSW Central Council for Education and Training in Social Work.

CCF Combined Cadet Force; Common Cold Foundation; Congress for Cultural Freedom; Conservative Centre Forward; congestive cardiac failure.

CCFA Caribbean Cane Farmers Association; Combed Cadet Force Association.

CCGB Cycling Council of Great Britain.

CCHE Central Council for Health Education.

CChem Chartered Chemist.

CCHF Children's Country Holidays Fund.

CCHH Churches Council for Health and Heating.

CCHMS Central Committee for Hospital Medical Services.

CCIA Commission of the Churches on International Affairs.

CCIS command control information system.

CCITU Co-ordinating Committee of Independent Trade Unions.

CCIVS Co-ordinating Committee for International Voluntary Service.

CCJ Council for Christians and Jews.

CCLGF Consultative Committee on Local Government Finance.

CCM Cornish Chamber of Mines.

CCMA Corrugated Case Materials Association; County and City Managers Association.

CCMP Coordinating Committee for the Moon and Planets.

CCN Community Computing Network; Cycle Campaign Network.

CCNR Consultative Committee on Nuclear Research.

CCOA County Court Officers' Association.

ccol Chartered Colourist.

CCPR Central Council for Physical Recreation.

CCS Centre for Child Study; Centre for Cognitive Science; Chocolate Chompers' Society; Corporation of Secretaries.

CCSC Central Consultants and Specialists Committee; Commercial Computer Security Centre.

CCSEM computer-controlled scanning electron microscope.

CCSS Cambridge Centre for Sixth Form Studies.

CCSU Council of Civil Service Unions.

CCT Chamber of Coal Traders; Cockburn Conservation Trust.

CCTA Central Computer and Telecommunications Agency.

CCTV closed circuit television.

CCU coronary care unit.

CCW Caribbean Church Woman; Council of Churches for Wales; Countryside Council for Wales; International Committee on Chemical Warfare.

CCWA Conservation Council of Western Australia.

CCWC Campaign for Cold Weather Credits.

CCWM Congregational Council for World Mission.

CD Christian Democracy (Poland); Co-operation for Development; compact disc; certificate of deposit; contagious disease; Civil Defence.

Cd cadmium (chemical element).

c/d carried down.

CDA Chemists Defence Association; Chinese Dancers' Association; Commonwealth Dental Association; Co-operative Development Association.

CDAA Churches Drought Action in Africa.

CDC Commonwealth Development Corporation; Control Data Corporation.

CDEE Chemical Defence Experimental Establishment.

CDEU Christian Democratic European Union.

CDH congenital disease of the heart.

CDipAF Certified Diploma in Accounting and Finance.

CDL central door locking.

CDMF Community Dance and Mime Foundation.

cDNA complementary DNA.

CDP Community Drug Project.

CD-ROM compact disk read-only memory.

CDSC Communicable Disease Surveillance Centre.

CDSE computer-driven simulation environment.

CDSO Companion of the Distinguished Service Order.

CDT Central Daylight Time.

CDTV compact disk television.

CDU Christian Democratic Union (political party in Germany).

CDV Civil Defence Volunteers; canine distemper virus.

CE Chancellor of the Exchequer; Church of England (*see also* C of E); Common Entrance; *Communauté Européenne*, French 'European Community', an EC safety approval mark; Council of Europe; civil engineer.

Ce cerium (chemical element).

ce caveat emptor, Latin 'let the buyer beware'.

CEA Cinematograph Exhibitors Association of Great Britain; Council for Educational Advance; Council of Economic Advisers.

CEBAR Chemical, Biological and Radiological Warfare.

CEBIS Centre for Environment and Business in Scotland.

CEC Catholic Education Council; Central Ethical Committee; Clarence Environment Centre; Commonwealth Engineers Council; Council for Exceptional Children (USA).

CECS Church of England Children's Society.

CEDA Canadian Electrical Distributors Association; Catering Equipment Distributors Association; Chinese Exploration and Design Association; Consumer Electronics Distributors' Association (Eire).

CEDO Centre for Education Development Overseas.

CEDR Centre for Dispute Resolution.

CEE Common Entrance Examination.

CEEC Council for European Economic Co-operation.

CEF College Employers Forum; Construction Employers' Federation.

CEFMR Campaign to End Fraudulent Medical Research.

CEG Computer Education Group.

CEGB Central Electricity Generating Board.

CEI Centre for Environmental Information; Committee for Environmental Information; Conference of the Electronics Industry; Council of Engineering Institutions; Cycling Engineers' Institute.

CEIM Conservative Evangelicals in Methodism.

CELS Centre for European Legal Studies; Coalition for Education in the Life Sciences.

CEMEP European Committee of Manufacturers of Electrical Machines and Power Electronics.

CEMS Church of England Men's Society.

CEMYC Council of Europe Minority Youth Committees.

CEng Chartered Engineer.

CEngFIProdE Fellow of the Institution of Production Engineers.

CEngMIProdE Member of the Institution of Production Engineers.

CENMAC Centre for Micro-Assisted Communication.

cent. *centum*, Latin 'a hundred'; century.

CENTA Combined Edible Nut Trade Association.

CENTO Central Treaty Organization.

CEO Centre for Earth Observation; Chief Executive Officer.

CEOS County Education Officers Society.

CEPO County Emergency Planning Officers Society.

CEPR Centre for Economic Policy Research.

CERC Chemical Energy Research Centre; Civil Engineering Research Council.

CERCI Centre for Educational Resources in the Construction Industry.

CERES Centre for the Education of Racial Equality in Scotland; Consumers for Ethics in Research Group.

CERN Conseil Européen pour la Recherche Nucleaire (European Organization for Nuclear Research).

CERT Charities Effectiveness Review Trust.

CertBDS Special Category Membership of the British Display Society Ltd.

CertBibKnowl Certificate of Bible Knowledge.

CertDesRCA Certificate of Designer of the Royal College of Art.

CertEd Certificate in Education.

CertHSAP Certificate in Health Services Administration Practice.

CertHSM Certificate in Health Services Management.

CertOccHyg Certificate of Operational Competence in Comprehensive Occupational Hygiene.

CES Centre for Environmental Studies; Charities Evaluation Studies; Christian Evidence Society.

CESA Catholic Ex-Servicemen's Association; Cultural Exchange Society of America.

CESC Conference on European Security and Co-operation.

CESDA Confederation of European Soft Drinks Associations.

CESPA Campaign for Equal State Pension Ages.

CESSAC Church of England Soldiers', Sailors' and Airmen's Clubs.

Cestr. *Cestrensis*, Latin 'of Chester'.

CET Central European Time; European Ceramic Tile Manufacturers Federation.

CETA Conference of Engineering Trades Associations.

CETHV Certificate of Education in Training as Health Visitor.

cet. par. *ceteris paribus*, Latin 'other things being equal'.

CF Chaplain to the Forces, Compassionate Friends; cystic fibrosis.

Cf californium (chemical element).

cf. confer, Latin 'compare'.

c/f carried forward.

CFA Chilled Food Association; Circus Fans Association of Great Britain; Commonwealth Forestry Association; Contract Flooring Association; Cookery and Food Association; Council for Acupuncture; Council of Ironfoundry Association.

CFAL current food additives legislation.

CFB Cavity Foam Bureau; Council of the Corporation of Foreign Bondholders.

CFBAC Central Fire Brigades Advisory Council of England and Wales.

CFC Caribbean Food Corporation; Conservative Family Campaign; chlorofluorocarbon.

CFCE Cathedrals Fabric Commission for England.

CFE College of Further Education.

CFFA Commonwealth Families and Friendship Association.

CFGB Canadian Foodgrains Bank.

CFHS Catholic Family History Society.

CFI Campaign for Freedom of Information; Campaign for Industry; Clothing and Footwear Institute; Confederation of Finishing Industries; Council of the Forest Industries of British Columbia.

cfi cost, freight and insurance.

CFIC Canned Food Information Centre.

CFL Creation for Liberation.

CFLP Central Fire Liaison Panel.

CFM Centre for Facilities Management; Centre for Franchise Marketing.

CFMA Chair Frame Manufacturers Association.

CFMEU Construction, Forestry, Mining and Energy Union.

CfN Council for Nature.

CFO Chief Fire Officer.

CFOA Chief Fire Officers' Association.

CFOCFA Commission For Our Common Future.

CFP Common Fisheries Policy.

CFPO Cornish Fish Producers Organisation.

CFPRA Campden Food Preservation Research Association.

CFR commercial fast reactor.

CFS Canadian Forestry Service; Centre for Fiscal Studies; Chinese Foot Society.

CFSA Charge Families' Support Association; Cornish Federation of Sea Anglers.

CFSL Central Forensic Science Laboratory.

CFT Campaign Free Tibet; Children's Family Trust; Circle Foundation Trust Co. Limited; Cystic Fibrosis Trust.

CFTA Celtic Film and Television Association.

CFTF Centre Technique Forestier Tropical; Children's Film and Television Foundation.

CFW Care For the Wild; Concern for Family and Womanhood.

CFWI County Federation of Women's Institutes.

CG Captain of the Guard; Coldstream Guards; Common Ground; Covent Garden; Commanding General; Coast Guard.

CGA Country Gentlemen's Association; Cyprus Geographical Association.

CGAT City Gallery Arts Trust.

CGB Commonwealth Geographic Bureau.

CGBAPS Cape Grim Baseline Atmospheric Pollution Station.

CGC Commonwealth Games Council.

CGCS Commonwealth Games Council for Scotland.

CGD Chronic Granulomatous Disease Research Trust and Support Group.

CGDEM Council of Gas Detection Equipment Manufacturers.

CGE Conservative Group for Europe.

CGF Commonwealth Games Federation.

cgh computer-generated hologram.

CGI Catholic Guides of Ireland; City and Guilds of London Institute.

CGLI City and Guilds of London Institute.

CGM Conspicuous Gallantry Medal.

CGMA Casein Glue Manufacturers Association.

CGP College of General Practitioners.

CGRA Canadian Good Roads Association; China and Glass Retailers Association.

CGS Carolina Geological Society; Cottage Garden Society; Chief of the General Staff.

CGT capital gains tax.

CH Companion of Honour; clearing house.

CHA Canadian Historical Association; Caribbean Hotel Association; Catholic Head-masters' Association (Eire); Commercial Horticultural Association; Community Hospitals Association; Countrywide Holidays Association.

CHAH Committee of Heads of Australian Herbaria.

CHAIS Consumer Hazards Analysis Information Service.

CHAPS Clearing House Automated Payment System.

CHAR Campaign for Homeless People (formerly Campaign for Homeless and Rootless).

CHAS Catholic Housing Aid Society; Children's Hospice Association Scotland.

CHB complete heart block.

ChB *Chirurgiae Baccalaureus*, Latin 'Bachelor of Surgery'.

CHCF Catholic Handicapped Children's Fellowship.

CHD Centre for Human Development; coronary heart disease.

ChD *Chirurgiae Doctor*, Latin 'Doctor of Surgery'.

CHDL computer hardware description language.

CHE Campaign for Homosexual Equality.

ChE Chemical Engineer.

CHEL Cambridge History of English Literature.

CHEMA Container Handling Equipment Manufacturers' Association.

ChemE Chemical Engineer.

CHF congestive heart failure.

CHIA Canadian Hovercraft Industries Association; Craft and Hobby Industry Association.

CHIPS Christian International Peace Service; Clearing House Inter-Bank Payments System.

CHIT Child Head Injury Trust.

CHIVE Council for Hearing-Impaired Visits and Exchanges.

ChJ Chief Justice.

CHLW commercial high-level waste.

CHM Choir-Training Diploma of the Royal College of Organists.

ChM *Chirurgiae Magister*, Latin 'Master of Surgery'.

CHME UK Standing Conference on Hospitality Management Education.

CHO Confederation of Healing Organizations.

CHOGM Commonwealth Heads of Government Meeting.

CHP Certificate in Hypnosis and Psychology; combined heat and power.

CHPA Combined Heat and Power Association.

CHQ Corps Headquarters.

CHRI Commonwealth Human Rights Initiative.

CHS Clarinet Heritage Society; Clydesdale Horse Society.

CHSA Chest, Heart and Stroke Association.

CHT Church Housing Trust.

CHULS Committee of Heads of University Law Schools.

CI Channel Islands; Chief Inspector; Combustion Institute; Commonwealth Institute.

CIA Cancer Information Association; Central Intelligence Agency (USA); Chemical Industries Association; Cigar Institute of America; Credit Insurance Association.

CIAC Ceramics Industry Advisory Committee; Construction Industry Advisory Council.

CIAgrE Companion of the Institution of Agricultural Engineers.

CIArb Chartered Institute of Arbitrators.

CIB Campaign for an Independent Britain; Chartered Institute of Bankers; Corporation of Insurance Brokers; corporate and institutional banking.

CIBS Chartered Institute of Building Societies.

CIC Capital Issues Committee; Caribbean Investment Corporation; Cinema International Corporation; Cognac Information Centre; Commander-in-Chief; Construction Industry Council; Council for International Contact.

CICB Criminal Injuries Compensation Board.

CICCA Committee for International Cooperation between Cotton Associations.

Cicestr. *Cicestrensis*, Latin 'of Chichester'.

CICF Cork International Choral Festival.

CICRA Crohn's in Childhood Research Association.

CID Criminal Investigation Department; Council of Industrial Design.

CIDIE Committee of International Development Institutions on the Environment.

CIDST Committee for Scientific and Technical Information and Documentation.

CIE Centre for International Economics; Choice in Education; Companion of the Order of the Indian Empire; *Córas Iompair Éireann*, Gaelic 'Transport Organization of Ireland'.

CIEC Chemical Industry Education Centre.

CIEE Companion of the Institution of Electrical Engineers.

CIEL Centre for International Environmental Law.

CIEx Companion of the Institute of Export.

CIF Construction Industry Federation (Eire).

cif cost, insurance and freight; charged in full.

CIFA Corporation of Insurance and Financial Advisers.

CIFC Council for the Investigation of Fertility Control.

cifc cost, insurance, freight and commission.

cifci cost, insurance, freight, commission and interest.

CIFE Colleges and Institutes of Further Education; Conference for Independent Further Education.

cife cost, insurance, freight and exchange.

CIFER Colorado Institute for Fuels and High Altitude Engine Research.

cifi cost, insurance, freight and interest.

CIFOR Centre for International Forestry Research.

CIG Cataloguing and Indexing Group; Conference Interpreters' Group; Conservative Integration Group.

CIGAS Cambridge Intercollegiate Graduate Application Scheme.

CIGS Chief of the Imperial General Staff.

CIH Commonwealth Institute of Helminthology.

CIHE Council for Industry and Higher Education.

CII Chartered Insurance Institute.

CIIA Council of Independent Inspecting Authorities.

CIID Communications and Information Industries Division.

CIIG Construction Industry Information Group.

CIIR Catholic Institute for International Relations.

CIJ Chartered Institute of Journalists.

CIL Centre for Independent Living; Commissioners of Irish Lights.

CILT Campaign to Improve London's Transport; Centre for Independent Transport Research in London; Centre for Information on Language Teaching.

CIM Chartered Institute of Marketing; Commission for Industry and Manpower; Cooperative Investigation in the Mediterranean.

CIMA Chartered Institute of Management Accountants.

CIMB Construction Industry Manpower Board.

CIMCLG Construction Industry Metric Change Liaison Group.

CIME Council of Industry for Management Education.

CIMgt Companion of the Institute of Management.

CIMGTechE Companion of the Institution of Mechanical and General Technician Engineers.

CIMM Canadian Institute of Mining and Metallurgy.

CIMO Confederation of Importers and Marketing Organizations in Europe of Fresh Fruit and Vegetables.

CIMP Committee on Igneous and Metamorphic Petrogenesis.

CIMS Centre for Innovation Management Studies.

C-in-C Commander-in-Chief.

CIntMC Companion of the International Management Centre.

CIO Church Information Office.

CIOB Chartered Institute of Building.

CIoH Chartered Institute of Housing.

CIP Caribbean Institute of Perinatology;

Centre for International Policy; Council of Iron Producers; Canadian Industrial Preparedness Association; Common Industrial Policy.

CIPA Chartered Institute of Patent Agents.

CIPFA Chartered Institute of Public Finance and Accountancy.

CIPS Chartered Institute of Purchasing and Supply; Choice in Personal Safety; Commonwealth International Philatelic Society.

CIR Commission for Industrial Relations.

CIRA Cast Iron Research Association; Confederation of Industrial Research Associations.

CIRC Centre for International Research Co-operation.

circ. *circa*, Latin 'about'.

CIRCLE Cultural and Information Research Centres in Europe.

CIRDAP Centre for Integrated Rural Development for Asia and the Pacific.

CIRET Centre for International Research on Economic Tendency.

CIRSE Cardiovascular and Interventional Radiological Society of Europe.

CIRSSE Center for Intelligent Robotic System for Space Exploration (USA).

CIS Centre for Institutional Studies; Centre for International Security; China Instrument Society; Coal Industry Society; Commonwealth of Independent States; Institute of Chartered Secretaries and Administrators; International Occupational Safety and Health Information Centre.

CISA Coach Industry Suppliers' Association.

CISC Citizens' Study Income Centre; complex instruction-set computer.

CISCO Civil Service Catering Organization.

CISE Council of the Institution of Structural Engineers.

CISOB Counsellor of the Incorporated Society of Organ Builders.

CISS Centre for International Sports Studies.

CISV Children's International Summer Villages.

CISWO Coal Industry Social Welfare Organisations.

CIT Centre for Information Technology; Coda International Training.

CITB Carpet Industry Training Board; Construction Industry Training Board.

CITES Campaign Against International Trade in Endangered Species; Convention on International Trade in Endangered Species of Wild Fauna and Flora.

CITG Coal Industry Tripartite Group.

CITHA Confederation of International Trading Houses Association.

cito disp. *cito dispensetur*, Latin 'let there quickly be dispensed'.

CIU Workingmen's Club and Institute Union.

CIUL Council for International Urban Liaison.

CIWF Compassion in World Farming.

CIYC Church of Ireland Youth Council.

CJ Chief Justice.

CJA & HSA Council of Justice to Animals and Humane Slaughter Association.

CJCC Commonwealth Joint Communications Committee.

CJD Creutzfeldt-Jakob disease.

CJEC Court of Justice of the European Communities.

CL Celtic League; Communist League.

Cl chlorine (chemical element).

cl centilitre.

CLA Canadian Lung Association; Cantonese Language Association; Commonwealth Lawyers Association; Computer Law Association (USA); Copyright Licensing Agency; Country Landowners' Association.

CLABE Centre for Language & Business in Europe.

CL(ADO) Diploma in Contact Lens Fitting of the Association of Dispensing Opticians.

CL&CGB Church Lads' and Church Girls' Brigade.

CLAPA Cleft Lip and Palate Association.

CLARA Centre for the Law of Rural Areas.

CLARNICO Clark, Nichols and Coombes Limited (confectioners).

CLASS Concrete Lintel Association.

CLAVA County Land Agents' and Valuers Association.

CLAW Consortium of Local Authorities in Wales.

CLAWS Community Land and Workspace Services Limited.

CLB Church Lads' Brigade; Communist League of Britain.

CLC Central Land Council; Children's Legal Centre; Commonwealth Liaison Committee.

CLCB Committee of the London Clearing Banks.

CLD Agency for Christian Literature Development; chronic liver disease.

CLE Centre for Languages in Education; Committee of Liberal Exiles; Council of Legal Education.

CLEA Commonwealth Legal Education Association; Council of Local Education Authorities.

CLEAR Campaign for Lead-Free Air; Center for Lake Erie Area Research (USA).

CLEPR Council on Legal education for Professional Responsibility.

CLES Centre for Local Economic Strategies.

CLIC Cancer and Leukaemia in Childhood Trust.

CLIMEX Information Exchange System on Country Activities on Climate Change.

CLISG Commonwealth Land Information Support Group.

CLit Companion of Literature.

CLL chronic lymphocytic leukaemia.

CLLR International Symposium on Computing in Literary and Linguistic Research.

CLMC Combined Loyalist Military Command (N. Ireland).

CLOA Chief Leisure Officers Association.

CLP Constituency Labour Party.

CLPA Common Law Procedure Acts.

CLR computer language recorder.

CLS Certificate in Library Science.

CLSB Committee of London and Scottish Bankers.

CLSP Community Landcare Support Programme.

CLSS Coast Life Saving Service (Eire).

CLT Campaign for Local Television; Cooperative League of Thailand; computer language translator.

CLU Chartered Life Underwriter.

CM *Chirurgiae Magister*, Latin 'Master of Surgery'; Corresponding Member.

Cm curium (chemical element).

cm centimetre.

CMA Cable Makers' Association; Carrot Marketing Association; Case Makers' Association; Castor Manufacturers' Association; Catering Managers Association of Great Britain; Centre for Management Agriculture; Certificate in Management Accountancy; Chinese Medical Association; Church Music Association; Communication Managers Association; Country Music Association.

CMAC Catholic Marriage Advisory Council.

CMB Christian Mission to Buddhists.

CMBHI Craft Member of the British Horological Institute.

CMC Catholic Media Council; Congregation of Mother of Carmel; Culture Ministers Council; Curriculum Ministers Council.

CMDA Cornish Mining Development Association.

CMDC Central Milk Distributive Committee.

CMF Cast Metal Federation; Coal Merchants' Federation.

CMG Companion of the Order of St Michael and St George.

CMHERA Community and Mental Handicap Educational and Research Association.

CMI Canadian Mediterranean Institute; Carmelites of Mary Immaculate; Cordage Manufacturers' Institute; computer-managed instruction.

CMIBCM Commercial Membership of the Institution of British Carriage and Automobile Manufacturers.

CMIM Centre for Measurement & Information Medicine.

CMIWHTE Companion Member of the Institution of Works and Highways Technician Engineers.

CMIWSc Member of the Institute of Wood Science.

CML Central Music Library; Council of Mortgage Lenders; chronic myeloid leukaemia; computer-managed learning.

CMO Chief Medical Officer.

CMOS complementary metal oxide semiconductor.

CMP Centre for Multiprocessors; Christian Movement for Peace; Commissioner of the Metropolitan Police.

CMPA Chinchilla Pelt Marketing Association.

CmpnIAP Companion of the Institution of Analysts and Programmers.

CMR Centre for Materials Research; cerebral metabolic rate.

CMRC Colonial Medical Research Committee.

CMRS Conference of Major Religious Superiors.

CMRSHR Chinese Medical Research Society of Health Recovery.

CMS Catholic Missionary Society; Centre for Mediterranean Studies; Certificate in Management Studies; Church Missionary Society; Church Monuments Society; Clay Minerals Society; Cricket Memorabilia Society; *cras mane sumendus*, Latin 'to be taken tomorrow morning'.

CMT Common Market Travel Association.

CMW Council of Museums in Wales.

CMU Communication Managers Union (Eire).

CMV cytomegalovirus.

C/N carbon/nitrogen.

CNAA Council for National Academic Awards.

CNAR compound net annual rate.

CNAUK Chemical Notation Association UK.

CNC Committee for Nature Conservancy (N. Ireland); computer numeric control.

CNCC Council for Nature Conservation and the Countryside; Czech National Committee for Chemistry.

CND Campaign for Nuclear Disarmament.

CNDA Cherished Numbers Dealers Association.

CNF Commonwealth Nurses' Federation.

CNG compressed natural gas.

CNHC Churches National Housing Coalition.

CNHS Cherokee National Historical Society.

CNIPA Committee of National Institutes of Patent Agents.

CNN Cable News Network; Certified Nursery Nurse.

CNO Council of National Organisations.

CNOOC China National Offshore Oil Corporation.

CNP Cornish National Party; Council for National Parks; Croatian National Party.

CNR Canadian National Railways.

CNS Centre for Neuroscience; Chief of Naval Staff; Chinese Nutrition Society; Cognitive Neuroscience Society; central nervous system; *cras nocte sumendus*, Latin 'to be taken tomorrow night'.

CNSA *Comhairle Nan Sgoiltean Araich* Gaelic Pre-School Council.

CNSF Cornell National Supercomputer Facility.

CNSLD chronic non-specific lung disease.

CNT Commission for the New Towns.

CNTMA Chinese National Traditional Medical Association.

Companion IEE Companion of the Institution of Electrical Engineers.

Companion IGasE Companion of the Institution of Gas Engineers.

CO Commanding Officer; Commissioner for Oaths; Commonwealth Office; Criminal Office; Crown Office; conscientious objector.

Co cobalt (chemical element).

Co. *or* **co.** company; county.

c/o care of; carried over.

COA Cathedral Organists' Association; China Orchid Association.

COBBA Council of Brass Bands Association.

COBCOE Council of British Chambers of Commerce in Continental Europe.

COBI Council on Biological Information.

COBOL Common Business-Oriented Language.

COCAST Council for Overseas Colleges of Arts, Science and Technology.

COCF Council for Our Common Future.

coch. *cochleare*, Latin 'spoonful'.

COCOS Co-ordinating Committee for Manufacturers of Static Converters in the Common Market Countries.

COCRIL Council of City Research and Information Libraries.

COCSU Council of Civil Service Unions.

COD cash on delivery.

cod. codex, codicil.

CODA Community Data.

Codasyl Conference on Data Systems Languages.

CODIR Campaign for the Defence of Iranian People's Rights.

CODOT Classification of Occupations and Directory of Occupational Titles.

COE Chamber Orchestra of Europe.

COED computer-operated electronic display.

COF Community Organising Foundation.

C of A Certificate of Airworthiness.

COFA Commonwealth and Overseas Families Association.

C of C Chamber of Commerce.

C of E Church of England; Council of Europe.

COFFER Coalition for Fair Electricity Regulation.

COFO Committee on Forestry.

COG Consultant Orthodontists' Group; Co-ordination Group of Non-Governmental Organisations in the field of the man-made environment.

COGDEM Council of Gas Detection Equipment Manufacturers.

C of I Church of Ireland.

C of S Chief of Staff; Church of Scotland.

COGB Certified Official Government Business.

COGENE Committee on Genetic Experimentation.

COGEODATA Committee on Storage, Automatic Processing and Retrieval of Geological Data.

COGMA Concrete Garage Manufacturers' Association.

COHSE Confederation of Health Service Employees.

COI Central Office of Information.

COID Council of Industrial Design; Council on International Development.

COIE Committee on Invisible Exports.

COIF Control of Intensive Farming.

COL computer-orientated language, cost of living.

COLA Camping and Outdoor Leisure Association.

COLD chronic obstructive lung disease.

COLING International Conference on Computational Linguistics.

coll' ott. *coll' ottava*, Italian 'in octaves' (music).

COLS communications for online systems.

COM Committee on Mutagenicity of Chemicals in Food, Consumer Products and the Environment; computer output on microfilm.

COMA Coke Oven Managers Association; Committee on Medical Aspects of Food Policy.

COMAL Common Algorithmic Language.

COMARE Committee on Medical Aspects of Radiation in the Environment.

COMATAS Committee for Monitoring Agreements on Tobacco Advertising and Sponsorship.

COMBAT Association to Combat Huntington's Chorea.

COMCIAM Climate Impacts Assessment and Management Program for Commonwealth Countries.

COMDA Canadian Office Machine Dealers Association.

COMEX Commonwealth Expedition; New York Commodity Exchange.

COMMET Council of Mechanical and Metal Trade Association.

COMPAC Commonwealth Trans-Pacific Telephone Cable.

COMPETA Computer and Peripherals Equipment Trade Association.

COMPIP Companion of the Institute of Plumbing.

COMPSAC International Computer Software and Applications Conference.

COMSAT communications satellite.

ComSec Commonwealth Secretariat.

COMSER Commission on Marine Science and Engineering Research (UN).

con. *conjunx*, Latin 'wife'; *contra*, Latin 'against'.

CONBA Council of National Beekeeping Associations of the United Kingdom.

CONCAWE Oil Companies European Organisation for Environmental and Health Protection.

con esp. *con expressione*, Italian 'with expression' (music).

con espr. *con expressione*, Italian 'with expression' (music).

CONGU Council of National Golf Unions.

CONIAC Construction Industry Advisory Committee.

cont. bon. mor *contra bonos mores*, Latin 'contrary to good manners'.

continuo *basso continuo*, Italian – in 17th century Baroque music the bass line on which a keyboard player could effect a harmonic accompaniment.

cont. rem. *continuantur remedia*, Latin 'let the remedies be continued'.

COPD chronic obstructive pulmonary disease.

COPEC Conference of Politics, Economics and Christianity.

COPOL Council of Polytechnic Librarians.

COPPSO Conference of Professional and Public Service Organizations.

COPRA Conference of Private Residents Associations.

COPUOS UN Committee on the Peaceful Uses of Outer Space.

COPUS Committee on the Public Understanding of Science.

COR The Club of Rome.

CORA Chemical and Oil Recycling Association.

CORAA Council of Regional Arts Associations.

CORAL Common Real-Time Application Language.

CORAS Centre for Operational Research & Applied Statistics.

CORAT Christian Organisations Research and Advisory Trust.

CORCA Committee of Registered Clubs Associations.

CORDA Coronary Artery Disease Research Association.

COREE Conference on Organic Environmental Economics.

CORGI Confederation for Registration of Gas Installers.

CORT Council of Regional Theatres; Council of Repertory Theatres.

COS Canadian Otolaryngological Society; Central Orchid Society; Cinema Organ Society.

CoS Chief of Staff.

cos cash on shipment; cosine (maths).

co. sa. *come sopra*, Italian 'as above' (music).

COSAWR Committee on South African War Resistance.

COSCO China Ocean Shipping Company.

COSFPS Commons, Open Spaces and Footpaths Preservation Society.

COSHH Control of Substances Hazardous to Health.

COSLA Convention of Scottish Local Authorities.

COSPOIR National Sports Council (Eire).

COSSEC Cambridge, Oxford and Southern School Examinations Council.

COSTA Council of Subject Teaching Associations.

COT Committee on Toxicity of Chemicals in Food, Consumer Products and the Environment.

COTS Childlessness Overcome through Surrogacy.

COYPSS Coalition on Young People and Social Security.

COZAC Conservation Zone Advisory Committee.

CP Common Prayer; *Congregatio Passionis*, Latin 'Congregation of the Passion' (RC monastic order); Court of Probate; Royal College of Preceptors; cerebral palsy.

cp candlepower; carriage paid; chemically pure.

cp. *compara*, Latin 'compare'.

CPA Canadian Postmasters Association; Carpet Planners Association; Centre for Policy on Ageing; Chartered Patent Agent; Chick Producers Association; China Photographers' Association; Chipboard Promotion Association; City Property Association; Cocoa Producers Alliance; Commonwealth Parliamentary Association; Concrete Pipe Association; Construction Plant-hire Association; Contractors Plant Association; Craftsmen Potters Association; Credit Protection Association; critical path analysis.

CPAC Consumer Protection Advisory Committee; Corrosion Prevention Advisory Centre.

CPAG Child Poverty Action Group.

CPB Communist Party of Britain; cardiopulmonary bypass.

CPBF Campaign for Press and Broadcasting Freedom.

CPBS Connemara Pony Breeders' Society (Eire).

CPC Campaign Against Pornography and Censorship; Caring Professions Concern; Centre for Peaceful Change (USA); Certificate of Professional Competence; Clerk of the Privy Council; Coffee Promotion Council; Commonwealth Palaeontological Collection; Conservative Political Centre.

CPCG Children's Panel Chairmen's Group.

CPDA Clay Pipe Development Association.

CPEA Confederation of Professional and Executive Associations; Cyprus Professional Engineers' Association.

CPFS Council for the Promotion of Field Studies.

CPG Coronary Prevention Group.

CPGB Communist Party of Great Britain.

CPI consumer price index.

CPIC Canadian Police Information Centre; Comprehensive Pig Information Centre.

CPIM Certificate in Production and Inventory Management.

CPISRA Cerebral Palsy International Sports and Recreation Association.

CPJ Committee to Protect Journalists.

CPL Cats' Protection League; commercial pilot's licence.

cpm characters per minute; cycles per minute.

CP/M Control Program for Microcomputers.

CPNA Community Psychiatric Nurses' Association.

CPO Chief Petty Officer; Crime Prevention Officer; compulsory purchase order.

CPPA Canadian Pulp and Paper Association; Coal Preparation Plant Association.

CPR cardiopulmonary resuscitation.

CPRE Council for the Protection of Rural England.

CPS Carnivorous Plant Society; Centre for Public Services; Certificate in Pastoral Studies and Applied Theology; Citizens Protection Society; Communist Party of Scotland; Crown Prosecution Service; *Custos Privati Sigilli*, Latin 'Keeper of the Privy Seal'.

CPSA Civil and Public Services Association; Clay Pigeon Shooting Association.

CPSR Computer Professionals for Social Responsibility.

CPsychol Chartered Member of the British Psychological Society.

CPT Confederation of British Road Passenger Transport.

CPTB Clay Products Technical Bureau.

CPU central processing unit (computing).

CPVE Certificate of Pre-Vocational Education.

CQM Chief Quartermaster; Company Quartermaster.

CQMS Company QuarterMaster-Sergeant.

CQSW Certificate of Qualification in Social Work.

Cr chromium (chemical element).

cr. *crescendo*, Italian 'growing' (music).

CRA Commercial Rabbit Association; Community Radio Association; Computing Research Association; Concrete Repair Association; County Registrars' Association (Eire); Crime Reporters' Association.

CRAB Centre for Research Aquatic Biology.

CRAC Careers Research and Advisory Centre.

CRAD Committee for Research into Apparatus for the Disabled.

CRAE Committee for the Reform of Animal Experimentation.

CRAG Cellular Radio Advisory Group.

CRAMRA Convention on the Regulation of Antarctic Mineral Resource Activities.

CRC Cancer Research Campaign; Chemical Rubber Company; Clinical Research Centre; Confederation of Roofing Contractors Limited; Cotton Research Corporation; camera-ready copy.

CRCC Canadian Red Cross Committee.

CRCI Car Rental Council of Ireland (Eire).

CRCP Certificant of the Royal College of Physicians.

CRCS Certificant of the Royal College of Surgeons.

CRD chronic respiratory disease.

CRE Campaign for Real Education; Coal Research Establishment; Commission for Racial Equality; Conference of the Regions of Europe; cumulative radiation effect.

CREG Centre for Research & Education on Gender.

CRES Chinese Rare Earth Society.

cres. *crescendo*, Italian 'growing' (music).

cresc. *crescendo*, Italian 'growing' (music).

CReSTeD Council for the Registration of Schools Teaching Dyslexic Pupils.

CRFA Canadian Restaurant and Foodservers Association.

CRI Centre for the Study of Regulated Industries; Children's Relief International.

CRIC Commercial Radio International Committee.

CRICT Centre for Research into Innovation & Culture Technology.

CRIMES Child Rape and Incest Merit Effective Sentencing.

CRIS command retrieval information system.

CRISA Car Radio Industry Specialists' Association.

CRJ Commission for Racial Justice.

CRL Certified Record Librarian; Certified Reference Librarian.

CRLS Coastguard Radio Liaison Station.

CRM counter-radar missile.

CRMF Cancer Relief Macmillan Fund.

CRMP Corps of Royal Military Police.

CRM Soc Charles Rennie Mackintosh Society.

CRN Co-op Reform Network; Countryside Recreation Network.

CRNA Campaign for the Restoration of the National Anthem and Flag.

CRNCM Companionship of the Royal Northern College of Music.

CRO Cave Rescue Organization of Great Britain; Citizens' Rights Office; Companies Registration Office; Criminal Records Office; cathode-ray oscillograph (or oscilloscope).

CRP Community Rights Project.

CRPB Clyde River Purification Board.

CRS Centre for Retail Studies (Eire); Cereals Research Station; Christian Rescue Service; Conflict Research Society.

CRSA Cold Rolled Sections Association.

CRSOA County Road Safety Officers Association.

CRT Ship Owners' Refrigerated Cargo Research Association; cathode-ray tube.

CRTC Clay Roofing Tile Council.

Cruse National Organisation for the Widowed and their Children.

CS Caesarean section; Cafe Society; Chocolate Society; Cliometric Society; Coleopterists Society; Concrete Society; Conservation Society; Cultural Survival; Cyclamen Society; Chemical Society; Civil Service; Court of Session.

Cs caesium (chemical element); cirrostratus (meteorology).

cs *come sopra*, Italian 'as above' (music).

CSA Campaign for a Scottish Assembly; Channel Swimming Association; Child Support Agency; Choir Schools' Association; Civil Service Alliance (Eire); Council for Scottish Archaeology; Creative Services Association.

CSAB Civil Service Appeal Board.

CSAC Catholic Scout Advisory Council.

CSB Central Statistical Board; Congregation of Saint Basil.

CSBF Civil Service Benevolent Fund.

CSBTA Civil Service Blind Telephonists' Association (Eire).

CSC Catholic Students Council; Christian Service Centre; Civil Service Commission; Conspicuous Service Cross; Construction Safety Campaign; Cuba Solidarity Campaign.

CSCAW Catholic Study Circle for Animal Welfare.

CSCB Committee of Scottish Clearing Bankers.

CSCFE Civil Service Council for Further Education.

CSD Centre for Sustainable Development; Chartered Society of Designers; Civil Service Department; Commonwealth Society for the Deaf.

CSE Campaign for State Education; Centre for Software Engineering; Certificate of Secondary Education (examination set at a lower level than the GCE 'O' level. In 1988 the GCSE examination was introduced, which replaced the two levels).

CSES Chinese Solar Energy Society.

CSEU Confederation of Shipbuilding and Engineering Unions.

CSF Coil Spring Federation; cerebrospinal fluid.

CSG Catholic Stage Guild; Chinese Society of Geriatrics.

CSGB Cartophilic Society of Great Britain.

CSI Chartered Surveyors Institution; Coeliac Society of Ireland; Construction Surveyors Institute.

CSII Centre for the Study of Industrial Innovation.

CSIP Committee for the Scientific Investigation of the Paranormal.

CSIR Council for Industrial and Scientific Research.

CSIRO Commonwealth Scientific and Industrial Research Organization.

CSL computer simulation language.

CSM Cambridge Society of Musicians; Christian Socialist Movement; Commission for Synoptic Meteorology; Committee on the Safety of Medicines; Company Sergeant-Major; Committee on the Safety of Medicines.

CSMA carrier-sensed multiple access.

CSS Certificate in Social Service.

CSO Central Selling Organisation of Diamond Producers; Central Statistical Office; Chief Scientist Office (Scotland); Committee of Senior Officials; community service order.

CSP Chartered Society of Physiotherapists; Council for Scientific Policy.

CSPA Congress of Catholic Secondary School Parents Associations.

CSPEC Confederation of the Socialist Parties of the European Community.

CSRA Committee of Secretaries of Research

Associations; Copper Smelters and Refiners Association.

CSRF Civil Service Retirement Fellowship.

CSS Clan Stewart Society; computer systems simulator.

CSSA Cactus and Succulent Society of America; Computer Society of South Africa.

CSSC Civil Service Sports Council.

CSSR *Congregatio Sanctissimi Redemptoris*, Latin 'Congregation of the Most Holy Redeemer'.

CST College of Science and Technology; College of Speech Therapists; central standard time; convulsive shock therapy.

CSTA Canadian Society of Technical Agriculturists; Catholic Secondary Teachers Association (N. Ireland).

Cstat Chartered Statistician.

CSU Civil Service Union; catheter specimen of urine.

CSV Community Service Volunteers.

CSW Central Scotland Woodlands.

CSWG Church of Scotland Women's Guild.

CSYS Certificate of Sixth Year Studies.

CT Cambodia Trust; Civic Trust; College of Technology; cerebral thrombosis; cerebral tumour; computer-aided axial tomography; coronary thrombosis.

ct carat; cent; court.

CTA Cable Television Association.

CTB comprehensive test ban.

CTBT comprehensive test ban treaty.

CTC Central Training Council; City Technical College; Clothing Technology Centre; Coach Tourism Council; Cyclists' Touring Club; carbon tetrachloride.

CTCC Central Transport Consultative Committee.

CTD classified telephone directory.

CTEB Council of Technical Examining Bodies.

CTF Catholic Teachers' Federation; Children's Tropical Forests UK.

CTFMA Copper Tube Fittings Manufacturers Association.

CTGA Ceylon Tea Growers Association.

CTGWE Christmas Tree Growers of Western Europe.

CTHCM Confederation of Tourism, Hotel and Catering Management.

CTMB Canal Transport Marketing Board.

CTMO Community Trade Marks Office.

CTOL conventional take-off and landing.

CTPA Cosmetic Toiletry and Perfumery Association.

CTS Incorporated Catholic Truth Society.

CTT capital transfer tax.

CTTH Cathedrals through touch and hearing.

CTU Conservative Trade Unionists.

CTVM Centre for Tropical Veterinary Medicine.

CU Cambridge University; Casualties Union; Church Union; Commercial Union; Customs Union.

Cu copper (chemical element).

CUA Conference of University Administrators; common user access.

CUAG Computer Users Association Group.

CUC Coal Utilization Council.

CUE Committee for University English.

CUEES Car User Entrapment Extrication Society.

CUEP Central Unit on Environmental Pollution.

CUEW Congregational Union of England and Wales.

CUG closed user group.

CUKT Carnegie United Kingdom Trust.

CUL Cambridge University Library.

CUM Cambridge University Mission.

CUNA Credit Union National Association.

CUNY City University of New York.

CUP Cambridge University Press.

CURB Campaign on the Use and Restriction of Barbiturates.

CURL Consortium of University Research Libraries.

CUT Chartered Union of Taxpayers.

CV Common Version (of the Bible); calorific value; cardiovascular; cerebrovascular; curriculum vitae.

cv *cras vespere*, Latin 'tomorrow evening'.

CVA cerebrovascular accident (stroke).

CVCP Committee of Vice Chancellors and Principals (of UK universities).

CVD cerebrosvascular disease.

CVE Certificate of Vocational Education.

CVI common variable immunodeficiency.

CVL Central Veterinary Laboratory.

CVNI Conservation Volunteers Northern Ireland.

CVO Centre for Voluntary Organisation; Chief Veterinary Officer; Commander of the Royal Victorian Order.

CVRTC Commercial Vehicle and Road Transport Club.

CVS cardiovascular system; chorionic villus sampling.

CVT Camphill Village Trust Limited.

CVWS combat vehicle weapons system.

CVWW Council of Voluntary Welfare Work.

CW chemical warfare; chemical weapons; child welfare; continuous wave.

CWA Campaign for a Welsh Assembly; Comedy Writers' Association of Great Britain; Crime Writers' Association.

CWBW chemical and biological warfare.

CWC Catering Wages Commission.

CWCC Children's World Community Chest.

CWCT Countrywide Workshops Charitable Trust.

CWD Caribbean Women for Democracy; Council of Welsh Districts; civilian war dead.

CWF Commonwealth Weightlifting Federation; Conservative Way Forward.

CWG Cooperative Women's Guild.

CWGC Commonwealth War Graves Commission.

CWI Clean World International.

CWL Catholic Women's League; Children with Leukaemia Charitable Trust.

CWM Council for World Mission.

CWMA Country Wool Merchants Association.

CWME Commission on World Mission and Evangelism.

CWN Catholic Women's Network; City Women's Network.

CWO Chief Warrant Officer.

cwo cash with order.

CWP Coordinating Working Party on Atlantic Fishery Statistics.

CWR Crusade for World Revival; continuous welded rail.

CWS Co-operative Wholesale Society.

cwt hundredweight (a unit of weight that is equal to 112 pounds/50.802 kg – from the Latin *centum* meaning 100).

CWU Communication Workers' Union (Eire).

CWVA Commonwealth Veterinary Association.

CWVYS Council for Wales Voluntary Youth Services.

CWWA Coloured Workers Welfare Association.

CXOI Xi'an Oils and Fats Research Institute.

CXR chest X-ray.

CXT Common External Tariff.

CYAC Commonwealth Youth Affairs Council.

CYL Communist Youth League.

CYM Centre for Young Musicians; Commonwealth Youth Movement.

CYMS Catholic Young Men's Society.

CYS Catholic Youth Services; Centre for Youth Studies.

CYSA Community Youth Services Association.

CYWU Community Youth Workers' Union.

CZ canal zone.

D

D 500 in Roman numerals; *Deus*, Latin 'God'; deuterium (chemical element); diamonds (cards); dinar (Tunisian currency); Director; *Dominus*, Latin 'Lord'; dong (Vietnamese currency); Duchess; Duke.

d. daughter; day; *dele*, Latin 'delete'; *denarius*, Latin 'penny', which was in use in the UK until decimalisation in 1971; depth; diameter; died; dividend; dose; duke.

3-D three-dimensional.

DA Depressives Anonymous; Despatch Association; Diploma in Anaesthetics; Diploma of Art; deposit account; developmental age; dopamine.

D/A digital-to-analogue.

d/a deposit account.

DAAG Deputy Assistant Adjutant-General.

DAC digital-to-analogue converter.

DACOR data correction.

DACS Design and Artists Copyright Society Limited.

DAES Diploma in Advanced Educational Studies.

DAF *Doorn Automobielfabriek*, Dutch for Doorn Car Factory.

DAFS Department of Agriculture and Fisheries for Scotland.

DAG Debendox Action Group; Deputy Adjutant-General; Divorce Action Group (Eire).

DAGMAR defined advertising goals for measured advertising results.

DAgr Doctor of Agriculture.

DAgrSc Doctor of Agricultural Science.

DAH disordered action of the heart.

DAI death from accidental injuries.

DALPA Danish Airline Pilots Association.

dal s. *dal segno*, Italian 'from the sign' (music).

DAN Direct Action Network.

D & B Dun and Bradstreet (financial reports).

D & C dilation and curettage.

d & d deaf and dumb; drunk and disorderly.

D & HAA Dock and Harbour Authorities Association.

d & p developing and printing.

d & s demand and supply.

D & V diarrhoea and vomiting.

DAP distributed array processor.

dap documents against payment.

DAppSc Doctor of Applied Science.

DAR Daughters of the American Revolution.

DArch Diploma in Architecture; Doctor of Architecture.

DAS data acquisition system.

das delivered alongside ship.

DASA Defence Analytical Services Agency; Domestic Appliance Service Association.

DASD direct-access storage device.

DASS Depressives Associated.

DAT dementia of the Alzheimer type; digital audio tape.

Datacom data communications.

Datanet data network.

Datastor data storage.

DATCO Disability Appeal Tribunal Central Office.

DATEC Art and Design Committee of the Technician Education Council.

Datel Data and telecommunications.

Datran data transmission.

Datrec data recording.

DAvMed Diploma in Aviation Medicine.

DAW Drama Association of Wales.

DB database; delayed broadcast.

Db dubnium (chemical element).

dB decibel.

db double bass; double bed; double-breasted.

DBA Dutch Barge Association; dihydro-dimethyl-benzopyranbutyric acid (for sickle-cell anaemia).

dba doing business as/at.

DBB dinner, bed and breakfast.

DBE Dame Commander of the Order of the British Empire.

DBM Diploma in Business Management.

DBMC Danish Bacon and Meat Council.

DBMS database management system.

DBNMA Disposable Baby Napkin Manufacturers Association.

DBO Diploma of the British Orthoptic Society.

DBS Donkey Breed Society; direct broadcast by satellite.

DBST Double British Summer Time.

DBW desirable body weight.

DC Daughters of Charity of Saint Vincent de Paul; Detective Constable; Diplomatic Corps; District Council; Doctor of Chiropractic; *da capo*, Italian 'from the beginning' (music); death certificate; depth charge; direct current.

DCAe Diploma of the College of Aeronautics.

DCAS Divorce Conciliation and Advisory Service.

DCB Dame Commander of the Order of the Bath.

DCBS Devon Cattle Breeders' Society.

DCC Diploma of Chelsea College; digital compact cassette.

DCCA Dessert and Cake Mixes Association.

DCCC Domestic Coal Consumers Council.

DCDH Diploma in Child Dental Health.

DCDSTF Digital Cartographic Data Standards Task Force.

DCE Doctor of Civil Engineering; data communications equipment.

DCF Disabled Christians Fellowship; discounted cash flow.

DCG Diploma in Careers Guidance.

DCH Diploma in Child Health.

DCh *Doctor Chirurgiae*, Latin 'Doctor of Surgery'.

DChD *Doctor Chirurgiae Dentalis*, Latin 'Doctor of Dental Surgery'.

DChE Doctor of Chemical Engineering.

DCHT Diploma in Community Health in Tropical Countries.

DCI Detective Chief Inspector.

DCIB Dry Cleaning Information Bureau.

DCL Distillers Company Limited; Doctor of Civil Law; Distillers Company Limited.

DCLF Diploma in Contact Lens Fitting.

DCLP Diploma in Contact Lens Practice.

DCM Distinguished Conduct Medal.

DCMG Dame Commander of the Order of St Michael and St George.

DCMS Department of Culture, Media and Sport.

DCnL Doctor of Canon Law.

DComL Doctor of Commercial Law.

DCompL Doctor of Comparative Law.

DCP Diploma in Clinical Pathology.

DCR(R) *or* **(T)** Diploma of the College of Radiographers.

DCS Deputy Clerk of Session; Diecasting Society.

DCT Drapers Chamber of Trade.

DCVO Dame Commander of the Royal Victorian Order.

DCW Dance Council for Wales.

DD *Divinitatis Doctor*, Latin 'Doctor of Divinity'; *Deco dedit*, Latin 'gave to God'; *dono dedit*, Latin 'gave as a gift'; dangerous drug; double density (of computer disk).

dd day's date; delayed delivery; direct debit; delivered to docks.

DDA Dangerous Drugs Act; Disabled Drivers' Association.

DDC Dewey Decimal Classification.

ddc direct digital control.

DDD *dat, dicat, dedicat*, Latin 'gives, devotes and dedicates'; *dono, dedit, dedicavit*, Latin 'gave and dedicated as a gift'.

DDE direct data entry.

DDH Diploma in Dental Health.

ddl data definition language; digital data link.

DDMC Disabled Drivers' Motor Club.

DDOrthRCPS Glas Diploma in Dental Orthopaedics of the Royal College of Physicians and Surgeons of Glasgow.

ddp distributed data processing.

DDPHRCSEng Diploma in Dental Public Health, Royal College of Surgeons of England.

DDRB Doctors' and Dentists' Review Body.

DDS Doctor of Dental Surgery; Dewey Decimal System; digital data storage.

DDSc Doctor of Dental Science.

DDT dichlorodiphenyltrichlorethane, an insecticide.

DE *Dáil Éireann*, Gaelic for Assembly of Representatives, the lower house of Irish parliament; Department of Employment.

DEA Dance Educators of America.

DEC Disasters Emergency Committee.

dec. *decrescendo*, Italian 'becoming softer' (music).

DEcon Doctor of Economics.

DEconSc Doctor of Economic Science.

decres. *decrescendo*, Italian 'decreasing' (music).

DECUS Digital Equipment Computer Users.

DED Department of Economic Development (N. Ireland).

DEd Doctor of Education.

DEEP Directly Elected European Parliament.

Defcon defence readiness condition.

del. delete, delegate; *delineavit*, Latin 'drew it'; deliver.

DemU Democratic Unionist.

DEN District Enrolled Nurse.

DENI Department of Education for Northern Ireland.

DEng Doctor of Engineering.

DEPCA International Study Group for the Detection and Prevention of Cancer.

DERE Dounreay Experimental Reactor Establishment.

DERV diesel-engined road vehicle.

DES Department of Education and Science; data encryption standard.

DET diethyltriptamine (a drug).

DEW distant early warning.

DF *Defensor Fidei*, Latin 'Defender of the Faith'; direction-finding.

DFAT Department of Foreign Affairs and Trade.

DFB Deciduous Fruit Board (South Africa).

DFC Distinguished Flying Cross; Duty Free Confederation.

DFD Dogs for Disabled; data function diagram.

DFE Department for Education.

DFFA Delicatessen and Fine Foods Association.

DFLP Democratic Front for the Liberation of Palestine.

DFM Diploma in Forensic Medicine; Distinguished Flying Medal.

DG *Dei gratia*, Latin 'by the grace of God'; *Deo gratias*, Latin 'thanks to God'; Director-General.

DGAA Distressed Gentlefolk's Aid Association.

DGAS Double Glazing Advisory Service.

DGCStJ Dame Grand Cross of the Order of St John of Jerusalem.

DGFMA Decorative Gas Fire Manufacturers' Association.

DGM Diploma in General Medicine.

DGO Diploma in Gynaecology and Obstetrics.

DGS Diploma in General Surgery; Diploma in Graduate Studies.

DH Department of Health.

DHA District Health Authority.

DHC Domestic Heating Council.

DHDS Dolmetsch Historical Dance Society.

DHE Diploma in Horticulture, Royal Botanic Garden, Edinburgh.

DHF Dag Hammarskjold Foundation.

DHI David Hume Institute.

DHM Daughters of the Heart of Mary.

DHMSA Diploma in the History of Medicine, Society of Apothecaries of London.

DHP Diploma in Hypnosis and Psychotherapy.

DHQ District Headquarters; Divisional Headquarters.

DHS Design History Society; Domestic Heating Society.

DHSA Diaphragmatic Hernia Support Association; Diploma of Health Service Administration.

DHSS Department of Health and Social Security.

DHT Disabled Housing Trust.

dhw domestic hot water.

DI Defence Intelligence; Detective Inspector; Dyslexia Institute; diabetes insipidus; donor insemination.

DIA Defence Industry Association; Diploma of Industrial Administration; Driving Instructors' Association.

DIANE Direct Information Access Network for Europe.

DIC Diamond Information Centre; Diploma of Membership of Imperial College of Science and Technology.

DICE Dairy and Ice Cream Equipment Association; Durrell Institute of Conservation and Ecology.

DIChem Diploma in Industrial Chemistry.

DIE Diploma in Industrial Engineering.

dieb. alt. *diebus alternis*, Latin 'every other day'.

DIG Disablement Income Group; Drinks Industry Group (Eire).

DIGS Disablement Income Group Scotland.

DIH Diploma in Industrial Health.

DIM Diploma in Industrial Management.

dim. *diminuendo*, Italian 'becoming softer' (music).

dimin. *diminuendo*, Italian 'becoming softer' (music).

DIMS data and information management system.

DIng *Doctor Ingeniariae*, Latin 'Doctor of Engineering'.

dinky dual income, no kids yet.

DIPA Diamond Industrial Products Association.

DipAD Diploma in Art and Design.

DipAE Diploma in Adult Education.

DipAgr Diploma in Agriculture.

DipAgrComm Diploma in Agricultural Communication.

DipALing Diploma in Applied Linguistics.

DipAppSc Diploma in Applied Science.

DipArch Diploma in Architecture.

DipASE(CofP) Graduate level Specialist Diploma in Advanced Study in Education.

DipAT Diploma in Accounting Technology.

DipBA Diploma in Business Administration.

DipCAM Diploma of the Communication Advertising and Marketing Education Foundation.

DipCD Diploma in Community Development.

DipCE Diploma in Civil Engineering.

DipChemEng Diploma in Chemical Engineering.

DipClinPath Diploma in Clinical Pathology.

DipCom Diploma in Commerce.

DipCOT Diploma of the College of Occupational Therapists.

DipCT Diploma in Corporate Treasury Management.

DipDS Diploma in Dental Surgery.

DipEd Diploma in Education.

DipEF Diploma in Executive Finance.

DipEH Diploma in Environmental Health.

DipEMA Diploma in Executive and Management Accountancy.

DipEng Diploma in Engineering.

DipEngLit Diploma in English Literature.

DipESL Diploma in English as a Second Language.

DipFD Diploma in Funeral Directing, National Association of Funeral Directors.

DipFS Financial Studies Diploma.

DipGAI Diploma of the Guild of Architectural Ironmongers.

DipGSM Diploma in Music, Guildhall School of Music and Drama.

DipHE Diploma of Higher Education.

DipISW Diploma of the Institute of Social Welfare.

DipLE Diploma in Land Economy.

DipLSc Diploma in Library Science.

DipM Diploma in Marketing, Institute of Marketing.

DipMechE Diploma in Mechanical Engineering.

DipMetEng Diploma in Meteorological Engineering.

DipN Diploma in Nursing.

DipOccHyg Diploma of Professional Competence in Comprehensive Occupational Hygiene.

DipPharmMed Diploma in Pharmaceutical Medicine.

DipPhil Diploma in Philosophy.

DipRADA Diploma of the Royal Academy of Dramatic Art.

DipRAM Diploma of the Royal Academy of Music.

DipRCM Diploma of the Royal College of Music, (Performer or Teacher).

DipRMS Diploma of the Royal Microscopical Society.

DipSc Diploma in Science.

DipSoc Diploma in Sociology.

DipSS Diploma in Social Studies.

DipSW Diploma in Social Work.

DipTCL Diploma of the Trinity College of Music.

DipTELF Diploma in Teaching English as a Foreign Language.

DipTESOL Diploma in Teaching of English to Speakers of Other Languages.

DipTh Diploma in Theology.

DipTHP Diploma in Therapeutic Hypnosis and Psychotherapy.

DipTM Diploma in Training Management, the Institute of Training and Development.

DipUniv Diploma of the University.

DipVen Diploma in Venereology, Society of Apothecaries of London.

DipWCF Diploma of the Worshipful Company of Farriers.

DipYD Diploma of Youth Development.

DIRA Danish Industrial Robot Association.

DIS Development Information System (UN); Diploma in Industrial Studies.

DISMAC digital scene-matching area correlation sensors.

DITB Distributive Industry Training Board.

DIY do-it-yourself.

DJ disc jockey; dinner jacket.

DJF Disc Jockeys Federation.

DJAG Deputy Judge Advocate General.

DJF Disc Jockeys Federation.

DJI Dow Jones Index (Stock Exchange in US).

DL Deputy Lieutenant.

D/L demand loan.

DLA Decorative Lighting Association; Dental Laboratories Association.

DLC Distance Learning Centre.

DLCC Disabled Living Centres Council.

DLCO-EA Desert Locust Control Organization for Eastern Africa.

DLF Disabled Living Foundation.

DLIS Desert Locust Information Service.

DLit(t) *Doctor Litterarum*, Latin 'Doctor of Letters' or 'Literature'.

DLO Diploma of Laryngology and Otology; dead letter office.

DLP Diploma in Legal Practice; Democratic Labour Party.

DLPA Dry Lining and Partition Association.

DLR Docklands Light Railway.

DLRI Dalian Diesel Locomotive Research Institute.

dls debt liquidation schedule.

DLSc Doctor of Library Science.

DLSRT Dunkirk Little Ships Restoration Trust.

DM Deutsche Mark or Deutschmark, the German unit of currency; Daughters of Our Lady of Mercy; Doctor of Medicine; Doctor of Music; diabetes mellitus; diastolic murmur.

DMA Dance Masters of America; Defence Manufacturers' Association; direct memory access.

dmc direct manufacturing costs.

DMD Duchenne muscular dystrophy.

DMedRehab Diploma in Medical Rehabilitation.

DMet Doctor of Metallurgy.

DMF Disabled Motorists Federation; decayed, missing and filled (teeth).

DMJ Daughters of Mary and Joseph.

DMJ(Clin) *or* **DMJ(Path)** Diploma in Medical Jurisprudence (Clinical or Pathological), Society of Apothecaries of London.

DML data manipulation language.

DMO District Medical Officer.

DMRD Diploma in Medical Radio-Diagnosis.

DMRT Diploma in Radiotherapy.

DMS Diploma in Management Studies; database management system.

DMSA Domestic Manufacturing Stationers' Association.

DMT dimethyltriptamine.

DMU Diploma in Medical Ultrasound; directly managed unit (hospital in National Health Service).

DMus Doctor of Music.

DMusCantuar The Archbishop of Canterbury's Doctorate in Music.

DMZ demilitarized zone.

DN Diploma in Nursing; *Dominus Noster*, Latin 'Our Lord'; debit note.

DNA District Nursing Association; deoxyribonucleic acid.

DNB Dictionary of National Biography.

DNC distributed numerical control.

DNF did not finish.

DNH Department of National Heritage.

DNJC *Dominus Noster Jesus Christus*, Latin 'Our Lord Jesus Christ'.

DNPP *Dominus Noster Papa Pontifex*, Latin 'Our Lord the Pope'.

DNR do not resuscitate.

DNS Department of National Savings; Domain Name System (of the Internet).

do. *ditto*, Italian 'the same'.

DO Diploma in Ophthalmology; District Office; deferred ordinary (shares).

DO Diploma in Osteopathy.

DOA dead on arrival; date of availability.

DOAE Defence Operational Analysis Establishment.

dob date of birth.

DOBETA Domestic Oil Burning Equipment Testing Association.

DObstRCOG Diploma in Obstetrics of the Royal College of Gynaecologists and Obstetricians.

DOC District Officer Commanding.

Docomomo International Working Party for the Documentation and Conservation of Buildings, Sites and Neighbourhoods of the Modern Movement.

dod date of death.

DoE Department of the Environment.

D of L Duchy of Lancaster.

DOG Directory of Opportunities for Graduates.

DoH Department of Health.

DOI died of injuries.

DoI Department of Industry.

dol. *dolce*, Italian 'sweet' (music).

dolciss. *dolcissimo*, Italian 'very sweetly' (music).

DOM *Deo optimo maximo*, Latin 'to God, the best and greatest'; *Dominus omnium magister*, Latin 'God the master of all'.

dom date of marriage.

DOMMDA Drawing Office Material Manufacturers and Dealers Association.

DOMO Dispensing Opticians Manufacturing Organisation.

DOMS Diploma in Ophthalmic Medicine and Surgery.

DOMSAT domestic communications satellite.

DOpt Diploma in Ophthalmic Optics.

DORA Defence of the Realm Act.

DOrth Diploma in Orthoptics.

DOrthRCSEdin Diploma in Orthodontics, Royal College of Surgeons of Edinburgh.

DOrthRCSEng Diplomate in Orthodontics, Royal College of Surgeons of England.

DOS Disk Operating System.

DoT Department of Tourism; Department of Transport.

DOT Department of Trade.

DOW died of wounds.

DP Diploma in Psychotherapy; data processing; displaced person; Democratic Party.

dp dual purpose; damp-proof.

DPA Dartmoor Preservation Association; Data Protection Agency; Diary Publishers Association; Diploma in Public Administration; Directory Publishers' Association; Duck Producers Association.

DPAA Draught Proofing Advisory Association.

DPAG Dangerous Pathogens Advisory Group.

DPAS Discharged Prisoners' Aid Society.

DPath Diploma in Pathology.

DpBact Diploma in Bacteriology.

DPC Defence Planning Committee (NATO).

dpc damp-proof course.

DPCM differential pulse-code modulation.

DPD(Dund) Diploma in Public Dentistry.

DPE Diploma in Physical Education.

DPH Diploma in Public Health.

DPh *or* **DPhil** Doctor of Philosophy.

DPHRCSEng Diploma in Dental Public Health, Royal College of Surgeons of England.

DPI Department of Public Information (UN).

dpi dots per inch.

DPM Diploma in Psychological Medicine; Deputy Prime Minister.

DPMI DOS/Protected Mode Interface.

DPP Director of Public Prosecutions.

DPR Data Protection Register.

DPRTF Drought Policy Review Task Force.

DPS Diploma in Pastoral Studies and Applied Theology; Dales Pony Society; Diploma in Professional Studies; Disabled Photographers' Society.

DPSE Diploma in Professional Studies in Education.

DPSPA Display Producers and Screen Printers Association.

DPSSC Drugs and Poisons Schedule Standing Committee.

DPT diphtheria, pertussis, tetanus (vaccine).

DPTAC Disabled Persons Transport Advisory Committee.

DPTRI Drilling and Production Technology Research Institute.

dpu data processing unit.

DQMG Deputy Quartermaster General.

Dr Doctor; driver; drummer.

dr debtor, drawer.

D/R deposit receipt.

DRA Danish Robot Association; Defence Research Agency.

DrAc Doctor of Acupuncture.

DRAM dynamic random access memory.

dram. pers. *dramatis personae*, Latin 'characters present in the drama'.

DRAW direct read after write.

DRC Dictionary Research Centre.

DRCOG Diploma of the Royal College of Obstetricians and Gynaecologists.

DRCPath Diploma of the Royal College of Pathologists.

DRD Diploma in Restorative Dentistry.

DRDW direct read during write.

DRE Diploma in Remedial Electrolysis.

DRI Diploma in Radionuclide Imaging.

DR(RCA) Doctor of the Royal College of Art.

DRSAM Diploma of the Royal Scottish Academy of Music and Drama.

DRT Disability Research Team.

DS Detective Sergeant; Doctor of Surgery; Down's syndrome; *dal segno*, Italian 'from the sign' (music); disseminated sclerosis; debenture stock.

D/S dextrose saline.

DSA Direct Selling Association; Door and Shutter Association; Down's Syndrome Association; Drilling and Sawing Association; Driving Standards Agency; Down's Syndrome Association; Driving Standards Agency.

DSAC Defence Scientific Advisory Council.

DSBA Dalesbred Sheep Breeders Association.

DSC Dangerous Sports Club; Desert Society of China; Distinguished Service Cross.

DSc *Doctor Scientiae*, Latin 'Doctor of Science'.

DScEcon Doctor in the Faculty of Economics and Social Studies.

DSc(Econ) Doctor of Science (Economics) or in Economics.

DSc(Eng) Doctor of Science (Engineering).

DSc(Social Sciences) Doctor of Science in the Social Sciences.

DScTech Doctor of Technical Science.

dsDNA double-stranded deoxyribonucleic acid.

DSM Distinguished Service Medal; deputy stage manager.

DSMA Door and Shutter Manufacturers Association.

DSMP Daughters of St Mary of Providence.

DSO Distinguished Service Order (British military decoration).

DSocSc Doctor of Social Science.

dsp *decessit sine prole*, Latin 'died without issue'; digital signal processing.

DSP Democratic Socialist Party.

DSPCA Dublin Society for the Prevention of Cruelty to Animals.

DSS Department of Social Security.

DSSA Dental System Suppliers' Association; Direct Sales and Service Association.

DSSc Doctor of Social Science.

DST Double Summer Time; daylight saving time.

DSTA Diploma Member of the Swimming Teachers' Association.

DSWA Dry Stone Walling Association of Great Britain.

DT Daily Telegraph; data transmission; delerium tremens.

DTA Development Trusts Association.

DTAG Development Training Advisory Group.

dtba date to be advised.

DTC Department of Technical Co-operation.

DTCD Diploma in Tuberculosis and Chest Diseases.

DTCH Diploma in Tropical Child Health.

DTD document type definition.

DTE data terminal equipment.

DTech Doctor of Technology.

DTF Dairy Trade Federation; Domestic Textiles Federation.

DTh *Doctor Theologiae*, Latin 'Doctor of Theology'.

DTI Department of Trade and Industry.

DTM&H Diploma in Tropical Medicine and Hygiene.

DTP desktop publishing.

DTp Department of Transport.

DTR double taxation relief.

DTRP Diploma in Town and Regional Planning.

DTs delerium tremens.

DTTAC Distributive Trades Technology Advisory Centre.

DU died unmarried; duodenal ulcer.

Dunelm. *Dunelmensis*, Latin 'of Durham'.

DUniv Doctor of the University.

DUP Democratic Unionist Party.

DV *Deo volente*, Latin 'God willing'; Douay version (of the Bible); defective vision; double vision.

DVA Dunkirk Veterans' Association.

DVE Diploma in Vocational Education.

DVetMed Doctor of Veterinary Medicine.

DVI digital video imaging.

DVLA Driver and Vehicle Licensing Agency.

DVM Doctor of Veterinary Medicine.

DVM&S Doctor of Veterinary Medicine and Surgery.

DVS Doctor of Veterinary Surgery.

DVSc Doctor of Veterinary Science.

DW Daughters of Wisdom.

DWA Drystone Walling Association; driving without awareness.

DWAS Doctor Who Appreciation Society.

dwc deadweight capacity.

dwt deadweight tonnage; pennyweight.

DXR deep X-ray.

DXRT deep X-ray therapy.

Dy dysprosium (chemical element).

E

E East; Ecstasy (slang term for the drug); English; earth (on electrical circuits); energy (in physics).

e European (concerning weights which comply with EC regulations).

EA East Anglia; Evangelical Alliance; enemy aircraft.

EAA Electrical Appliance Association; Entertainments Agents Association; European Aluminium Association; European Athletic Association.

EAACI European Academy of Allergology and Clinical Immunology.

EAAE European Association of Agricultural Economists.

e & e each and every.

E & OE errors and omissions excepted.

EAAS East Anglian Aviation Society.

EAC Elderly Accommodation Counsel; Engineering Applications Centre; Evangelical Association of the Caribbean.

EACC Edinburgh Airport Consultative Committee.

EACE European Association for Cognitive Ergonomics.

EACN European Air Chemistry Network.

EACRO European Association of Contract Research Association.

EADA Eastern Dredging Association.

EAECMI Export Association of the Electric Cable Making Industry.

EAEE European Association of Earthquake Engineering.

EAES European Atomic Energy Society.

EAFA European Aluminium Foil Association.

EAHF eczema, asthma, hay fever.

EAG Environmental Assessment Group; European Atherosclerosis Group.

EAGB Executives Association of Great Britain; Eyecare Association of Great Britain.

EAGLE European Association for Grey Literature Exploitation.

EAGO European Association of Gynaecologists and Obstetricians.

EAHP European Association for Humanistic Psychology; European Asssociation of Hospital Pharmacists.

EAHTMA Engineers and Allied Hand Tool Makers Association.

EAIA Early American Industries Association.

EAN European Academic Network; European Article Number (computer coding on retail items); effective atomic number.

EANI Energy Action Northern Ireland.

EAP Environment Action Plans.

EAPA English Apples and Pears Association; European Ashphalt Pavement Association.

EAPAC Eggs Authority Producer Advisory Committee.

EARN European Academic and Research Network.

EAROM electrically alterable read-only memory.

EAS Energy Action Scotland; Epilepsy Association of Scotland; European Aquaculture Society; equivalent air speed; electronic article surveillance.

EAT Employment Appeals Tribunal (Eire); Environmental Awareness Trust.

EATA East Asia Travel Association.

EATB East Anglia Tourist Board.

EAVA Ethnographic Audio Visual Archive.

EAW Electrical Association for Women.

EAX electronic automatic exchange.

EB Encyclopaedia Britannica; Epstein-Barr (virus); epidermolysis bullosa (skin disease).

EBA Electric Boat Association; English Basketball Association; English Bowling Association; European Boardsailing Association.

EBAA Eye Bank Association of America.

EBBS European Brain and Behaviour Society.

EBC English Bowls Council; European Brewery Convention.

EBCIDIC extended binary coded decimal interchange code (computing).

EBEA Economics and Business Education Association; Electronic and Business Equipment Association.

EBF English Bowling Federation; European Baptist Federation.

EBOA Export Buying Offices Association.

Ebor. *Eboracensis*, Latin 'of York'; *Eboracum*, Latin for York.

EBRD European Bank for Reconstruction and Development.

EBS Emergency Bed Service; European Book Society; European Business School; emergency broadcast system.

EBSA Estuarine and Brackish-Water Sciences Association.

EBSC Equine Behaviour Study Circle.

EBSC European Bird Strike Committee.

EBU English Bridge Union; European Badminton Union; European Boxing Union; European Broadcasting Union.

EBV Epstein-Barr Virus.

EC Engineering Council; Episcopal Church; Established Church; European Community; European Council of Ministers; Executive Committee.

ECA Economic Commission for Africa; Educational Centres Association; Electrical

Contractors Association; Employment Conditions Abroad; English Clergy Association; English Curling Association; Environmental Contaminants Authority; European Cockpit Association; European Commission on Agriculture.

ECAMA European Citric Acid Manufacturers' Association.

ECAT emission computerized axial tomography.

ECATRA European Car and Truck Rental Association.

ECAZA European Community Association of Zoos and Aquaria.

ECBC European Carbon Black Centre.

ECBO European Community Baroque Orchestra; European Conference of British Bus and Coach Operators.

ECC Electricity Consumers Council; English Ceramic Circle; European Crystallographic Committee.

ECCA European Coil Coating Association.

ECCC English Country Cheese Council.

ECCM electronic counter-countermeasures.

ECCO European Culture Collections' Organization.

ECCP European Committee on Crime Problems.

ECCU English Cross-Country Union.

ECDU European Christian Democratic Union.

ECE Economic Commission for Europe.

ECF East China Fair; Eastern Counties Farmers; European Caravan Federation; European Coffee Federation; European Commission on Forestry and Forest Products; European Cyclists Federation.

ECG Ecosystem Conservation Group; Export Credit Guarantee; electrocardiogram; electrocardiograph.

ECGD Export Credits Guarantee Department.

ECHG English Churches Housing Group; Equipment for Charity Hospitals Overseas.

ECHR European Court of Human Rights; European Commission on Human Rights.

ECIMOT European Central Inland Movements of Transport.

ECJ European Court of Justice.

ECMA European Collectors and Modellers Association; European Computer Manufacturers Association.

ECMWF European Centre for Medium-Range Weather Forecasting.

ECNC Economic Committee of the Nordic Council; European Centre for Nature Conservation.

ECO English Chamber Orchestra; English Channel Organisation; Irish Environmental Conservation Organisation for Youth; Malta Ecological Society.

ECoG electrocorticogram.

E. coli Escherichia coli (type of bacteria).

ECOM electronic computer-originated mail.

Ecovast European Council for the Village and Small Town.

ECP English Collective of Prostitutes; European Confederation for Plant Protection Research.

ECPS European Centre for Population Studies.

ECR electronic cash register.

ECS European Communications Satellite.

ECSA Estuarine and Coastal Studies Association; European Chips and Snacks Association.

ECSC Energy Conservation and Solar Centre; European Coal and Steel Community.

ECST European Convention on the Suppression of Terrorism.

ECT electroconvulsive therapy.

ECTA Electrical Contractors' Trading Association.

ECTF Edinburgh Centre for Tropical Forests.

ECTG European Channel Tunnel Group.

ECTMAC East Coast Trawl Management Advisory Committee.

ECTU European Confederation of Trade Unions.

ECU English Church Union; European Chiropractors Union; European Customs Union.

Ecu European Currency Unit.

ECWS English Civil War Society.

ECY European Conservation Year.

ECYO European Community Youth Orchestra.

EDA Eating Disorders Association; Ecological Design Association; English Draughts Association; European Dyslexia Association.

EDANA European Disposables and Nonwovens Association.

EdB Bachelor of Education.

EDBS expert database system.

EDC Early Dance Circle; Education Development Centre; European Defence Community; ethylene dichloride; expected date of confinement (medical).

EDD expected date of delivery (medical); English Dialect Dictionary.

EdD Doctor of Education.

EDF European Development Fund.

EDLS European Divine Life Society.

EdM Master of Education.

edoc effective date of change.

EDP electronic data processing.

EDS English Dialect Society.

Edsat educational television satellite.

EE Early English; English Estates; errors excepted.

EEA Employment Equality Agency (Eire); European Energy Association; European Evangelical Alliance.

EE & MP Envoy Extraordinary and Minister Plenipotentiary.

EEBB East Europe Boxing Bureau.

EEC English Electric Company; European Economic Community.

EED electro-explosive device.

EEF Engineering Employers' Federation.

EEG Essence Export Group; electroencephalogram; electroencephalograph.

EEIBA Electrical and Electronics Industries Benevolent Association.

EENT eye, ear, nose and throat.

EEO Energy Efficiency Office.

EEOC Equal Employment Opportunities Commission.

EEPROM electrically erasable programmable memory (computing).

EEROM electrically erasable read-only memory.

EES European Exchange System.

EET Eastern European Time.

EETPU Electrical, Electronic, Telecommunications and Plumbing Union.

EETS Early English Text Society.

EEZ exclusive economic zone.

EF! Earth First!.

EFA Electrical Floorwarming Association; Eton Fives Association; European Free Alliance; European Fighter Aircraft; essential fatty acids.

EFAA English Field Archery Association.

EFDSS English Folk Dance and Song Society.

EFEC European Fashion Export Council.

EFFTA European Fishing Tackle Trade Association.

EFG Economic Forestry Group.

EFGA English Farmers Growers Association.

EFH Elizabeth Fitzroy Homes.

EFI Electronic Forum for Industry; Equestrian Federation of Ireland.

EFL English as a foreign language.

EFT electronic funds transfer.

EFTA European Free Trade Association.

EFTPOS electronic funds transfer at point of sales (the transfer of monies by electronic means from one bank account to another).

EFTU Engineering and Fastener Trade Union.

EFTS electronic funds transfer system.

EFU European Football Union.

EG Engineers' Guild.

e.g. *exempli gratia*, Latin 'for the sake of example'.

EGA enhanced graphics adapter.

EGI Edward Grey Institute of Field Ornithology.

EGM extraordinary general meeting.

EGS English Goethe Society.

EGSF Equine Grass Sickness Fund.

EGU English Golf Union.

EHA Economic History Association; European Helicopter Association.

EHB European Homograft Bank.

EHF European Hockey Federation; extremely high frequency.

EHIA European Herbal Infusions Association.

EHO Environmental Health Officer.

EHPS Endurance Horse and Pony Society of Great Britain.

EHS Ecclesiastical History Society.

EHT extra high tension.

EIA environmental impact assessment.

EIB European Investment Bank.

EIBA English Indoor Bowling Association.

EICA East India Cotton Association.

EIG Ethical Investors' Group.

E-in-C Engineer-in-Chief.

EIIR *Elizabeth Secunda Regina*, Latin for Queen Elizabeth the Second.

EIS Epidemic Intelligence Service.

EJCS English Jersey Cattle Society.

EJMA English Joinery Manufacturers' Association.

ejusd. *ejusdem*, Latin 'of the same'.

ELBS English Language Book Society.

ELDO European Launcher Development Organization.

ELF Earth Liberation Front; Elimination of Leukaemia Fund; Environmental Law Foundation; extra/extremely low frequency.

ELFA Educational Film Library Association; Electric Light Fittings Association.

Elien. *Eliensis*, Latin 'of Ely' (bishop's see).

Elint electronic intelligence.

ELMA Electric Lamp Manufacturers' Association; European Association for Length Measuring Instruments and Machines.

ELO European Leisure Organisation.

ELSS emergency life support system.

ELT English Language Teaching.

ELU English Lacrosse Union.

ELV expendable launch vehicle.

ELWW European Laboratory Without Walls.

EM electromagnetic; electromotive; electron microscope; evening meal.

EMA European Monetary Agreement; European Motorcycle Association; Excavator Makers Association; Executives and Managers Association of Great Britain and Ireland.

EMAC Extra-Mural Activity Association.

email *or* **e-mail** electronic mail.

EMC Early Music Centre; European Muscle Club.

EMF European Monetary Fund.

emf electromotive force (term used in physics).

EMFEC East Midland Further Education Council.

EMI Electrical and Musical Industries.

emi electromagnetic interference.

EMLC Ethnic Minorities Law Centre.

EMP European Member of Parliament; electromagnetic pulse.

EMPA European Marine Pilots Association.

EMR electronic magnetic resonance.

EMS European Monetary System; Emergency Medical Service; expanded memory specification.

EMU European Monetary Union; economic and monetary union; electromagnetic unit.

EN English Nature; Enrolled Nurse.

ENA English Newspaper Association; European Needlemakers Association.

ENB English National Board.

ENE east-northeast.

ENG electronic news gathering.

EN(G) Enrolled Nurse (General).

EngTech Engineering Technician.

EN(M) Enrolled Nurse (Mental).

EN(MH) Enrolled Nurse (Mental Handicap).

ENO English National Opera.

Enrich European Network for Research in Global Change.

ENS European Nuclear Society.

ENSA Entertainments National Services Association.

ENT ear, nose and throat (mainly hospital departments or specialist clinics).

ENWRAC European Network for Women's Right to Abortion and Contraception.

EO Education Officer; Education Otherwise; Equal Opportunities; Executive Officer.

eo *ex officio*, Latin 'by right of office'.

EOA examination, opinion and advice.

EOAAD Wildpeace - European Organization for Aid to Animals in Distress.

EOC Equal Opportunities Commission.

EODC Earth Observation Data Centre.

EORTC European Organization for Research into the Treatment of Cancer.

EOSC Employments Occupational Standards Council.

EP European Parliament; electroplate; extended play (record).

ep *en passant*, French 'while passing' (chess).

EPA Emergency Powers Act; Employment Protection Act; English Pool Association; European Productivity Agency.

EPACT European Promotion Association for Composite Tanks and Tubulars.

EPC Educational Publishers Council; Emergency Preparedness Canada; European Pancreatic Club; Export Publicity Council.

EPCC Edinburgh Parallel Computing Centre.

EPCIA Expanded Polystyrene Cavity Insulation.

EPDA Emergency Powers Defence Act.

EPG Eminent Persons' Group.

EPI European Peace Initiative.

Epic European Philosophical Inquiry Centre.

EPL European Petrochemical Luncheon.

EPNS English Place-Name Society; electroplated nickel silver.

EPO Earthnet Programme Office.

EPOCH End Physical Punishment of Children.

EPOS electronic point of sale.

EPP European People's Party.

EPPAPA European Pure Phosphoric Acid Producers' Association.

EPPO European and Mediterranean Plant Protection Organisation.

EPROM erasable programmable memory.

EPS Emergency Planning Society; European Palm Society; European Pineal Society; Experimental Psychology Society.

EPSF European Paintball Sports Federation.

EPSG Epiphytic Plant Study Group; European Pineal Study Group; European Production Study Group.

EPT Environmental Protection Technology; Exploring Parenthood Trust.

EPTA Electrophysiological Technologists Association; European Paltrusion Technology Association; European Piano Teachers Association; European Power Tool Association.

EPU European Payments Union; European Picture Union.

EQA European Quality Alliance.

ER *Elizabeth Regina*, Latin for Queen Elizabeth.

Er erbium (chemical element).

ERA Education Reform Act; Eritrean Relief Association; European Renal Association; European Rifle Association (Luxembourg).

ERAD Eradication of Animal Diseases Board (Eire).

ERASMUS European Community Action Scheme for the Mobility of University Students.

ERBM extended-range ballistic missile.

ERC Earth Resources Centre.

ERES European Rare Earth and Actinide Society.

ERF European Rotorcraft Forum.

ERM exchange rate mechanism.

ERMA Ernest Read Music Association; European Resin Manufacturers' Association.

ERMCO European Ready Mixed Concrete Organization.

ERNIE Electronic Randon Number Indicator Equipment. A machine used to draw random winning numbers of premium bonds.

ERO Ethiopian Relief Organization.

EROM erasable read-only memory.

ERR Earth Resources Research.

ERRA European Recovery and Recycling Association (Belgium).

ERS Electoral Reform Society; Electric Railway Society; European Respiratory Society.

ERU English Rugby Union.

Es einsteinium (chemical element).

ESA Economic Science Association; Electrolysis Society of America; Environmentally Sensitive Area; Euratom Supply Agency; European Sightseeing and Tours Association; European Space Agency; European Spice Association.

ESAA English Schools Athletic Association.

ESAG Escalator Safety Action Group.

ESB English-Speaking Board; European Settlement Board; electrical stimulation of the brain.

ESC English Ski Council; Entomological Society of Canada; Ethiopi Solidarity Campaign; European Shippers' Council; Executive Secretaries Club.

ESCA East of Scotland College of Agriculture; English Schools Cricket Association; European Speech Communication Association; electronic spectroscopy for chemical analysis.

ESCB European System of Central Banks.

ESD European Society of Dacryology.

ESE Engineering Associate of the Society of Engineers (Incorporated); east- southeast.

ESF European Script Fund; European Social Fund; European Surfing Federation.

ESFA English Schools Football Association.

ESG Euphorbia Study Group; European Seal Group.

ESGA English Schools Gymnastics Association.

ESH European Society of Hypnosis.

ESI Ecological Studies Institute; electricity supply industry.

ESL English as a second language.

ESMG Electric Steel Makers' Guild.

ESN educationally subnormal.

ESOP employee share ownership plan.

ESOT European Society for Organ Transplantation.

ESP extrasensory perception; English for special purposes.

esp. *espressivo*, Italian 'expressive' (music).

ESPRIT European Strategic Programme of Research into Information Technology.

Esq. Esquire.

ESQA English Slate Quarries Association.

ESRA European Safety and Reliability Association; European Synthetic Rubber Association.

ESRC Economic and Social Research Council.

ESRO European Space Research Organization.

ESRS European Sleep Research Society.

ESS evolutionarily stable strategy.

ESSC European Society for Soil Conservation.

ESSE European Society for Surgery of Shoulder and Elbow.

Esso Standard Oil (from the initials SO).

est. estimate(d).

EST electric shock treatment.

ESTA European Security Transport Association; European String Teachers Association.

ESTEC European Space Technology Centre.

ESTOC European Smokeless Tobacco Council.

ESTRA English Speaking Tape Respondents Association.

ESU Endangered Species Unit; Energy Studies and Sustainable Technology Unit Scotland); English Speaking Union; European Showmen's Union.

esu electrostatic unit.

ESV earth satellite vehicle; emergency shutdown valve.

ESVA English Schools Volleyball Association.

ET extra-terrestrial; Employment Trainee; Employment Training; embryo transfer.

ETA Entertainment Trades' Alliance; Environment Teachrs' Association; Esperanto Teachers Association; European Tallying Association; European Tennis Association; European Truckowners Association; estimated time of arrival.

et al. *et alii*, Latin 'and others', used in bibliography.

ETB English Tourist Board.

etc. *et cetera*, Latin 'and the rest'.

ETD estimated time of departure.

ETF electronic transfer of funds.

ETFRN European Tropical Forest Research Network.

ETRA European Textile Rental Association.

ETSA English Table Soccer Association.

et seq. *et sequens*, Latin 'and the following'.

ETSMA European Tyre Stud Manufacturers Association.

ETTA English Table Tennis Association.

ETTU European Table Tennis Union.

ETU Electrical Trades Union.

ETUC European Trade Union Confederation.

EU Evangelical Union; European Union.

Eu europium (chemical element).

EURABIA European Coordinating Committee of Friendship Societies with the Arab World.

EURATOM European Atomic Energy Community.

EURING European Union for Bird Ringing.

EuroACE European Association for the Conservation of Energy.

EURORAD European Association of Manufacturers of Radiators.

EUROSAG European Salaried Architects Group.

EUVEPRO European Vegetable Protein Federation.

EUW European Union of Women.

EUWEP European Union of Wholesale Trade in Eggs, Egg-Products, Poultry and Game.

EV electronic volt; English version (of Bible).

eV electron-volt.

EVA Electric Vehicle Association of Great Britain; English Vineyards Association; English Volleyball Association; extravehicular activity (astronautics).

EVR electronic video recording and reproduction.

EW early warning; electronic warfare.

EWA European Welding Association.

EWAC Effluent and Water Advisory Committee; European Wheat Aneuploid Co- operative.

EWBA English Women's Bowling Association.

EWEA European Wind Energy Association.

EWF European Wax Federation; European Weightlifting Federation.

EWIA External Wall Insulation Association.

EWN Education Workers Network.

EWO European Women's Orchestra.

EWPCA European Water Pollution Control Association.

EWRS European Weed research Society. .

EWS English Westerners Society.

ex. aq. *ex aqua*, Latin 'from water'.

EXCO Express Coach Operators' Association (Eire).

ex lib. *ex libris*, Latin 'from the library of'.

ex. off. *ex officio*, Latin 'by virtue of office'.

ex p *ex parte*, Latin 'in the interests of one party' (legal terminology).

EXPS Exmoor Pony Society.

EYC European Young Conservatives.

EYE European Youth Exchange.

EYFA European Youth Forest Action.

EYHG European Young Homeless Group.

F

F Fahrenheit; Father; Fellow: Finance; fluorine (chemical element); farad; fathom.

f fathom; feet; female; filly; fine; *forte*, Italian 'loud' (music); formula; frequency; furlong.

FA Faculty of Actuaries; Families Anonymous; Family Allowance; Flora of Australia; Football Association; Freedom Association; field artillery.

FAA Federal Aviation Administrations; Film Artistes Association; Finnish Aerosol Association; Fleet Air Arm.

FAACE Fight Against Animal Cruelty in Europe.

FAB Farm Apprenticeship Board (Eire); Feline Advisory Board; Feminist Audio Books; Flour Advisory Board.

FABAC Fellow of the Association of Business and Administrative Computing.

FABE Fellow of the Association of Business Executives.

FAC Feminists Against Censorship; Food Aid Convention.

FACB Fellow of the Association of Certified Book-keepers.

FACE Fight Against Cuts in Education; International League of Folk Arts for Communication and Education.

FACP Fellow of the Association of Computer Professionals.

FACT Federation Against Copyright Theft; Food Additives Campaign Team.

FADO Fellow of the Association of Dispensing Opticians.

FAFPIC Forestry and Forest Products Industry Council.

FAFS Farm and Food Society.

FAG Friedreich's Ataxia Group.

FAIA Fellow of the Association of International Accountants.

FAIE Fellow of the British Association of Industrial Editors.

FAM Free and Accepted Masons.

FAMEM Federation of Associations of Mine Equipment Manufacturers.

FAMS Fellow of the Association of Medical Secretaries, Practice Administrators and Receptionists.

FAMW Federation of African Media Women.

f & a fore and aft.

f & f fixtures and fittings.

F & M foot and mouth.

F & T fire and theft.

FANY First Aid Nursing Yeomanry.

FAO Food and Agriculture Organization.

fao for the attention of.

FAPA Federation of Asian Pharmaceutical Associations.

FAQ frequently asked question.

FAS Federation of Astronomical Societies; Fellow of the Anthropological Society; foetal alcohol syndrome; Fellow of the Antiquarian Society; Fellow of the Society of Arts; Funding Agency for Schools.

f.a.s. free alongside ship.

FASL Farm Assured Scotch Livestock.

FASI Fellow of the Ambulance Service Institute.

FASI Fellow of the Architects and Surveyors Institute.

FASP Fellow of the Association of Sales Personnel.

FASS Federation of Associations of Specialists and Sub-contractors.

FASST Farming for Agriculturally Sustainable Systems in Tasmania; Friends of Aerospace Supporting Science and Technology.

FAST Federation Against Software Theft.

FAUNA Friends of Animals Under Abuse.

FAW Federation of Army Wives.

FAWC Farm Animal Welfare Council.

FB Faculty of Building; Federation of Bakers; Fenian Brotherhood; Free Baptist; fire brigade.

fb full back; freight bill.

FBA Farm Buildings Association; Federation of Bloodstock Agents; Federation of British Astrologers; Fellow of the British Academy; Freshwater Biological Association; Fur Breeders Association.

FBA Fellow of the British Academy; Fellow of the British Arts.

FBAA Fellow of the British Association of Accountants and Auditors.

FBAS Federation of British Aquatic Societies.

FBAE Fellow of the British Academy of Experts.

FBCM Federation of British Carpet Manufacturers.

FBCO Fellow of the British College of Ophthalmic Opticians.

FBCS Fellow of the British Computer Society.

FBDO Fellow of the Association of British Dispensing Opticians.

FBDO(Hons) Fellow of the Association of British Dispensing Opticians with Honours Diploma.

FBDO(Hons)CL Fellow of the Association of British Dispensing Opticians with Honours Diploma and Diploma in Contact Lens Fitting.

FBEI Fellow of the Institution of Body Engineers.

FBEng Fellow of the Association of Building Engineers.

FBG Federation of British Growers.

FBHA Fellow of the British Hypnotherapy Association.

FBHI Fellow of the British Horological Institute.

FBHS Fellow of the BritishHorse Society.

FBHTM Federation of British Hand Tool Manufacturers.

FBI Federal Bureau of Investigation (US); Federation of British Industries.

FBIBA Fellow of the British Insurance Brokers' Association.

FBID Fellow of the British Institute of Interior Design.

FBIE Fellow of the British Institute of Embalmers.

FBIM Fellow of the British Institute of Management.

FBIPP Fellow of the British Institute of Professional Photography.

FBIS Fellow of the British Interplanetary Society.

FBIST Fellow of the British Institute of Surgical Technologists.

FBM fleet ballistic missile.

FBMA Finnish Boat and Motor Association; Food and Beverage Managers Association.

FBOA Fellow of the British Optical Association.

FBPP Federation of British Plant Pathologists.

FBPSS Fellow of the British Psychological Society.

FBR fast-breeder reactor.

FBT Fellow of the Association of Beauty Teachers.

FBTO Federation of British Trawler Officers.

FBW fly by wire.

FC Fighter Command; Football Club; Forestry Commission; Free Church.

FCA Fellow of the Institute of Chartered Accountants; Fishing Clubs of Australia; Food Casings Association.

FCAM Fellow of the Communication Advertising and Marketing Education Foundation.

FCBSI Fellow of the Chartered Building Societies Institute.

FCCA Fellow of the Chartered Association of Certified Accountants.

FCDRC Family & Community Dispute Research Centre.

FCEA Fellow of the Association of Cost and Executive Accountants.

FCES Fellow of the Faculty of Executive Secretaries.

FCF Fellow of the Faculty of Community Finance; Footwear Components Federation.

FCFC Free Church Federal Council.

FCH Flower Council of Holland.

FCFI Fellow of the Clothing and Footwear Institute.

FCGI Fellow of the City and Guilds of London Institute.

FCHS Fellow of the Society of Chiropodists.

FCI Factors Chain International; Foreign and Commonwealth Institute; Fellow of the Institute of Commerce; Finance Corporation for Industry.

FCIA Fellow of the Corporation of Insurance Agents.

FCIArb Fellow of the Chartered Institute of Arbitrators.

FCIB Fellow of the Chartered Institute of Bankers.

FCIBS Fellow of the Chartered Institute of Bankers in Scotland.

FCIBSE Fellow of the Chartered Institution of Building Services Engineers.

FCII Fellow of the Chartered Insurance Institute.

FCILA Fellow of the Chartered Institute of Loss Adjusters.

FCIM Fellow of the Chartered Institute of Marketing.

FCIMA Fellow of the Chartered Institute of Management Accountants.

FCIOB Fellow of the Chartered Institute of Building.

FCIPS Fellow of the Chartered Institute of Purchasing and Supply.

FCIS Fellow of the Institute of Chartered Secretaries and Administrators.

FCIT Fellow of the Chartered Institute of Transport.

FCJ Faithful Companions of Jesus.

FCM Friends of Cathedral Music.

FCMA Fellow of the Institute of Cost and Management Accountants.

FCO Foreign and Commonwealth Office.

FCollP Ordinary Fellow of the College of Preceptors.

FCOphth Fellow of the College of Ophthalmology.

FCP Fellow of the College of Preceptors.

FCPM Fellow of the Confederation of Professional Management.

FCPWA Fellow of the Faculty of Community, Personal and Welfare Accounting.

FCS Federation of Conservative Students.

FCSA Fellow of the Institute of Chartered Secretaries and Administrators.

FCSD Fellow of the Chartered Society of Designers.

FCSP Fellow of the Chartered Society of Physiotherapy.

FCST Fellow of the College of Speech Therapists.

FCT Fellow of the Association of Corporate Treasurers.

FCYW Fellow of the Community and Youth Work Association.

FCTHCM Fellow of the Confederation of Tourism, Hotel and Catering Management.

FD *Fidei Defensor*, Latin 'Defender of the Faith'; Financial Director.

fd flight deck; focal distance; free delivery; free dispatch.

FDA First Division Association (union for senior civil servants); Food and Drugs Administration (US).

FDC first-day cover; *fleur de coin*, French 'excellent impression' (referring to coins in mint condition).

FDF Food and Drink Federation.

FDFU Federation of Documentary Film Units.

FDPA Furniture Design Protection Association.

FDR Franklin Delano Roosevelt (US President); *Freie Demokratische Republik*, German for Free Democratic Republic (formerly West Germany).

FDS Fellow in Dental Surgery.

FDSRCPSGlas Fellow in Dental Surgery of the Royal College of Physicians and Surgeons of Glasgow.

FDSRCSEd Fellow in Dental Surgery of the Royal College of Surgeons of Edinburgh.

FDSRCSEng Fellow in Dental Surgery of the Royal College of Surgeons in England.

FDTF Food, Drink and Tobacco Federation (Eire).

FE further education.

Fe *ferrum*, Latin 'iron' (chemical element).

FEC Fair Employment Commission (N. Ireland); Fluid Engineering Centre; Free Europe Committee.

fec. *fecit*, Latin 'he made' or 'she made'.

FEDA Further Education Development Association.

FEDC Federation of Engineering Design Consultants.

FECI Fellow of the Institute of Employment Consultants.

FEEM Federation of European Explosive Manufacturers.

FEFG Far East Fracture Group.

FEIS Fellow of the Educational Institute of Scotland.

FELASA Federation of European Laboratory Animal Science Associations.

FEMC Federation of Earth Moving Contractors.

FEPOW Far East Prisoners of War Association.

FES Federation of Engineering Societies; foil, épée and sabre (fencing); Fellow of the Entomological Society; Fellow of the Ethnological Society.

FET Future of Europe Trust; field-effect transistor.

FETA Federation of Environmental Trade Associations; Fire Extinguishing Trades Association.

FEU Further Education Unit.

FEW Freemen of England and Wales.

FF *Fianna Fáil*, Gaelic for Warriors of Ireland, an Irish political party; Feminist Forum.

ff *fortissimo*, Italian 'very loud' (music); *fecerunt*, Latin 'made it'; fixed focus; fully fashioned; fully furnished/fitted.

ff. folios; and the following, used in references and bibliography.

FFA Fellow of the Faculty of Actuaries; Fellow of the Institute of Financial Accountants; Future Farmers of America; South Pacific Forum Fisheries Agency.

FFARCSEng Fellow of the Faculty of Anaesthetists of the Royal College of Surgeons of England.

FFARCSIrel Fellow of the Faculty of Anaesthetists, Royal College of Surgeons in Ireland.

FFAS Fellow of the Faculty of Architects and Surveyors (Architects).

FFB Fellow of the Faculty of Bulding.

FFBA Fellow of the Faculty of Business Administrators.

FFCA Fellow of the Association of Financial Controllers and Administrators.

FFCC Farms For City Children.

FFCI Fellow of the Faculty of Commerce and Industry Ltd.

FFCS Fellow of the Faculty of Secretaries.

FFDO Fellow of the Faculty of Dispensing Opticians.

FFF Fish Friers' Federation.

fff *fortissimo*, Italian 'as loud as possible' (music).

FFHC Freedom from Hunger Campaign.

FFHS Federation of Famaily History Societies.

FFHom Fellow of the Faculty of Homoeopathy.

FFMA Flavour and Fragrance Manufacturers' Association (Japan).

FFP Forests for the People (Sri Lanka); Fund for Peace (USA).

FFPHM Fellow of the Faculty of Public Health Medicine,.

FFPHMIrel Fellow of the Faculty of Public Health Medicine, Royal College of Physicians of Ireland.

FFPS Fauna and Flora Preservation Society; Fellow of the Faculty of Physicians and Surgeons.

FFR Fellow of the Faculty of Radiologists.

FFRC Food Freezer Refrigeration Council.

FFRRCSIrel Fellow of the Faculty of Radiologists, Royal College of Surgeons in Ireland.

FFS Fellow of the Faculty of Architects and Surveyors (Surveyors); Farm & Food Society.

FFTA Finnish Foreign Trade Association.

FFTCom Fellow of the Faculty of Teachers in Commerce.

FFVIB Fresh Fruit and Veetable Information Bureau.

FFVMA Fire Fighting Vehicle Manufacturers Association.

FG *Fine Gael*, Gaelic for Tribe of the Gaels, an Irish politish party; Federal Government.

FGA Fellow of the Gemmological Association.

FGB Federation of Associations of Wholesale Dealers in Building Materials (Netherlands).

FGBI Federation of Soroptimist Clubs of Great Britain and Ireland.

FGC Flat Glass Council.

FGCL Fellow of the Guild of Cleaners and Launderers.

FGCM Field General Court Martial.

FGI Fellow of the Greek Institute.

FGO Fleet Gunnery Officer.

FGS Fellow of the Geological Society.

FGSM Fellow of the Guildhall School of Music and Drama.

FH fire hydrant.

f/h freehold; fly half; foghorn.

FHA Family Heart Association; Finance Houses Association; Future Homemakers of America.

FHB Farm Holiday Bureau.

FHC Food Hygiene Centre.

FHF Federation of Hardware Factors.

FHFS Fellow of the Council of Health Fitness and Sports Therapists.

FHFW Federation of High Frequency Welders.

FHG Fellow of the Institute of Heraldic and Genealogical Studies.

FHH foetal heart heard.

FHNH foetal heart not heard.

fhp friction horsepower.

FHR foetal heart rate; Federal House of Representatives.

FHS Fellow of the Heraldry Society.

FHSM Fellow of the Institute of Health Services Management.

FI Falkland Islands; Fiji Islands; Faeroe Islands.

FIA Fellow of the Institute of Actuaries; Fitness Industry Association; Friends of Israel Association; Fruit Importers Association.

FIAB Fellow of the International Association of Book-keepers.

FIAEA Fellow of the Institute of Automotive Engineer Assessors.

FIAgrE Fellow of the Institution of Agricultural Engineers.

FIAP Fellow of the Institution of Analysts and Programmers.

FIAT *Fabbrica Italiana Automobili Torino*, Italian for Italian Motor Works, Turin; Fellow of the Institute of Animal Technicians; Fellow of the Institute of Asphalt Technology; Forest Industries Association of Tasmania.

FIB Fellow of the Institute of British Foundrymen; Fellow of the Institute of Bankers.

FIBA Fellow of the Institution of Business Agents.

FIBC Fellow of the Institute of Building Control.

FIBCM Fellow of the Institute of British Carriage and Automobile Manufacturers.

FIBCO Fellow of the Institution of Building Control Officers'.

FIBiol Fellow of the Institute of Biology.

FIBP Fellow of the Institute of British Photographers.

FICA Forest Industries Campaign Association; Formula 1 Constructors Association.

FICE Fellow of the Institution of Civil Engineers.

FIChemE Fellow of the Institution of Chemical Engineers.

FIChor Fellow of the Benesh Institute of Choreology.

FICM Fellow of the Institute of Credit Management.

FICO Fellow of the Institute of Careers Officers.

FICorr Fellow of the Institute of Corrosion.

FICS Fellow of the Institute of Chartered Shipbrokers.

FICSA Federation of International Civil Servants' Associations.

FICW Fellow of the Institute of Clerks of Works of Great Britain Incorporated.

FID Falkland Island Dependencies; Field Intelligence Department; Fellow of the Institute of Directors.

FIDA Falkland Islands Development Agency; Federation of Industrial Development Association.

FIDASE Falkland Islands and Dependencies Aerial Survey Expedition.

FIDO Film Industry Defence Organisation; Forklift Independent Distributors Organisation; Frazer Island Defenders Organisation.

FIDTA Fellow of the International Dance Teachers' Association.

FIED Fellow of the Institution of Engineering Designers.

FIEE Fellow of the Institution of Electrical Engineers.

FIEIE Fellow of the Institution of Electrical and Electronics Incorporated Engineers.

FIELD Foundation for International Environmental Law and Development.

FIEM Fellow of the Institute of Executives and Managers.

FIEx Fellow of the Institute of Export.

FIExpE Fellow of the Institute of Explosives Engineers.

FiF Forward in Faith.

fi. fa. *fieri facias*, Latin 'see that it is done' (legal).

FIFA *Fédération Internationale de Football Association*, French for International Association Football Federation.

FIFF Fellow of the Institute of Freight Forwarders.

FIFireE Fellow of the Institution of Fire Engineers.

FIFO first in, first out.

FIFST Fellow of the Institute of Food Science and Technology.

FIGA Fretted Instrument Guild of America.

FIGasE Fellow of the Institution of Gas Engineers.

FIGD Fellow of the Institute of Grocery Distribution.

FIGeol Fellow of the Institution of Geologists.

FIH Fellow of the Institute of Housing.

FIHEC Fellow of the Institute of Home Economics Ltd.

FIHIE Fellow of the Institute of Highway Incorporated Engineers.

FIHT Fellow of the Institution of Highways and Transportation.

FIIM Fellow of the Institution of Industrial Managers.

FIIMR Fellow of the Institute of Investment Management and Research.

FIInfSc Fellow of the Institute of Information Scientists.

FIIRSM Fellow of the International Institute of Risk and Safety Management.

FIISE Fellow of the International Institute of Social Economics.

FIISec Fellow of the Institute of Industrial Security.

FIL Fellow of the Institute of Linguists.

FILAM Fellow of the Institute of Leisure and Amenity Management.

FILO first in, last out.

FIM Fellow of the Institute of Materials.

FIMA Fellow of the Institute of Mathematics and its Applications.

FIMBRA Financial Intermediaries, Managers and Brokers Regulatory Association.

FIManf Fellow of the Institute of Manufacturing.

FIMarE Fellow of the Institute of Marine Engineers.

FIMBM Fellow of the Institute of Maintenance and Building Management.

FIMBRA Financial Intermediaries, Managers and Brokers Regulatory Association.

FIMC Fellow of the Institute of Management Consultants.

FIMechE Fellow of the Institution of Mechanical Engineers.

FIMechIE Fellow of the Institution of Mechanical Incorporated Engineers.

FIMF Fellow of the Institute of Metal Finishing.

FIMgt Fellow of the Institute of Management.

FIMI Fellow of the Institute of the Motor Industry.

FIMinE Fellow of the Institution of Mining Engineers.

FIMIT Fellow of the Institute of Musical Instrument Technology.

FIMLS Fellow of the Institute of Medical Laboratory Sciences.

FIMatM Fellow of the Institute of Materials Management.

FIMM Fellow of the Institute of Massage and Movement; Fellow of the Institution of Mining and Metallurgy.

FIMS Fellow of the Institute of Management Specialists.

FIMunE Fellow of the Institution of Municipal Engineers.

FIN Food Irradiation Network.

fin. *ad finem*, Latin 'towards the end'.

FINNPAP Finnish Paper Mills' Association.

FInstAEA Fellow of the Institute of Automotive Engineer Assessors.

FInstAM Fellow of the Institute of Administrative Management.

FInstBA Fellow of the Institute of Business Administration.

FInstBB Fellow of the Institute of British Bakers.

FInstBCA Fellow of the Institute of Burial and Cremation Administration.

FInstBRM Fellow of the Institute of Baths and Recreation Management.

FInstD Fellow of the Institute of Directors.

FInstCh Fellow of the Institute of Chiropodists.

FInstE Fellow of the Institute of Energy.

FInstP Fellow of the Institute of Physics.

FInstMC Fellow of the Institute of Measurement and Control.

FIntMC Fellow of the International Management Centre.

FInstNDT Fellow of the British Institute of Non-Destructive Testing.

FInstP Fellow of the Institute of Physics.

FInstPet Fellow of the Institute of Petroleum.

FInstPkg Fellow of the Institute of Packaging.

FInstPM Fellow of the Institute of Professional Managers.

FInstPS Fellow of the Institute of Purchasing and Supply.

FInstR Fellow of the Institute of Refrigeration.

FInstRS Fellow of the Institute of Road Safety Officers.

FInstSMM Fellow of the Institute of Sales and Marketing Management.

FInstTA Fellow of the Institute of Transport Administration.

FInstWM Fellow of the Institute of Wastes Management.

FInstWM(Hon) Honorary Fellowship of the Institute of Wastes Management.

fio for information only.

FIOC Fellow of the Institute of Carpenters.

FIOFMS Fellow of the Institute of Financial and Management Studies.

FIOP Fellow of the Institute of Plumbing.

FIOP Fellow of the Institute of Printing.

FIOSH Fellow of the Institution of Occupational Safety and Health.

FIPA Fellow of the Institute of Practitioners in Advertising.

FIPC Fellow of the Institute of Production Control.

FIPHE Fellow of the Institution of Public Health Engineers.

FIPI Fellow of the Institute of Professional Investigators.

FIPlantE Fellow of the Institution of Plant Engineers.

FIPM Fellow of the Institute of Personnel Management.

FIPR Fellow of the Institute of Public Relations.

FIQ Fellow of the Institute of Quarrying.

FIQA Fellow of the Institute of Quality Assurance.

FIQS Fellow of the Institute of Quantity Surveyors.

FIR Fellow of the Institute of Population Registration; fuel indicator reading.

FIRA Furniture Industry Research Association.

FIRSE Fellow of the Institute of Railway Signal Engineers.

FIRSO Fellow of the Institute of Road Safety Officers.

FIRTE Fellow of the Institute of Road Transport Engineers.

FIS Fellow of the Institute of Statisticians; Family Income Supplement; Federation of Irish Societies.

fis flight information service.

FISA Federation of Insurance Staffs Associ-

ationsFellow of the Incorporated Secretaries Association.

FISC Foundation for International Scientific Coordination; Fund for International Student Cooperation.

FISCC Fruit Industry Sugar Concession Committee (Australia).

FISM Fellow of the Institute of Supervisory Management.

FISOB Fellow of the Incorporated Society of Organ Builders.

FIST Fellow of the Institute of Science Technology.

FISTD Fellow of the Imperial Society of Teachers of Dancing.

FIStructE Fellow of the Institution of Structural Engineers.

FISVA Fellow of the Incorporated Society of Valuers and Auctioneers.

FISW Fellow of the Institute of Social Welfare.

FIT Federation of International Traders.

FITC Foundry Industry Training Committee.

FITD Fellow of the Institute of Training and Development.

FITSA Fellow of the Institute of Trading Standards Administration.

FIWEM Fellow of the Institution of Water and Environmental Management.

FFI Fellow of the Institute of Journalists.

FKC Fellow of King's College, London.

FL Flight/Flag Lieutenant.

fl *falsa lectio*, Latin 'erroneous reading'.

fl. *floruit*, Latin 'he/she flourished'; florin (former unit of currency); floor; fluid.

FLA Fellow of the Library Association; Fiji Library Association; Film Laboratory Association; Finance and Leqsing Association; Free Lebanese Army; Future Large Aircraft (future EC 'plane project).

FLAC Free Legal Advice Centres (Eire).

FLAMES Fabrication Labour and Material Estimating Service.

FLBA Family Law Bar Association.

FLCM Fellow of the London College of Music.

FLCSP(Phys) Fellow of the London and Counties Society of Physiologists.

FLD Friends of the Lake District.

FLI Fellow of the Landscape Institute.

FLS Fellow of the Linnean Society; Folklore Society.

FLSPT Fellowship of the London School of Polymer Technology.

FM frequency modulation, as used in physics; Field Marshal.

Fm fermium (chemical element).

fm *fiat mistura*, Latin 'let a mixture be made'.

FMA Family Mediators Association; Fan Manufacturers' Association; Fellow of the Museums Association; Fertilizer Manufacturers' Association; Football Membership Authority.

FMB Federation of Master Builders.

FMBRA Flour Milling and Baking Research Association.

FMC Families of Murdered Children; Fatstock Marketing Corporation; Finnish Management Council.

FMD foot and mouth disease.

FMDIYR Federation of Multiple DIY Retailers.

FMDM Franciscan Missionaries of the Divine Motherhood.

FMDV foot and mouth disease virus.

FME Foundation for Management Education.

FMF Food Manufacturers Federation; Forest Management Foundation; foetal movements felt.

FMG Food Machinery Group.

FMO Fleet/Flight Medical Officer.

FMOB Federation of Master Organ Builders.

FMPA Fellow of the Master Photographers Association.

FMR Fellow of the Association of Health Care Information and Medical Records Officers; field maintenance request.

FMS Family Mediation Scotland; Fellow of the Institute of Management Services; Fellow of the Medical Society; flight management system.

FMSE Federation of Medium and Small Employers.

FMSPA Fish and Meat Spreadable Products Association.

FMT Federation of Merchant Tailors.

FMTA Farm Machinery and Tractor Trade Association of New South Wales.

FNAEA Fellow of the National Association of Estate Agents.

FNAEAHonoured Honoured Fellow of the National Association of Estate Agents.

FNCP Fellow of the National Council of Psychotherapists.

FNI Fellow of the Nautical Institute.

FNIMH Fellow of the National Institute of Medical Herbalists.

FNSSA Field Naturalists Society of South Australia.

FNO Fleet Navigation Officer.

FO Faculty of Ophthalmologists; Field Officer; Flag Officer; Flying Officer; Foreign Office (department of the British Government).

FOAA Flying Optometrists Association of America.

FOAL Friends of Animals League.

FOAS Friends of Afghanistan Society.

FOB Friends of Blue; faecal occult blood.

fob free on board.

FOBS fractional-orbit bombardment system.

FOC Father of the Chapel (union official).

foc free of charge.

FOE Friends of the Earth.

FOFA follow-on forces' attack.

FOH front of house (theatre).

FOI Freedom of Information.

FOIC Flag Officer in Charge.

FOP forward observation post.

FoR Fellowship of Reconciliation.

FORC Financial Options Research Centre.

FORDS Floating Ocean Research and Development Station.

FOREST Freedom Organization for the Right to Enjoy Smoking Tobacco.

FORTRAN Formula Translation (computing).

FORWARD Foundation for Women's Health Research and Development.

forz. *forzando*, Italian 'forcing' (music).

fos free on ship; free on station.

Fosdic film optical sensing device (computing).

FOSFA Federation of Oils, Seeds and Fats Associations.

fot free of tax.

FOWP Fertilisers from Organic Wastes Programme.

Fox Futures and Options Exchange.

FP freezing point.

FPA Family Planning Association; Film Production Association of Great Britain; Fire Protection Association; Flexible Packaging Association; Flowers and Plants Association; Free Pacific Association.

fp *forte piano*, Italian 'loud and then immediately soft' (music); *fiat pilula*, Latin 'let a pill be made'; *fiat potio*, Latin 'let a drink be made'; fine paper; fixed price; footpath; freezing point; frontispiece; fully paid.

FPAS Frank Patterson Appreciation Society.

FPB Forum of Private Business.

fpb fast patrol boat.

FPC Family Practitioner Committee; Flowers Publicity Council.

FPCS Farm Planning Computer Service.

FPD Forum of People with Disabilities (Eire).

FPFC Fair Play For Children.

FPIA Family Planning International Assistance.

fpm feet per minute.

FPMI Forest Pest Management Institute (Canada).

FPO field post office.

FPPTE Federation of Public Passenger Transport Employers.

FPRC Flying Personnel Research Committee.

FPRI Fellow of the Plastics and Rubber Institute.

FProfBTM Fellow of Professional Business and Technical Management.

FPS Federation of Petroleum Suppliers; Federation of Piling Specialists; Fell Pony Society; Free Painters and Sculptors.

FPSC Family Policy Studies Centre.

fps feet per second; frames per second (photography).

FPTP first past the post (voting system).

Fr francium (chemical element).

Fr. *frater*, Latin 'brother'; Father; France; Friar; Friday.

f.r. *folio recto*, Latin 'right-hand page'.

FRAD Fellow of the Royal Academy of Dancing.

FRAeS Fellow of the Royal Aeronautical Society.

FRAI Fellow of the Royal Anthropological Institute.

FRAM Fellow of the Royal Academy of Music.

FRAME Fund for the Replacement of Animals in Medical Experiments.

FRAS Fellow of the Royal Astronomical Society; Fellow of the Royal Asiatic Society.

FRB Federal Reserve Bank (US).

FRBS Fellow of the Royal Botanic Society; Fellow of the Royal Society of British Sculptors.

FRCA Fellow of the Royal College of Anaesthetists; Fellow of the Royal College of Art.

FRCAB Flat Roofing Contractors Advisory Board.

FRCC Fell and Rock Climbing Club.

FRCGP Fellow of the Royal College of General Practitioners.

FRCM Fellow of the Royal College of Music.

FRCO Fellow of the Royal College of Organists.

FRCO(CHM) Fellow of the Royal College of Organists (Choir-training Diploma).

FRCOG Fellow of the Royal College of Obstetricians and Gynaecologists.

FRCP Fellow of the Royal College of Physicians.

FRCPath Fellow of the Royal College of Pathologists.

FRCPEdin Fellow of the Royal College of Physicians of Edinburgh.

FRCPS Fellow of the Royal College of Physicians and Surgeons.

FRCPsych Fellow of the Royal College of Psychiatrists.

FRCR Fellow of the Royal College of Radiologists.

FRCS Fellow of the Royal College of Surgeons.

FRCSEd Fellow of the Royal College of Surgeons of Edinburgh.

FRCSEd(C/Th) Fellow of the Royal College

of Surgeons of Edinburgh, specialising in Cardiothoracic Surgery.

FRCSEd(Orth) Fellow of the Royal College of Surgeons of Edinburgh, specialising in Orthopaedic Surgery.

FRCSEd(SN) Fellow of the Royal College of Surgeons of Edinburgh, specialising in Surgical Neurology.

FRCSEng Fellow of the Royal College of Surgeons of England.

FRCSGlasg Fellow of the Royal College of Physicians and Surgeons of Glasgow.

FRCS(Irel) Fellow of the Royal College of Surgeons in Ireland.

FRCVS Fellow of the Royal College of Veterinary Surgeons.

FREconS Fellow of the Royal Economic Society.

FRED Fast Reactor Experiment, Dounreay.

FREGG Free Range Egg Association.

FRG Federal Republic of Germany.

FRGS Fellow of the Royal Geographical Society.

FRHB Federation of Registered House Builders.

FRHistS Fellow of the Royal Historical Society.

FRHS Fellow of the Royal Horticultural Society.

FRI Federation of Reclamation Industries; Flowers Research Institute (China).

FRIBA Fellow of the Royal Institute of British Architects.

FRICS Fellow of the Royal Institution of Chartered Surveyors.

FRIN Fellow of the Royal Institution of Navigation.

FRINA Fellow of the Royal Institution of Naval Architects.

FRIPHH Fellow of the Royal Institute of Public Health and Hygiene.

FRLSU Forum for Research into the Languages of Scotland and Ulster.

FRMedSoc Fellow of the Royal Medical Society.

FRMetS Fellow of the Royal Meteorological Society.

FRMS Fellow of the Royal Microscopical Society.

FRN Furniture Recycling Network.

FRNCM Fellow of the Royal Northern College of Music.

FRNS Fellow of the Royal Numismatic Society.

FRO Fire Research Organisation.

FRPharms Fellow of the Royal Pharmaceutical Society of Great Britain.

FRPS Fellow of the Royal Photographic Society.

FRS Fellow of the Royal Society; Federal Reserve System.

FRSA Fellow of the Royal Society of Arts.

FRSC Fellow of the Royal Society of Chemistry.

FRSCM Fellow of the Royal School of Church Music.

FRSE Fellow of the Royal Society of Edinburgh.

FRSH Fellow of the Royal Society of Health.

FRSL Ffestiniog Railway Society.

FRSM Fellow of the Royal Society of Medicine.

FRTPI Fellow of the Royal Town Planning Institute.

FRTRA Federation of Radio and Television Retailes Association.

FRU Free Representation Unit.

frust. *frustillatim*, Latin 'in small portions'.

FRVA Fellow of the Rating and Valuation Association.

FS Fabian Society; Faraday Society; Fertiliser society; Flight Sergeant; Fountain Society; Friendly Society; Free State; feasibility study.

FSA Fellow of the Society of Antiquaries; Football Supporters Association.

FSAA Fellow of the Society of Incorporated Accountants and Auditors.

FSAO Fellow of the Scottish Association of Opticians.

FSAPP Fellow of the Society of Advanced Psychotherapy Practitioners.

FSAS Family Squatting Advisory Service.

FSAW Federation of South African Women.

FSB Federation of Small Businesses.

FSBI Fisheries Society of the British Isles.

FSBP Fellow of the Society of Business Practitioners.

FSC Field Studies Council; Fiji Sugar Corporation; Forest School Camps; Forestry Stewardship Council.

FSBTH Fellow of the Society of Health and Beauty Therapists.

FSCA Fellow of the Institute of Company Accountants.

FSCT Fellow of the Society of Cardiological Technicians.

FSDC Fellow of the Society of Dyers and Colourists.

FSE Fellow of the Society of Engineers (Inc).

FSElec Fellow of the Society of Electroscience.

FSG Factoring Services Group; Fellow of the Society of Genealogists; Fortress Study Group.

FSGT Fellow of the Society of Glass Technology.

FSH follicle-stimulating hormone.

FSI International Society of Fire Service Instructors; Financial Services Industry Association (Eire).

FSIAD Fellow of the Society of Industrial Artists and Designers.

FSID Foundation for the Study of Infant Deaths.

FSK Frequency Shift Keying (computing).

FSL First Sea Lord; Folger Shakespeare Library.

FSMA Fellow of the Society of Sales Management Administrators Ltd.

FSMF Furniture Spring Makers Federation.

FSMGB Federation of Small Mines of Great Britain.

FSNNA Fellow of the Society of Nursery Nursing Administrators.

FSPG Fire Service Preservation Group.

FSPS Federation of Sailing and Powerboat Schools.

FSPYOA Farm Shop and Pick Your Won Association.

FSS Fellow of the Finnish Sauna Society; Fellow of the Royal Statistical Society.

FSSCH Fellow of the School of Surgical Chiropody.

FSSU Federated Superannuation Scheme for Universities.

FSTA Fellow of the Swimming Teachers' Association.

FSVA Fellow of the Incorporated Society of Valuers and Auctioneers.

FT Financial Times; full term (pregnancy).

ft *fiat*, Latin 'let there be made'; foot, feet (Imperial measure of distance equal to 30.48 cm); fort.

FTA Fair Trials Abroad; Flotation Tank Association; Freight Transport Association; Free Trade Area.

FTAT Furniture, Timber and Allied Trades Union.

FTA Index Financial Times Actuaries Share Index.

FTAM file transfer, access and management.

FTASI Financial Times Actuaries All-Share Index.

FTAT Fair Trials Abroad Trust; Furniture, Timber and Allied Trades Union.

FTB first-time buyer.

FTBD full-term, born dead.

FTC Feed the Children; Forestry Training Council.

FTCD Fellow of Trinity Collee, London.

FTCL Fellow of the Trinity College of Music, London.

FTF Fibre Trade Federation.

fth. *or* **fthm.** fathom.

FTI Fellow of the Textile Institute.

FT Index Financial Times Ordinary Share Index.

FT-IR Fourier-transform infra-red.

FTIT Fellow of the Institute of Taxation.

FTND full-term, normal delivery.

FT-NMR Fourier-transform nuclear magnetic resonance.

FT Ord. Financial Times Industrial Ordinary Share Index.

FTP File Transfer Protocol (computing).

FTSC Fellow in the Technology of Surface Coatings.

FT-SE 100 Financial Times Stock Exchange 100-Share Index.

FTSKO Federation of Textile Societies and Kindred Organisations.

FTT failure to thrive.

FTWN Farmers' Third World Network.

FTZ Free Trade Zone.

FUGB Federation of Ukrainians in Great Britain.

FULS Federation of Ulster Local Studies.

FUMIST Fellow of the University of Manchester Institute of Science and Technology.

FUN Friends United Network.

FUO fever of uncertain origin.

FURC Foundation for Underdeveloped Regions in China.

f.v. *folio verso*, Latin 'left-hand page'.

FVE Federation of Veterinarians of the EEC.

FVPC Federation of Visual Planning Consultants.

FVPG Film and Video Press Group.

FVPRA Fruit and Vegetable Preservation Research Association.

FWA Family Welfare Association; Free Wales Army.

FWAG Farming and Wildlife Advisory Group.

FWB Free-Will Baptists.

fwd. four/front-wheel drive.

FWeldI Fellow of the Welding Institute.

fwh flexible working hours.

FWN Farmers' World Network.

FWT Farming and Wildlife Trust.

fwt fair wear and tear.

FWVFA Federation of World Volunteer Firefighters Associations.

FWWCP Federation of Worker Writers and Community Publishers.

fya first-year allowance.

FYC Family & Youth Concern.

FYD Fellowship of the Youth Development Association.

FYDA Associate Fellowship of the Youth Development Association.

FYF Find Your Feet.

fyi for your information.

FX sound effects; special effects.

Fx fracture.

fz *forzando*, Italian 'to be strongly accentuated' (music).

FZS Fellow of the Zoological Society.

FZY Federation of Zionist Youth.

G

G Great; Gulf; £1000 (slang); German; gravitational constant (physics).

g gram; gallon; goal; good; guinea (former UK unit of currency); gravitational acceleration (physics).

G3 Group of Three (most powerful Western economies).

G5 Group of Five (nations taking part in exchange-rate stabilisation).

G7 Group of Seven (the leading industrialised nations).

G10 Group of Ten (the nations that are lending money to the IMF).

G24 Group of Twenty-Four (the industrialised nations).

G77 Group of Seventy-Seven (developing nations).

GA Galvanizers Association; Gamblers Anonymous; Gemmological Association of Great Britain; General Agent; General Assembly; Giftware Association; Green Alliance; Greening Australia; gestational age.

Ga gallium (chemical element).

g/a ground to air.

GAA Gaelic Athletic Association; Greenhouse Action Australia.

GAFTA Grain and Free Trade Association.

GAI General Assembly of International Sports Federations; Guild of Architectural Ironmongers.

GALHA Gay and Lesbian Humanist Association.

GAN Green Academic Network.

G & AE general and administrative expenses.

G & O gas and oxygen.

G & SS Gilbert & Sullivan Society.

g and t gin and tonic.

GAP Girls Alone Project; great American public; gross agricultural product.

GAS Glasgow Archaeological Society.

GASCO General Aviation Safety Committee.

GASI Graduate Member of the Ambulance Service Institute.

GASP Group Against Smog Pollution.

GATB General Aptitude Test Battery.

GATCO Guild of Air Traffic Control Officers.

GATT General Agreement on Tariffs and Trade.

GAUFCC General Assembly of Unitarian and Free Christian Churches.

GAV gross annual value.

GAVA Guild of Aviation Artists.

GAW Gay Authors Workshop; Global Atmosphere Watch.

GB Girls' Brigade; Gas Board; Great Britain; gunboat.

gb gall bladder.

GBA Governing Bodies Association; Alderney.

GBC Gibraltar Broadcasting Corporation.

GBE Dame Grand Cross of the British Empire; Knight Grand Cross of the British Empire.

gbe gilt-bevelled edge.

GBG Guernsey.

GBH grievous bodily harm.

GBJ Jersey.

GBM Isle of Man.

GBMPC Great Britain Map Postcard Club.

GBNE Guild of British Newspaper Editors.

gbo goods in bad order.

GBP Gay Bereavement Project; great British Public.

GBRMPA Great Barrier Reef Marine Park Authority.

GBSM Graduate of the Birmingham School of Music.

GBZ Gibraltar.

GC Gas Council; George Cross; Grand Cross; Golf Club; gas chromatography.

gc going concern; gigacycle; good condition.

GCA Garden Centre Association; Global Commission on AIDS; Grains Council of Australia; ground controlled approach (aircraft landing system).

GCB Dame Grand Cross of the Order of the Bath; Greyhound Consultative Council; Guernsey Cattle Breeders' Association; Knight Grand Cross of the Order of the Bath.

GCBS General Council of British Shipping.

GCC Gas Consumers' Council; Game Conservancy Council; Gulf Co-operation Council.

GCCA Greeting Card and Calendar Association.

GCCF Governing Council of the Cat Fancy.

GCD greatest common divisor.

GCE General Certificate of Education, an examination formerly taken at Ordinary and Advanced levels ('O' and 'A' levels) but latterly replaced by the GCSE.

GCF greatest common factor.

GCFR gas-cooled fast reactor.

GCH Knight Grand Cross of Hanover; gas central heating.

GCHQ Government Communications Headquarters.

GCI ground-controlled interception.

GCIC Gifed Children's Information Centre.

GCL ground-controlled landing.

GCLH Grand Cross of the Legion of Honour.

GCM General Court-Martial; greatest common measure/multiple.

GCMG Dame Grand Cross of the Order of St Michael and St George; Knight Grand Cross of the Order of St Michael and St George.

GCMS gas-chromatography mass spectroscopy.

GCR gas-cooled reactor; ground controlled radar.

GCRN General Council and Register of Naturopaths.

GCRO General Council and Register of Osteopaths.

GCSE General Certificate of Secondary Education, an examination in the UK for 16 year old children which replaced the CSE and GCE 'O' level.

GCVO Dame Grand Cross of the Royal Victorian Order; Knight Grand Cross of the Royal Victorian Order.

GCWT Golf Course Wildlife Trust.

GD Grand Duchess; Grand Duke; Grand Duchy.

Gd gadolinium (chemical element).

GDBA Guide Dogs for the Blind Association.

GDC General Dental Council.

GDP gross domestic product.

GDPA General Dental Practitioners' Association.

GDR German Democratic Republic (the former East Germany).

gdt graphic display terminal.

gdu graphic display unit.

GE gastroenterology.

Ge germanium (chemical element).

ge gilt edges.

GEBCO General Bathymetric Chart of the Oceans.

GEC General Electric Company.

GED general educational development.

GEF Global Environment Facility.

Gemcos Generalized Message Control System.

GEMS Global Environment Monitoring System.

GEO geostationary earth orbit.

GEON gyro-erected optical navigation.

Georef. World Geographic Reference System.

GEOS geodetic orbiting satellite.

GEP Grasslands Ecology Program.

Gerbil Great Education Reform Bill (GB 1988).

GES Global Epidemiological Surveillance and Health Situation.

GESM Group for Educational Services in Museums.

Gestapo *Geheime Staatspolizei*, German for State Secret Police (in Nazi Germany and her conquests during 1933–45).

GET gastric emptying time.

GeV giga-electronvolt.

GEW gram equivalent weight.

GF General Foods; growth factor.

gf glass fibre; girlfriend.

GFCH gas-fired central heating.

GFG Good Food Guide.

GFOF Geared Futures and Options Funds.

GFR German Federal Republic.

GFS Girls' Friendly Society.

GFSA Gold Fields of South Africa.

GG Girl Guides; Grenadier Guards; Governor General.

gg gas generator; gamma globulin.

GGA Good Gardeners Association; Guernsey Growers Association.

GGE Guild of Glass Engravers.

GGGS Golden Guernsey Goat Society.

GGSM Graduate of Guildhall School of Music.

GH General Hospital; Guild of Hairdressers; growth hormone.

GHI Good Housekeeping Institute.

GHMS Graduate in Homoeopathic Medicine and Surgery.

Ghost global horizontal sounding technique.

GHQ general headquarters.

GHRF growth hormone releasing factor.

GHS Garden History Society; Girls' High School.

Ghz gigahertz.

GI Gideon's International; Government Issue (US slang for ordinary servicemen); gastrointestinal.

gi galvanised iron.

GIB Gibraltar Information Bureau.

GIBCM Graduate of the Institute of British Carriage and Automobile Manufacturers.

GIBiol Graduate of the institute of Biology.

GIE Graduate of the Institute of Engineers.

GIF Garden Industry Federation; growth-hormone inhibiting factor.

GIFT gamete intra-Fallopian transfer.

GIMechE Graduate of the Institution of Mechanical Engineers.

GIMI Graduate of the Institute of the Motor Industry.

Gino graphical input/output.

GInstP Graduate of the Institute of Physics.

GInstT Graduate of the Institute of Transport.

GIntMC Graduate of the International Management Centre.

GINucE Graduate of the Institution of Nuclear Engineers.

GIPME Global Investigation of Pollution in the Marine Environment.

GISS Goddard Institute for Space Studies.

GITB Gas Industry Training Board.

gj gigajoule.

gk goalkeeper.

GKA Garter King of Arms.

GKN Guest, Keen and Nettlefold.

GL *grande luxe*, French 'great luxury'; ground level.

Gl. *Gloria Patri*, Latin 'glory be to the Father'.

g/l grams per litre.

GLAAS Greater London Association of Alcohol Services.

glam greying, leisured, affluent, married.

GLB Girls' Life Brigade.

GLC Greater London Council; gas-liquid chromatography.

GLCM Graduate Diploma of the London College of Music; ground-launched cruise missile.

GLIAS Greater London Industrial Archaeological Society.

Globecom Global Commnications System.

GM Geiger-Müller counter; George Medal; Grand Master; general manager; General Motors; guided missile.

gm² grams per square metre.

GMA Glasgow Mathematical Association; Gospel Music Association; Grocery Manufacturers of Australia.

GMAG Genetic Manipulation Advisory Group.

GMB General, Municipal and Boilermakers Union; Grand Master of the Order of the Bath.

gmb good merchantable brand.

GMBE Grand Master of the Order of the British Empire.

GmbH *Gesellschaft mit beschränkter Haftung*, German 'limited liability company'.

GMC General Medical Council; General Management Committee.

GMFA Gay Men Fighting AIDS.

GMO genetically modified organism.

gmq good merchantable quality.

GMR ground-mapping radar.

GMS Grant-Maintained Status.

GMSC General Medical Services Committee.

GMST Grant-Maintained Schools Trust; Greenwich Mean Sidereal Time.

GMT Greenwich Mean Time.

GMusRNCM Graduate in Music of the Royal Northern College of Music, (Hons).

GMW gram-molecular weight.

GMWU General and Municipal Workers Union.

GNAS Grand National Archery Society.

GNC General Nursing Council.

GNP gross national product.

GNRS Great Northern Railway Society.

GNSM Graduate of the Northern School of Music.

GNTC Girls Nautical Training Corps.

GNVQ General National Vocational Qualification.

GO Group Officer; general office; general order.

goa gone on arrival.

gob good ordinary brand.

GOC General Officer Commanding.

GOC-in-C General Officer Commanding-in-Chief.

GOCO Government-owned, contractor-operated.

GODA Guild of Drama Adjudicators.

GOE General Ordination Examination.

GOETO Grand Order of European Tour Operators.

GOFTA Golf Facilities Trades Association.

GOM Grand Old Man.

GOONS Guild of One-Name Studies.

GP General Practitioner; Gallup Poll; *Gloria Patri*, Latin 'glory to the Father'; Government Property; Grand Prix; graduated pension; gross profit; general paresis (medical).

GPA Garden Products Association; Garlic Processors Association; Global Programme of Action; Goat Producers Association.

GPALS Global Protection against Limited Strikes.

GPC General Purposes Committee.

gpc good physical condition.

gpd gallons per day.

GPDST Girls' Public Day School Trust.

gph gallons per hour.

GPh Graduate in Pharmacy.

GPHI Guild of Public Health Inspectors.

GPI general paralysis of the insane.

gpm gallons per minute.

GPMU Graphical, Paper and Media Union.

GPO General Post Office.

GPP Guild of Pastoral Psychology.

GPS Graduated Pension Scheme; global positioning system.

gps gallons per second.

GPWM Guild for the Promotion of Welsh Music.

GQ general quarters.

GR *Georgius Rex*, Latin for King George; Green Realignment; *Gulielmus Rex*, Latin for King William; gamma ray.

GRA Greyhound Racing Association.

GRACE group routeing and charging equipment.

GradBHI Graduate of the British Horological Institute.

GradIAE Graduate of the Institution of Automobile Engineers.

GradIAP Graduate of the Institution of Analysts and Programmers.

GradIElecIE Graduate of the Institution of Electrical and Electronics Incorporated Engineers.

GradISec Graduate of the Institute of Industrial Security.

GradIM Graduate of the Institute of Metals.

GradIMA Graduate Member of the Institute of Mathematics and its Applications.

GradIManf Graduate Member of the Institute of Manufacturing.

GradIMechIE Graduate of the Institution of Mechanical Incorporated Engineers.

GradIMF Graduate of the Institute of Metal Finishing.

GradIMS Graduate of the Institute of Management Specialists.

GradInstBE Graduate Member of the Institute of British Engineers.

GradInstNDT Graduate of the British Institute of Non-Destructive Testing.

GradInstP Graduate of the Institute of Physics.

GradInstPS Graduate of the Institute of Purchasing and Supply.

GradIOP Graduate of the Institute of Printing.

GradIPM Graduate of the Institute of Personnel Management.

GradIS Graduate Member of the Institute of Statisticians.

GradISCA Graduate of the Institute of Chartered Secretaries and Administrators.

GradPRI Graduate of the Plastics and Rubber Institute.

GradRSC Graduate of the Royal Society of Chemistry.

GradSE Graduate of the Society of Engineers.

GradStat Graduate Statistician.

GraduateIEIE Graduate of the Institution of Electrical and Electronics Incorporated Engineers.

GradWeldI Graduate of the Welding Institute.

GRAS generally recognised as safe.

GRB Gas Research Board; gamma-ray burst.

GRBI Gardeners' Royal Benevolent Institution.

GRBS Gardeners' Royal Benevolent Society.

GRCM Graduate of the Royal College of Music.

GRDF Gulf Rapid Deployment Force.

GRE Guardian Royal Exchange Assurance PLC.

GRI *Georgius Rex Imperator*, Latin 'George, King and Emperor'.

GRIC Graduate Membership of the Royal Institute of Chemistry.

GRID Global Resource Information Database; gay-related immunodeficiency.

GRN goods received note.

GRNCM Graduate of the Royal Northern College of Music.

GRO General Register Office; Greenwich Royal Observatory.

GROBDM General Register Office of Briths, Deaths and Marriages.

GRP glass-reinforced plastic (a plastic material that is made stronger by the addition of glass fibres, often incorrectly known as fibreglass).

GRSC Graduate of the Royal Society of Chemistry.

GRSM Graduate of the Royal Schools of Music.

GRSM(Hons) Graduate of the Royal Schools of Music.

GRT gross registered tonnage.

gry gross redemption yield.

GS General Staff/Secretary; Genetical Society; Grammar School.

gs ground speed.

GSA Girls' School Association.

GSC gas-solid chromatography.

GSD General Supply Depot; Law Society Group for Solicitors with Disabilities.

GSG Guild of St Gabriel.

GSGB Geological Survey of Great Britain; Golf Society of Great Britain.

GSM General Sales Manager; Guildhall School of Music and Drama.

gsm grams per square metre; good sound merchantable.

GSMA Graduate of the Society of Sales Management Administrators Ltd.

GSNNA Graduate of the Society of Nursery Nursing Administrators.

GSO General Staff Officer.

GSOH good sense of humour.

GSP glass fibre-strengthened polyester.

GSR galvanic skin response.

GSS Government Statistical Service; global surveillance system; geostationary satellite.

GST Greenwich Sidereal Time.

GSW gunshot wound.

GT gas turbine; gas-tight; gran turismo (Grand Tourer); gross tonnage.

gt. *gutta*, Latin 'a drop'.

GTA Gibraltar Teachers Association; Glass Textile Association; Gun Trade Association; gas-tungsten arc.

GTC Government Training Centre; General Teaching Council.

GTCL Graduate of Trinity College of Music, London.

GTH gonadotrophic hormone.

GTI Gran Turismo (Grand Tourer), Injection.

GTO *Gran Turismo Omologato*, Italian 'certified Gran Turismo' (Grand Tourer).

GTR *Gran Turismo* (Grand Tourer), Racing.

GTS gas-turbine ship; *Gran Turismo* (Grand Tourer), Special/Sport; Greenwich Time Signal.

GU genito-urinary; gastric ulcer.

GUI Golfing Union of Ireland.

gui graphics user interface.

gulag *Glavnoye Upravleniye Lagerei*, Russian 'Principal Administrative Camp' (a Soviet labour camp).

GUM genito-urinary medicine; *Gosudarstvenni Universalni Magazin*, Russian 'Universal State Store'.

GUS Great Universal Stores.

GV *grande vitesse*, French 'high speed'.

gv gravimetric volume.

GVA Gin and Vodka Association of GB.

GVC Girls Venture Corps.

GVH graft-versus-host.

GVHD graft-versus-host disease.

GVS Goat Veterinary Society.

GVW gross vehicle weight.

GW gigawatt; gross weight.

GWH gigawatt hour.

GWIS German Wine Information Service.

GWP gross world product.

GWR Great Western Railway.

GWS Great Western Society.

GWUCC Garment Workers Union Consultative Committee.

H

H hydrogen (chemical element) hard (pencils); hearts (cards); henry (physics); hospital; heroin.

h hand; hecto-; hot; husband; hour.

HA Health Authority; Herpes Association; Historical Association; Hockey Association; high altitude.

Ha hahnium (chemical element).

ha hectare; hardy annual; heir apparent; *hoc anno*, Latin 'in this year'.

HAA Historic Aircraft Association; Homeless Action and Accommodation Limited; hepatitis-associated antigen.

HAB high altitude bombing.

hab. corp. *habeas corpus*, Latin 'may you have the body'.

HAC Honourable Artillery Company; Horticultural Advisory Council for England and Wales; high-alumina cement.

HACSG Hyper Active Children's Support Group.

HACT Housing Association Charitable Trust.

HAD high altitude deterioration.

HADC Helen Arkell Dyslexic Centre.

HAE Hire Association Europe.

HAFRA British Hat and Allied Feltmakers Research Association.

HAHP Health Action for Homeless People.

HAI Health Action International; Helicopter Association International; Help Age International; Historical Association of Ireland; hospital-acquired infection.

HAIA Hearing Aid Industry Association.

HAIL Hague Academy of International Law.

HALOW Help and Advice Line for Offenders' Wives.

HANA Halibut Association of North America.

h & c hot and cold (water).

h & f heated and filtered (swimming pool).

h & j hyphenation and justification.

h & t hardened and tempered; hospitalisation and treatment.

H & W Harland and Wolff; Hereford & Worcester.

HAPA Handicapped Adventure Playground Association.

HAS Headmasters' Association of Scotland Health Advisory Service.

HASAWA Health and Safety at Work Act.

HASTE Helicopter Ambulance Service to Emergencies.

HAT Housing Association Trust; History of Advertising Trust; housing action trust.

HATIS Hide and Allied Trades Improvement Society.

HATRA Hosiery and Allied Trades Research Association.

HAV hepatitis A virus.

HB hard black (pencil); housing benefit.

Hb haemoglobin.

hb half-back; handbook; hardbook; hardy biennial; homing beacon; human being.

HBA Herring Buyers Association.

HbA adult haemoglobin.

HBAB hepatitis B antibody.

HBAg hepatitis B antigen.

HBC Historic Buildings Council; Hudson's Bay Comapny.

HBD has been drinking.

HBEF Health and Beauty Employers Federation.

HBES Human Behaviour and Evolution Society.

HBF House-Builders Federation; hepatic blood flow.

HbF foetal haemoglobin.

HBJ Harcourt Brace Jovanovich.

HBLB Horse Racing Betting Levy Board.

HBLV human B-lymphotropic virus.

HBM Her/His Britannic Majesty.

HBMC Historic Buildings and Monuments Commission for England.

HBO hyperbaric oxygen.

H-bomb hydroen bomb.

HBP high blood pressure.

HBPF High Blood Pressure Foundation.

HBS Harvard Business School; Havergal Brian Society; Hawaiian Botanical Society; Historic Brass Society.

HbS sickle-cell haemoglobin.

HBSA Historical Breechloading Smallarms Association.

HBV hepatitis B virus.

HBWB Home Beer and Winemaking Bureau.

HBWTA Home Brerwing and Winemaking Trade Association.

HC Hairdressing Council; Headmasters Conference; Heralds' College; High Commission/er; High Court; Higher Certificate; Hockey Club; Holy Communion; House of Commons; highly commended; housing corporation.

HCA Hospital Caterers Association; Hypertrophic Cardiomyopathy Association.

HCAAS Homeless Children's Aid and Adoption Society.

HCC Hospital Chaplaincies Council; Housing Consultative Council for England; Hovermail Collectors' Club.

hcd high current density.

HC Deb. House of Commons Debates.

hce human-caused error.

HCEC Hospital Committee of the European Community.

HCF Honorary Chaplain to the Forces; high carbohydrate and fibre; highest common factor.

HCFC hydrochlorofluorocarbon.

HCG Hoverclub of Great Britain; human chorionic gonadotrophin.

HCGB Helicopter Club of Great Britain; Hoverclub of Great Britain.

HCH hexachlorocyclohexane.

HCHD Diploma in Higher Chiropodial Theory of the Institute of Chiropodists.

HCI Hotel and Catering Institute; human-computer interaction/interface.

HCIL Hague Conference on International Law.

HCIMA Hotel Catering and Institutional Management Association.

HCITB Hotel and Catering Industry Training Board.

HCJ High Court of Justice; High Court Judge.

HCJA High Court Journalists' Association.

HCO Higher Clerical Officer.

HCOPIL The Hague Conference on Private International Law.

HCP Healthy Cities Project.

HCPT Handicapped Childrens Pilgrimage Trust; Historic Churches Preservation Trust.

HCM Her/His Catholic Majesty.

HCRC Hotel and Catering Research Centre.

HCT Herpetological Conservation Trust.

HCTA Health Careers Tutors' Association.

HCVC Historic Commercial Vehicle Club.

HCVD hypertensive cardiovascular disease.

HD Higher Diploma; Hodgkin's Disease; heavy duty; high density.

hd *hora decubitus*, Latin 'at bedtime'.

HDA Hodgkin's Disease Association; Holistic Dental Association; Horticultural Dealers Association; Hospital Doctors' Association.

HDATZ high-density air traffic zone.

HDC high-dose chemotherapy.

HDCR(R) *or* **(T)** Higher award in Radiodiagnosis *or* Radiotherapy, College of Radiographers.

HDD Higher Dental Diploma.

HDK husbands don't know.

HDL hardware description language; high-density lipoprotein.

HDLC high-density lipoprotein cholesterol; high-level data link control.

HDN haemolytic disease of the newborn.

HDR high dose rate.

HDRA Henry Doubleday Research Association.

HDS Historical Diving Society.

HDTV high-definition television.

HDU haemodialysis unit.

HDV heavy-duty vehicle.

HE His Eminence; His Excellency; higher education; high explosive.

He helium (chemical element).

HEA Hairdressing Employers Association; Health Education Authority; Heating Engineering Association; Higher Education Authority (Eire); Horticultural Education Association.

HEBA Home Extension Building Association.

HEBS Health Education Board for Scotland.

HEC Health Education Council.

HECTOR heated experimental carbon thermal oscillator reactor.

HEF high-energy fuel.

HEFA Human Embryo and Fertilization Authority.

HEFC Higher Education Funding Council.

HEH Her/His Exalted Highness.

HEI Health Effects Institute.

hei high-explosive incendiary.

HEIC Honourable East India Company.

HEIST Higher Education Information Services Trust.

HeLa Helen Lake (tumour cell line).

HELIOS Handicapped People in Europe Living Independently in Open Society.

HELP Holiday Endeavour for Lone Parents; helicopter electronic landing path.

HEO Higher Executive Officer.

HEOS high-ecliptic-inclined-orbit satellite.

Herald Highly-Enriched Reactor, Aldermaston.

HERE Hotel Employees and Restaurant Employees International Union.

Hereford. *Herefordensis*, Latin 'of Hereford'.

HERI Higher Education Research Institute.

HERU Higher Education Research Unit.

HET Heritage Education Trust; Holocaust Education Trust.

HETMA Heavy Edge Tool Manufacturers' Association.

HEU highly-enriched uranium.

Hex hexadecimal notation.

HF high frequency, used in physics; hard firm (pencils).

Hf hafnium (chemical element).

HFC high frequency current; hydrofluorcarbon.

HFDA High Fidelity Dealers Association.

HFFF Hungarian Freedom Fighters Federation.

HFH Home from Hospital.

hfm hold for money.

HFRA Honorary Fellow of the Royal Academy.

HFRO Hill Farming Research Organization.

HFT Home Farm Trust.

HFVOA Hull Fishing Vessel Owners' Association.

HFW Housing for Women.

HG Her/His Grace; Home Guards; High German; Horse Guards.

Hg mercury (chemical element).

HGA Hop Growers of America.

HGCA Home Grown Cereals Authority.

HGDH Her/His Grand Ducal Highness.

HGG human gamma-globulin.

HGH human growth hormone.

HGHSC Home Grown Herbage Seeds Committee.

HGTAC Home Grown Timber Advisory Committee.

HGTMC Home Grown Timber Marketing Corporation.

HGV heavy goods vehicle.

HH Her/His Highness; His Holiness; His/Her Honour; double hard (pencils).

HHA Historic Houses Association.

hha half-hardy annual.

hhb half-hardy biennial.

HHH Hash House Harriers International; triple hard (pencil).

HHIA Headway Head Injuries Association.

HHLA Handkerchief & Household Linens Association.

HHMT Helene Harris Memorial Trust.

hhp half-hardy perennial.

HHS Historical Harp Society.

HHW household hazardous waste.

HI Hawaiian Islands; hearing impaired; *hic iacet*, Latin 'here lies'.

HIA Housing Improvement Association.

hia hold in abeyance.

HIB Herring Industry Board.

HICAT high-altitude clear air turbulence.

HIDB Highlands and Islands Development Board.

HIE Highlands and Islands Enterprise.

HIH Her/His Imperial Highness.

HIP Homeless Information Project.

HIPA Honey Importers and Packers Association.

HIS Hospital Infection Society; Hunters' Improvement and National Light Horse Breeding Society; *hic iacet sepultus*, Latin 'here lies buried'.

HISHA Highlands and Islands Sheep Health Association.

HITA Hamper Industry Trade Association.

HIT Scotland Hospitality Industry Trust Scotland.

HIV human immunodeficiency virus.

HJ *hic jacet*, Latin 'here lies'.

HJS hic jacet sepultus, Latin 'here lies buried'.

HJSC Hospital Junior Staff Council (BMA).

HK House of Keys.

HKCW Hong Kong Council of Women.

HKI Helen Keller International.

HKJSMA Hong Kong Jade and Stone Manufacturers Association.

HL House of Lords; Honours List.

hl hectolitre.

HLA human lymphocyte antigen.

HLCas House of Lords Cases.

HLDeb House of Lords Debates.

HLE high-level exposure.

HLG Historic Landscapes Group.

HLI Highland Light Infantry.

HLL high-level language.

HLNW high-level nuclear waste.

HLPR Howard League for Penal Reform.

HLRW high-level radioactive waste.

HLS Harvard Law School.

HM Her/His Majesty; Her/His Majesty's; harbourmaster; hazardous material; headmaster/headmistress; heavy metal (music).

hm hallmark; hectometre.

HMA Head Masters' Association; Hop Merchants Association; high-memory area.

HMAC Her/His Majesty's Customs; Hospital Management Committee; Royal Commission on Historical Manuscripts.

HMC Royal Commission on Historical Manuscripts.

HMCA Hospital and Medical Care Association.

HMCG Her/His Majesty's Coast Guard.

HMCIC Her/His Majesty's Chef Inspector of Constabulary.

HMCIF Her/His Majesty's Chief Inspector of Factories.

HMCSC Her/His Majesty's Civil Service Commissioners.

HMD Her/His Majesty's Destroyer.

HMF Her/His Majesty's Forces.

HMFI Her/His Majesty's Factory Inspectorate.

HMG Her/His Majesty's Government.

HMHS Her/His Majesty's Hospital Ship.

HMI Her/His Majesty's Inspectorate (of schools); human-machine interface.

HMIC Her/His Majesty's Inspectorate of Constabulary.

HMIP Her/His Majesty's Inspectorate of Pollution.

HMIT Her/His Majesty's Inspector of Taxes.

HMLR Her/His Majesty's Land Registry.

HMML Her/His Majesty's Motor Launch.

HMMS Her/His Majesty's minesweeper.

HMOCS Her/His Majesty's Overseas Civil Service.

HMP Her/His Majesty's Prison; *hoc monumentum posuit*, Latin 'erected this monument'.

HMRS Historical Model Railway Society.

HMS Her/His Majesty's Ship; Her/His Majesty's Service.

HMSO Her/His Majesty's Stationery Office.

HMT Her/His Majesty's Treasury.

HMV His Master's Voice.

HMW high molecular weight.

hn *hac nocte*, Latin 'tonight'.

HNC Higher National Certificate.

HND Higher National Diploma.

HNHIA Headway National Head Injuries Association.

hnRNA heterogeneous nuclear ribonucleic acid.

hnRNP heterogenerous nuclear ribonucleoprotein.

HO Home Office.

Ho holmium (chemical element).

HOCRE Home Office Central Research Establishment.

HoD Head of Department.

H of C House of Commons.

H of K House of Keys.

H of L House of Lords.

H of R House of Representatives.

HOI! Hands off Ireland!.

HOLLAND hope our love lasts and never dies.

HOLMES Home Office large major enquiry system (central crime-investigation computer).

HonARAM Honorary Associate of the Royal Academy of Music.

HonASTA Honorary Associate of the Swimming Teachers' Association.

HonDrRCA Honorary Doctorate of the Royal College of Art.

HonFBID Honorary Fellow of the British Institute of Interior Design.

HonFBIPP Honorary Fellow of the British Institute of Professional Photography.

HonFCP Charter Fellow of the College of Preceptors.

HonFEIS Honorary Fellow of the Educational Institute of Scotland.

HonFHCIMA Honorary Fellow of the Hotel, Catering and Institutional Management Association.

HonFIEE Honorary Fellow of the Institution of Electrical Engineers.

HonFIGasE Honorary Fellow of the Institution of Gas Engineers.

HonFIIM Honorary Fellow of the Institution of Industrial Managers.

HonFIMarE Honorary Fellow of the Institute of Marine Engineers.

HonFIMechE Honorary Fellow of the Institution of Mechanical Engineers.

HonFIMM Honorary Fellow of the Institution of Mining and Metallurgy.

HonFInstD Honorary Fellow of the Institute of Directors.

HonFInstE Honorary Fellow of the Institute of Energy.

HonFInstMC Honorary Fellow of the Institute of Measurement.

HonFInstNDT Honorary Fellow of the British Institute of Non-Destructive Testing.

HonFIQA Honorary Fellow of the Institute of Quality Assurance.

HonFIRSE Honorary Fellow of the Institution of Railway Signal Engineers.

HonFIRTE Honorary Fellow of the Institute of Road Transport Engineers.

HonFPRI Honorary Fellow of the Plastics and Rubber Institute.

HonFRAM Honorary Fellow of the Royal Academy of Music.

HonFRINA Honorary Fellow of the Royal Institution of Naval Architects.

HonFRPS Honorary Fellow of the Royal Photographic Society.

HonFSE Honorary Fellow of the Society of Engineers (Inc).

HonFSGT Honorary Fellow of the Society of Glass Technology.

HonFWeldI Honorary Fellow of the Welding Institute.

HonGSM Honorary Member of the Guildhall School of Music and Drama.

HonMInstNDT Honorary Member of the British Institute of Non-Destructive Testing.

HonMRIN Honorary Member of the Royal Institute of Navigation.

HonMWES Honorary Member of the Women's Engineering Society.

HonRAM Honorary Member of the Royal Academy of Music.

HonRCM Honorary Member of the Royal College of Music.

HonRNCM Honorary Member of the Royal Northern College of Music.

HonRSCM Honorary Member of the Royal School of Church Music.

HOPE Help Organise Peaceful Energy.

hor. dec. *hora decubitus*, Latin 'at bedtime'.

HORU Home Office Research Unit.

HOST Hosting for Overseas Students.

HOT Hawk and Owl Trust.

Hotol horizontal take-off and landing.

HOV high-occupancy vehicle.

HOW Hands off Our Water.

HP Handley Page; Hewlett Packard; High Priest; Houses of Parliament; high pressure; house physician; hire purchase; horse power.

hp hardy perennial; half pay; horsepower; heir presumptive; hybrid perpetual.

HPA Handley Page Association; Hen Packers Association; Hospital Physicists Association; Hurlingham Polo Association; Hospital Physicists' Association.

HPC Horticultural Policy Council; history of present complaint.

HPLC high-pressure liquid chromatography.

HPMA Heat Pump Manufacturers Association.

HPPA Horses and Ponies Protection Association.

HPRU Handicapped Persons Research Unit.

HPS Hardy Plant Society; Highland Pony Society; high-pressure steam.

HPTA High Pressure Technology Association; Hire Purchase Trade Association.

HPV human papilloma virus.

HQ headquarters.

HR Highland Regiment; Home Rule; House of Representatives; human resources.

HRA Horse Rangers' Association.

HRC Highland Regional Council; high-resolution chromatography.

HRCT high-resolution computerized tomography.

HRE Holy Roman Empire; Holy Roman Emperor.

HREM high-resolution electron microscopy.

HRG high resolution graphics.

HRGB Handbell Ringers of Great Britain.

HRGC high-resolution gas chromatography.

HRH Her/His Royal Highness.

HRIP *hic requiescit in pace*, Latin 'here rests in peace'.

HRMS high-resolution mass spectrometry.

HRP human remains pouch.

HRS Human Rights Society.

HRT hormone replacement therapy.

HRW heated rear window.

HS High School; Home Secretary; house surgeon; hospital ship.

Hs hassium (chemical element).

hs *hoc sensu*, Latin 'in this sense'; *hic sepultus*, Latin 'here is buried'.

HSA Hospital Saving Association; Humane Slaughter Association; Hunt Saboteurs Association; human serum albumin.

HSBA Herdwick Sheep Breeders Association.

HSBS Hunt Servants Benefit Society.

HSC Higher School Certificate; Health and Safety Commission.

HSE Health and Safety Executive; *hic sepultus est*, Latin 'here lies buried'.

HSDU hospital sterilisation and disinfection unit.

HSF Hospital Saturday Fund.

HSH Her/His Serene Highness.

HSI human-system interface; human-system interaction.

HSLA high strength, low alloy (steel).

HSM Her/His Serene Majesty.

HSN Hysterectomy Support Network.

HSS Henry Sweet Society for the History of Linguistic Ideas.

HSSU hospital sterile supply unit.

HST high speed train.

HSV herpes simplex virus.

HT heat-treated/treatment; high tension; high tide.

ht half-time.

HTA Harris Tweed Association; Help the Aged; Horticultural Trades Association.

HTB high-tension battery.

HTC Higher Technical Certificate.

HTGR high-temperature gas-cooled reactor.

HTLV human T-cell lymphotrophic virus.

HTML Hypertext Markup Language.

HTOL horizontal take-off and landing.

HTR high-temperature reactor.

HTS high-temperature superconductor/superconductivity; high-tensile steel.

HTT heavy tactical transport.

HTV Harlech Television.

HU Harvard University.

Hugo Human Genome Organization.

Humint human intelligence.

Humv human light vehicle.

Huridocs International Human Rights Information and Documentation System.

Husat Human Science and Advanced Technology Research Institute.

HV Health Visitor; high velocity; high voltage.

HVAC heating, ventilation and air conditioning; high-voltage alternating current.

HVACMA Heating, Ventilating & Air Conditioning Manufacturers' Association.

HVAR high-velocity aircraft rocket.

HVDC high voltage direct current.

HVEM high-voltage electron microscope.

HVP hydrolysed vegetable protein.

HW hazardous waste.

hw hot water; hit wicket (cricket).

h/w herewith; husband and wife.

HWL high water line.

HWLB high water, London Bridge.

HWM high water mark.

HWR heavy-water reactor.

HWS hot water system.

Hz hertz, used in physics.

I

I iodine (chemical element); independence; institute; island.

IA Ileostomy Association of Great Britain; Indian Army; Institute of Actuaries; International Alert; International Ångström; infected area.

IAA International Advertising Association; International Aerosol Association; International Association for Aerobiology; Ireland-Australia Association; Irish Architectural Archive; indoleacetic acid.

IAAA Irish Amateur Athletic Association.

IAAC International Antarctic Analysis Centre.

IAAF International Agricultural Aviation Foundation; International Amateur Athletic Federation.

IAAI International Association of Arson Investigators.

IAAS Immigrant Appeals Advisory Service; Incorporated Association of Architects and Surveyors; Institute of Auctioneers and Apprentices in Scotland.

IAATM International Association for Accident and Traffic Medicine.

IAB International Aquatic Board; Internet Architecture Board; Irish Association for the Blind.

IABA International Association of Aircraft Brokers and Agents; Irish Amateur Boxing Association.

IABSOIW International Association of Bridge, Structural and Ornamental Iron Workers.

IAC International Aerobatic Club; International Alpine Conference.

IACA Independent Air Carriers' Association; Irish American Cultural Association.

IACB International Advisory Committee on Bibliography.

IADR International Association for Dental Research.

IAE International Association of Egyptologists.

IAEA International Atomic Energy Agency.

IAF International Archery Federation; International Association of Falconry and Conservation of Birds of Prey; International Astronautical Federation.

IAFF International Art Film Federation; International Association of Fire Fighters.

IAFT International Association of Forensic Toxicologists.

IAGLP International Association of Great Lakes Ports.

IAgrE Institution of Agricultural Engineers.

IAHM Incorporated Association of Headmasters.

IAI Institute of Architectural Ironmongers; International Apple Institute (USA); International Association for Identification; Israel Aviation Authorities.

IAL International Algebraic Language.

IAM Institute of Administrative Management; Institute of Advanced Motorists.

IAMA International Abstaining Motorists Association; Irish Association of Municipal Authorities.

IAMPTH International Association of Master Penmen and Teachers of Handwriting.

IANA Internet Assigned Numbers Authority.

I & D incision and drainage.

I & O intake and output.

IANE Institute of Advanced Nursing Education.

IAOC International Athletic Olympic Committee.

IAP Institute of Animal Physiology; International Academy of Poets; International Association of Planetology.

IAPA Irish Airline Pilots Association.

IAPP Irish Association of Pigmeat Producers.

IAPS Incorporated Association of Preparatory Schools.

IAPSC International Association of Pipe Smokers Clubs.

IAR instruction address register.

IARU International Amateur Radio Union.

IARW International Association of Refrigerated Warehouses.

IAS immediate access store; instrument approach system; indicated air speed.

IASA International Air Safety Association.

IASMAL International Academy of Social and Moral Sciences, Arts and Letters.

IASP International Association for the Study of Pain.

IASS International Association for Scandinavian Studies.

iat inside air temperature.

IATA International Air Transport Association.

IATEFL International Association of Teachers of English as a Foreign Language.

IAVS Irish Association for Victim Support.

iaw in accordance with.

IAWA International Animal Welfare Alliance; International Association of Wood Anatomists.

IAWCM International Association of Wiping Cloth Manufacturers.

IAWE International Association for Wind Engineering.

IAWM Industrial Association of Wales and Monmouthshire.

IAWQ International Association on Water Quality.

IAWRT International Association of Women in Radio and Television.

IB International Baccalaureate; Institute of Brewing; Intervention Board; incendiary bomb.

ib. *ibidem*, Latin 'in the same place'.

IBA Independent Broadcasting Agency (now Independent Television Commission, the UK regulatory body for commercial radio and television; Institute of British Architects; International Banana Association; International Bartenders Association; International Bridge Academy; Irish Brewers Association.

IBB Institute of British Bakers; International Bowling Board; Invest in Britain Bureau.

IBBA Irish Basket Ball Association; Irish Break Bakers' Association; Irish-Belgian Business Association.

IBBR interbank bid-rate.

IBCAM Institute of British Carriage and Automobile Manufacturers.

IBCC International Bird Census Committee.

IBD inflammatory bowel disease.

IBE Institute of British Engineers; International Bureau of Education.

IBDISFS Institute of British Detective, Investigative Security and Forensic Specialists.

IBF International Badminton Federation; International Bandy Federation; International Bodysurfing Federation; International Boxing Foundation; Irish Bankers Federation.

IBFAN International Baby Food Action Network.

IBI invoice book, inward.

Ibid international bibliographical description.

ibid. *ibidem*, Latin 'in the same place'.

Ibiol Institute of Biology.

IBK Institute of Bookkeepers.

IBL Institute of British Launderers; International Brotherhood of Longshoremen.

IBM Indian Bureau of Mines; International Business Machines; intercontinental ballistic missile.

IBMBR interbank market bid rate.

IBO invoice book, outward.

IBP Institute for Business Planning; Institute of British Photographers; initial boiling point.

IBRD International Bank for Reconstruction and Development.

IBS irritable bowel syndrome.

IBSA International Blind Sports Association; International Board Sailing Association; Irish Building Society Association.

IBTA International Baton Twirling Association of America and Abroad.

IBTS International Beer Tasting Society.

IBWM International Bureau of Weights and Measures.

IC Industrial Court; Institute of Carpenters; Intelligence Corps; International Chapters; integrated circuit; internal combustion.

I/c in charge; in command.

ICA Ice Cream Alliance; Institute of Consumer Advisers; Institute of Contemporary Arts; International Caribbean Airways; International Chefs Association; International Claim Association; International Confederation of Accordionists; International Congress of Acarology; International Copper Association; Invalid Care Allowance; Irish Countrywomen's Association; Islamic Cement Association.

ICAN International Commission for Air Navigation; Invalid Children's Aid Nationwide.

ICAO International Civil Aviation Organization.

ICAS Institute of Chartered Accountants of Scotland; International Conference on Acoustics, Speech and Signal Processing; International Council of Air Shows; International Council of Associations of Surfing.

ICBB International Commission for Bee Botany.

ICBBA International Cornish Bantam Breeders Association.

ICBD International Council of Ballroom Dancing.

ICBM intercontinental ballistic missile.

ICBN International Code of Biological Nomenclature.

ICBP International Council for Bird Preservation.

ICC International Association of Cereal Science and Technology; International Chamber of Commerce; International Coffee Council; International Corrosion Council; International Cricket Conference; Inuit Circumpolar Conference; Irish Council of Churches.

ICCA International Corrugated Case Association.

ICCBC International Committee for Colorado Beetle Control.

ICCE International Commission on Continental Erosion.

ICCG International Conference on Crystal Growth.

ICCM International Committee for the Conservation of Mosaics.

ICCPR International Covenant on Civil and Political Rights.

ICCU International Cross-Country Union.

ICD International Classification of Diseases.

ICDA International Catholic Deaf Association.

ICE Institute for Consumer Ergonomics; Institution of Civil Engineers; International Congress of Ecology; International Cultural Exchange; internal combustion engine.

ICEATCA Icelandic Air Traffic Controllers Association.

ICED Interprofessional Council on Environmental Design.

ICEH International Centre for Eye Health.

ICEPHEW Institution of Civil Engineers Panel for Historical Engineering Works.

ICES International Council for the Exploration of the Sea.

ICET International Centre for Earth Tides.

ICF Ice Cream Federation; Industrial Careers Foundation; Institute of Chartered Foresters; International Canoe Federation; International Chess Federation; International Crane Federation; International Cremation Federation; International Curling Federation.

ICFC International Council of Fan Clubs.

ICFG International Commission on Fungal Genetics.

ICFM Institute of Charity Fundraising Managers.

ICFPW International Confederation of Former Prisoners of War.

ICFS Ireland-Cuba Friendship Society.

ICFTU International Confederation of Free Trade Unions.

ICGA Imperial Continental Gas Association; International Carnival Glass Association; International Classic Guitar Association; Irish Craft and Giftware Association.

IChemE Institution of Chemical Engineers.

Ichthys *Iesous Christos, Theou Uios, Soter*, Greek 'Jesus Christ, Son of God, Saviour' (persecuted members of the early Church used a drawing of a fish, *ichthys* in Greek, as a secret sign).

ICI Imperial Chemical Industries.

ICJ International Commission of Jurists; International Court of Justice.

ICJW International Council of Jewish Women.

ICL International Computers Limited.

ICLA International Committee on Laboratory Animals.

ICLD International Commission on Large Dams.

ICLPA Irish Cream Liqueur Producers' Association.

ICM International Conference of Midwives.

ICMA International Christian Maritime Association; International City Management Association; International Congresses for Modern Architecture; Irish Cable Makers Association.

ICMR International Committee for Mountain Racing.

ICMSA Irish Creamery Milk Suppliers Association.

ICMT International Commission on Mycotoxicology.

ICMUA International Commission on the Meteorology of the Upper Atmosphere.

ICN *in christi nomine*, Latin 'in the name of Christ'; International Communes Network; International Council of Nurses.

ICNAF International Council for North West Atlantic Fisheries.

ICNB International Code of Nomenclature of Bacteria.

ICNCP International Code of Nomenclature of Viruses.

ICO International Coffee Organization; International Commission on Oceanography; Irish Chiropodists Association; Islamic Circle Organization.

ICOBA International Confederation of Book Actors.

ICOM International Council of Museums.

ICOMOS International Council on Monuments and Sites.

ICOSI International Committee on Smoking Issues.

ICPL International Centre for Protected Landscapes; International Committee of Passenger Lines.

ICPO International Criminal Police Organisation.

ICPS International Cerebral Palsy Society; International Conference on the Properties of Steam.

ICR Institute of Cancer Research; International Collective Resistance; Irish Consumer Research Limited; intelligent character recognition.

ICRC International Committee of the Red Cross.

ICRF Imperial Cancer Research Fund.

ICRP International Commission on Radiological Protection.

ICRUM International Commission on Radiation Units and Measurements.

ICS Imperial College of Science and Technology; Institute of Chartered Shipbrokers; Institute of Cornish Studies; Intensive Care Society; International Camellia Society; International Crocodilian Society (USA); Irish Concrete Society; investors' compensation scheme.

ICSA Institute of Chartered Secretaries and Administrators; International Council of Securities Associations.

ICS/CI International Clarinet Society/Clari-Network International.

ICSF Intermediate Certificate of the Society of Floristry.

ICSH interstitial-cell-stimulating hormone.

ICSLS International Convention for Safety of Life at Sea.

ICSU International Council of Scientific Unions.

ICT Institute of Clay Technology; Institute of Concrete Technology.

ICTP International Centre for Theoretical Physics.

ICTU Irish Congress of Trade Unions.

ICU International Code Use; intensive care unit.

ICUMSA International Commission for Uniform Methods of Sugar Analysis.

ICW Institute of Clayworkers; Institute of Clerks of Works of Great Britain.

icw in connection with.

ICWA Institute of Cost and Works Accountants; International Coil Winding Association.

ICYYLM International Commission on Yeasts and Yeast-like Microorganisms.

ICZN International Code of Zoological Nomenclature.

ID identity; identity card; infectious diseases; information/intelligence department.

id inside diameter.

IDA International Dark-Sky Association; International Desalination Association; International Development Association; International Drapery Association; International Drummers Association; Irish Diabetic Association; Israeli Dental Association.

IDAS Implanted Defibrillator of Scotland.

IDB illicit diamond buyer/buying.

IDBRA International Drivers Behaviour Research Association.

IDC International Dance Council; International Diamond Council; International Drycleaners Congress.

IDCA International Diving Coaches Association; International Dragon Class Association.

IDCCC International Dredging Conference Coordinating Committee.

IDD International Direct Dialling; Institute for Design and Disability (Eire); insulin-dependent diabetes.

IDDD International Direct Distance Dialling.

IDF International Dairy Federation; International Dental Federation.

IDHS(GB) Irish Draught Horse Society (Great Britain).

IDI International Disaster Institute.

IDL International Date Line.

IDLG Infant Drinks Litigation Group.

IDMS integrated data management system.

IDN *in Dei nomine*, Latin 'in the name of God'; integrated data network.

IDP International Driving Permit; integrated data processing.

IDPM Institute of Data Processing Management.

IDPT International Donkey Protection Trust.

IDR International Dental Relief.

IDS Income Data Services; Industry Department for Scotland; International Dostoevsky Society; Irish Deaf Society.

IDSA Infectious Diseases Society of America; Irish Deaf Sports Association.

IDT Industrial Design Technology.

IE Indo-European.

i.e. *id est*, Latin 'that is'.

IEA International Emergency Action; International Energy Agency; International Entrepreneurs Association; International Ergonomics Association; Irish Epilepsy Association.

IEC International Egg Commission; International Everesters Club; Irish Equine Centre.

IECA International Erosion Control Association.

IEE Institution of Electrical Engineers.

IEEE Institute of Earth Education; Institute of Electrical and Electronic Engineers; Institute of Explosives Engineers.

IEF International Eye Foundation; Irish Equine Foundation.

IEHO Institute of Environmental Health Officers.

IEM inborn error of metabolism.

IEng Incorporated Engineer.

IEngAMIMM Associate Member of the Institution of Mining and Metallurgy.

IESBS Institute of Engineers and Ship Builders in Scotland.

IIExE Associate Member of the Institution of Incorporated Executive Engineers.

IERE Institution of Electronic and Radio Engineers.

IF Institute of Foresters; Institute of Fuel; intermediate frequency.

if information feedback.

I-f in flight.

IFA Independent Film Makers Association; Institute of Field Archaeologists; Institute of Foresters of Australia; International Federation of Airworthiness; International Federation on Ageing; International Florists Association; International Footprint Association; Irish Farmers Association.

IFAA Independent Financial Advisers Association.

IFAD International Fund for Agricultural Development.

IFAW International Fund for Animal Welfare.

IFB International Film Bureau; International Fire Buff Associates; invitation for bid.

IFBB International Federation of Body Builders.

IFC International Finance Corporation.

IFE Institute of Fence Engineers; Institute of Freshwater Ecology; Institution of Fire Engineers.

IFEAT International Federation of Essential Oils and Aroma Trades.

IFES International Flat Earth Society.

IFF Institute of Freight Forwarders.

IFHOH International Federation of the Hard of Hearing.

IFIP International Federation for Information Processing.

IFL Institute of Fluorescent Lighting; International Federation of Lithographers, Process Workers and Kindred Trades; International Friendship League.

IFM International Falcon Movement; International Federation of Musicians; International Fund for Monuments.

IFMA Independent Furniture Manufacturers' Association; International Farm Management Association; International Federation of Margarine Associations; Irish Fireplace Manufacturers' Association.

IFMS International Federation of Magical Societies.

IFN International Feminist Network.

IFO International Farmers Organization.

IFOAD International Federation of Original Art Diffusers.

IFOG International Federation of Olive Growers.

IFR instrument flying regulations.

IFRB International Frequency Registration Board.

IFS Institute for Fiscal Studies; Irish Free State.

IFSA Instock Footwear Suppliers Association; International Federation of Sports Acrobatics; International Fuzzy Systems Association; Intumescent Fire Seals Association; Irish Federation of Sea Anglers.

IFSMP International Federation of Serious Music Publishers.

IFSSH International Federation of Societies for Surgery of the Hand.

IFST Institute of Food Science and Technology.

IG Indo-Germanic; Institution of Geologists; Irish Guards.

Ig immunoglobulin.

IG&GA International Grooving and Grinding Association.

IGA International Gay Association; International Geographical Association; International Glaucoma Association; International Goat Association; International Gold Association; International Golf Association; Irish Grassland Association.

IgasE Institute of Gas Engineers.

IGC Institute for Global Communications; International Garden Club; International Green Cross; International Guides Club.

IGD illicit gold dealer.

IGF International Gymnastic Federation.

IGLD International Grand Lodge of Druidism.

IFLYO International Lesbian and Gay Youth Organization (Netherlands).

IGM International Grand Master (chess).

ign. *ignotus*, Latin 'unknown'.

IGO intergovernmental organization.

I-GOOS IOC Committee for Global Oxean Observing System.

IGS Imperial General Staff; International Geoxtextile Society; International Geranium Society; International Glaciological Society; Irish Georgian Society; Israel Geographical Society.

IGY International Geophysical Year.

IH Institute of Horticulture.

IHA Independent Hospitals Association; International H-Boat Association; International Horse Association; Irish Hardware Association; Issuing Houses Association.

IHBS Irish Hereford Breed Society.

IHC International Health Council; International Help for Children.

IHD ischaemic heart disease.

IHF International Hockey Federation; Irish Heart Foundation.

IHGS Institute of Heraldic and Genealogical Studies.

IHP indicated horsepower.

IHRA Indonesian Hotel and Restaurant Association; International Hot Rod Association.

IHS International Headache Society; International Horn Society; International Hydrofoil Society.

IHSGB Icelandic Horse Society of Great Britain.

IHVE Institute of Heating and Ventilation Engineers.

II Ikebana International; Institute of Inventors.

IIA Information Industry Association; Institute of Industrial Archaeology; International Imagery Association; Irish Insurance Association.

IIBA Irish Indoor Bowling Association; Irish-Italian Business Association.

IID insulin-independent diabetes.

IIHF International Ice Hockey Federation.

III Insurance Institute of Ireland; International Isocyanates Institute (USA); Investors in Industry.

IIP International Ice Patrol; Irish Independence Party.

IIS Institute of Industrial Selling; International Institute of Stress (Canada); Institute of Information Scientists.

IIW Indian Institute of Welders; International Inner Wheel.

IJJF International Ju Jitsu Federation.

IJMA Indian Jute Mills Association.

IJS Institute of Jazz Studies (USA).

IJVS International Jewish Vegetarian Society.

IKA International Kitefliers Association.

IKBS intelligent knowledge-based system.

IL Institute of Linguists; inside left.

il inside leg.

ILA Independent Living Alternatives; Insolvency Lawyers Association; International Laundry Association; International Law Association; International Leprosy Association; International Longshoremen's Association; International Lupin Association; Israel Library Association.

ILAE International League Against Epilepsy.

ILAM Institute of Leisure and Amenity Management.

ILAMA International Life-Saving Appliance Manufacturers Association.

ILC Inner Light Consciousness; International Life-Boat Conference.

ILCA International Lightning Class Association.

ILCS International Liquid Crystal Society.

ILCTA International League of Commercial Travellers and Agents.

ILD interstitial lung disease.

ILDA International Lutheran Deaf Association.

ILDAV International League of Doctors Against Vivisection.

ILE Institute of Legal Executives; Institution of Locomotive Engineers.

ILEA Inner London Education Authority.

ILESA International Law Enforcement Stress Association.

ILF Industrial Leathers Federation; International Lifeboat Federation; International Loan Fund.

ILMB Irish Livestock and Meat Board.

ILN Illustrated London News.

ILO International Labour Organization.

ilo in lieu of.

ILP Independent Labour Party.

ILPH International League for the Protection of Horses.

ILR independent local radio.

ILRI International Institute for Land Reclamation and Improvement (Netherlands).

ILS Incorporated Law Society; Industrial Locomotive Society; International Latitude Service; International Lilac Society; International Lunar Society (USA); Irish Literary Society; instrument landing system.

ILTTA International Light Tackle Tournament Association.

ILW intermediate-level waste.

ILWC International League of Women Composers.

ILZSG International Lead and Zinc Study Group.

IM Institute of Metals; International Master (chess); International Missions; intramuscular/ly.

IMA Independent Midwives Association; Indonesian Mining Association; Industrial Marketing Association; International Magnesium Association; International Military Archives; International Mohair Association; International Music Association; Irish Medical Association.

IMarE Institute of Marine Engineers.

Imarsat International Maritime Satellite Organization.

IMAS International Marine and Shipping Conference.

IMASA Irish Match Angling and Surfcasting Association.

IMB Institute of Marine Biology.

IMBA Irish-Mexican Business Association.

IMBEX International Mens and Boys Exhibition.

IMC Institute of Measurement and Control; Institute of Motorcycling; International Mailbag Club; International Materials Conference; International Meteorological Committee; Irish Manuscripts Commission.

IMCO Intergovernmental Maritime Consultative Organization.

IMCoS International Map Collectors Society.

IMDA International Magic Dealers Association.

IME Institute of Medical Ethics.

IMechE Institute of Mechanical Engineers.

IMet Institute of Metals.

IMF International Monetary Fund.

IMH International Medical Help.

IMI Imperial Metal Industries; Institute of Medical Illustrators; Institute of the Motor Industry.

IMinE Institution of Mining Engineers.

IMLA International Maritime Lecturers Association.

IMM Institute of Massage and Movement; Institute of Master Mariners (Eire); Institution of Mining and Metallurgy.

IMMRAN International Meeting of Marine Radio Aids to Navigation.

IMO International Maritime Organization; International Mennonite Organisation; International Meteorological Organisation; International Miners' Organization.

Imp. *Imperatrix*, Latin 'Empress'; *Imperator*, Latin 'Emperor'.

imp. *imprimatur*, Latin 'let it be printed'.

IMPA International Maritime Pilots Association; International Master Printers Association; International Motor Press Association; International Myopia Prevention Association (USA).

IMR infant mortality rate.

IMRA Irish Mountain Rescue Association.

IMRO Investment Management Regulatory Organization.

IMS Information Management System; Institute of Management Services; Institute on Man and Science; International Meditation Society; International Mountain Society; International Multihull Society.

IMU International Mathematical Union.

IMunE Institution of Municipal Engineers.

In indium (chemical element).

in inch (Imperial unit of length equal to 2.54 cm).

Inbucon International Business Consultants.

Inc. Incorporated.

INCA Independent National Computing Association; International Committee for Andean Aid.

Incpen Industry Committee for Packaging and the Environment.

IND *in nomine Dei*, Latin 'in the name of God'.

ind *in dies*, Latin 'each day'.

INEOA International Narcotic Enforcement Officers Association.

INF intermediate-range nuclear forces, as named in the Intermediate Nuclear Forces Treaty; International Naturist Federation.

inf. *infra*, Latin 'below'; *infusum*, Latin 'infusion'.

INFA International Federation of Aestheticians.

INFACT Irish National Federation Against Copyright Theft.

infra dig. *infra dignitatem*, Latin 'beneath one's dignity'.

Ingo International non-governmental organization.

INJ *in nomine Jesu*, Latin 'in the name of Jesus'.

INLA Irish National Liberation Army.

in loc. *in loco*, Latin 'in its place'.

in loc. cit *in loco citato*, Latin 'in the place cited'.

Inmarsat International Maritime Satellite.

INN International Negotiation Network.

INO Irish Nurses Organisation.

INPA International Newspaper Promotion Association.

INRI *Jesus Nazarenus Rex Iudaeorum*, Latin 'Jesus of Nazareth, King of the Jews'.

INS International Neuromodulation Society; International News Service; inertial navigation system.

INSA International Shipowners' Association.

INSCA International Sausage Casing Association.

Inset in-service education and training.

Intelsat International Telecommunications Satellite Organization.

Internet International Network (of computers).

Interpol International Criminal Police Organization.

in trans. *in transitu*, Latin 'in transit'.

INTROP Information Centre of Tropical Plant Protection.

INTS International Nuclear Track Society.

INucE Institution of Nuclear Engineers.

inv. *invenit*, Latin 'designed it'.

INWAT International Network of Women Against Tobacco.

Io ionium (chemical element).

IOB Institute of Brewing; Insurance Ombudsman Bureau.

IOC Indian Ocean Commission; Institute of Carpenters; International Olympic Committee; International Ornithological Congress; International Ozone Commission.

IOD Institute of Directors, injured on duty.

IoF Institute of Fuel.

IOF Independent Order of Foresters.

IOFB intraocular foreign body.

IOFGA Irish Organic Farmers and Growers Association.

IOGT Independent Order of Good Templars.

IoJ Institute of Journalists.

IOOC International Olive Oil Council (Spain).

IOOF Independent Order of Odd Fellows.

IOOTS International Organisation of Old Testament Scholars.

IOM Isle of Man.

IOP Institute of Painters in Oil Colours; Institute of Plumbing; Institute of Pyramidology; Iranian Oil Participants; intraocular pressure.

IoP Institute of Physics.

IOPC Institute of Paper Conservation.

IOPCW International Organization for the Prohibition of Chemical Weapons.

IOQ Institute of Quarrying.

IOR Independent Order of Rechabites; Institute of Roofing.

IOS integrated office system.

IOU I owe you.

IOW Isle of Wight.

IP india paper; in-patient; instalment plan; International Pharmacopoeia; Internet Protocol.

IPA Independent Petroleum Association; Insolvency Practitioners Association; Institute of Practitioners in Advertising; India

Pale Ale; International Association for the Child's Right to Play; International Peace Academy; International Peach Academy; International Phonetic Alphabet/Association; International Pinball Association; International Psychogeriatric Association; International Publishers' Association; Involvement and Participation Association.

IPAA International Prisoners' Aid Association.

IPARS International Programmed Airline Reservation System.

IPBA Irish Paper Box Association.

IPBM interplanetary ballistic missile.

IPC Indicative Planning Council; Institute of Pure Chiropractic; International Paralympic Committee; International Pepper Community; International Press Centre; International Prison Commission; International Publishing Corporation.

IPCA International Petroleum Co-operative Alliance; International Postcard Collectors Association.

IPCC Intergovernmental Panel on Climatic Change; Irish Peatland Conservation Council.

IPCS Institution of Professional Civil Servants.

IPE Incorporated Plant Engineers.

IPF International Peace Forest; International Pen Friends (Ireland); International Powerlifting Federation; International Prayer Fellowship.

IPFA Member of Chartered Institute of Public Finance and Accountancy.

IPGS International Philatelic Golf Society.

IPGSA International Plant Growth Substance Association.

IPHC International Pacific Halibut Commission.

IPI Institute of Patentees and Inventors; Institute of Professional Investigators; International Pesticide Institute; International Press Institute; Irish Planning Institute.

IPM Institute of Personnel Management; Institute of Psychosexual Medicine.

IPMI International Precious Metals Institute.

ipm inches per minute.

IPMS Institution of Professionals, Managers

and Specialists; International Plastic Modellers Society.

IPO input, processing, output.

IPPA Indo-Pacific Prehistory Association (Australia); International Paediatric Pathology Association; International Peat Society; International Pectin Producers' Association; International Prisoners Aid Association; Irish Pre-School Playgroups Association.

IPPF International Planned Parenthood Federation.

IPS Incorporated Phonographic Society; Institute for Policy Studies; International Palm Society; International Planetarium Society; Intractable Pain Society of Great Britain and Northern Ireland.

ips inches/instructions per second.

IPTPA International Professional Tennis Players' Association.

IPTS International Practical Temperature Scale.

IPU Interparliamentary Union.

IPVS International Pig Veterinary Society.

IPWH International Organisation for the Provision of Work for Handicapped Persons.

IQ intelligence quotient.

iq *idem quod*, Latin 'the same as'.

IQA Institute of Quality Assurance; Irish Quality Association.

IQS Institute of Quantity Surveyors.

IR Industrial Relations; Inland Revenue; information retrieval; infra red.

Ir Iridium (chemical element).

ir inside radius.

IRA International Raquetball Association; International Rodeo Association; International Rubber Association; Irish Republican Army.

IRASA International Radio Air Safety Association.

IRATA Industrial Rope Access Trades Association.

IRBM intermediate range ballistic missile.

IRC International Red Cross; International Relations Club; International Rescue Committee; International Rubber Conference; Internet Relay Chat.

IRCS Irish Red Cross Society.

IRF International Reform Federation; International Religious Fellowship; International Rowing Federation.

IRFB International Rugby Football Board.

IRL Institute of Rural Life at Home and Overseas.

IRLA Independent Record Labels Association; International Religious Liberty Association.

IRLCOCSA International Red Locust Control Organisation for Central and Southern Africa.

IRN Independent Radio News.

IRO Industrial Relations Officer; Inland Revenue Office; Institute of Rent Officers; International Refugee Organization.

IRRS Irish Railway Records Society.

IRS International Rhinologic Society; information retrieval system.

IRSO Institute of Road Safety Officers.

IRTA International Reciprocal Trade Association; International Road Racing Teams Association (Switzerland).

IRU International Railway Union; International Rugby Union.

IS Industrial Society; International Socialists; International Society of Sculptors, Painters and Gravers; information science; internal security.

ISA Individual Savings Account; Instrument Society of America; International Schools Association; International Seaweed Association; International Settlement Authority; International Shakespeare Association; International Silk Association; International Skating Association; International Society of Arboriculture; International Sunflower Association; International Surfing Association; Irish Society for Archives.

ISAM index sequential access method.

ISB Institute of Small Business; International Society of Bassists; International Society of Biorheology.

ISBA Incorporated Society of British Advertisers; Independent Schools Bursars Association; International Seabed Authority; Irish-Swedish Business Association.

ISBN International Standard Book Number

(an individual reference allocated to each book title).

ISBRA International Society for Biomedical Research on Alcoholism.

ISC Imperial Service College; Institute for the Study of Conflict; International Sculpture Centre; International Society of Citriculture; International Sporting Commission; International Student Conference; International Supreme Council of World Masons; International Surfing Committee.

ISCh Incorporated Society of Chiropodists.

ISCM International Society for Contemporary Music.

ISD international subscriber dialling.

ISDD Institute for the Study of Drug Dependence.

ISDN integrated services digital network.

ISF International Science Foundation; International Shipping Federation; International Society for Fat Research; International Solidarity Fund; International Spiritualist Federation.

ISFL International Society of Family Law.

ISGA Irish Salmon Growers' Association.

ISI International Statistical Institute; Iron and Steel Institute.

ISIS Independent Schools Information Service.

ISLEWTT International Post Conference Symposium on Low Cost and Energy Saving Wastewater Treatment Technologies.

ISM Imperial Service Medal; Incorporated Society of Musicians; Institute of Spiritualist Mediums; International Society for Mesotherapy; Irish Sovereignty Movement.

ISMS International Society for Mushroom Science.

ISO Imperial Service Order; International Organization for Standardization.

ISO7 International Organization for Standardization 7-bit code.

ISOA International Support Vessel Owners' Association.

ISOB Incorporated Society of Organ Builders; International Society of Barristers.

ISOC Internet Society.

ISP Internet Service Provider; Institute of Sales Promotion; Institute of Sewage Purification.

ISPA International Screen Publicity Association; International Skat Players Association; International Society of Parametric Artists; International Squash Players Association.

ISPCA Irish Society for the Prevention of Cruelty to Animals; Ironmaking and Steelmaking Plant Contractors Association.

ISPCAN International Society for Prevention of Child Abuse and Neglect.

ISP Internet service provider.

ISQ *in statu quo*, Latin 'unchanged'.

ISR information storage and retrieval.

ISRN Incorporated Society of Registered Naturopaths.

ISRS International Society for Reef Studies.

ISS Inn Sign Society; International Seaweed Symposium; International Social Services; International Society of Surgery; International Student Service (USA); International Sunshine Society.

ISSM Institute of Sterile Services Management.

ISSN International Standard Serial Number.

ISSO International Self-Service Organisation; International Side-Saddle Organisation.

ISSOL International Society for the Study of the Origin of Life.

IST insulin shock therapy.

ISTA International School of Theatre Anthropology; International Schools Theatre; International Seed Testing Association; International Sight-Seeing and Tours Association; International Special Tooling Association.

ISTC Institute of Scientific and Technical Communicators; Iron and Steel Trades Confederation.

ISTRA Interplanetary Space Travel Research Association.

ISTRC International Society for Tropical Root Crops.

ISTRO International Soil Tillage Research Organisation.

IStructE Institution of Structural Engineers.

ISU Immigration Services Union; International Salvage Union; International Shooting Union; International Skating Union; International Stereoscopic Union.

ISV International Scientific Vocabulary.

ISVA Incorporated Society of Valuers and Auctioneers.

ISVBM International Society of Violin and Bow Makers.

ISVR Institute of Sound & Vibration Research.

ISWA International Science Writers Association; International Solid Wastes and Public Cleansing Association.

ISWG Imperial Standard Wire Gauge.

IT Information Technology; Inner Temple; Institute of Trichologists; income tax; industrial tribunal.

ITA Independent Television Authority; Indian Tea Association; Initial Teaching Alphabet Association; Institute of Transport Administration; Institute of Travel Agents; International Tape Association; International Turquoise Association; International Twins Association; Ireland-Taiwan Association.

ita initial teaching alphabet.

ITAI Institute of Traffic Accident Investigators.

ITALY I trust and love you.

ITAR Information Telegraph Agency of Russia.

ITAS Industrial Training Association (Scotland).

ITB Industry Training Board.

ITC Imperial Tobacco Company; Independent Television Commission; Independent Theatre Council; Indian Tobacco Company; Industrial Training Council; Inland Transport Commission; International Tea Committee; International Thyroid Conference; International Trade Centre; International Translations Centre; International Tribology Council; International Trotsky Committee; International Typeface Corporation; Irish Timber Council.

itc installation time and cost.

ITF International Tennis Federation; International Trampoline Federation; Irish Textiles Federation.

ITG International Trumpet Guild.

ITI Indian Telephone Industries; Institute of Translation and Interpreting; International Theatre Institute; International Thrift Institute; Irish Timber Industries.

ITMA Imported Tyre Manufacturers Association; Institute of Trade Mark Agents; Irish Transport Manufacturers' Association (Eire); *It's That Man Again* (former radio programme).

ITN Independent Television News.

ITO International Trade Organization.

ITS Institute for Transport Studies; International Telecommunications Society; International Thespian Society; International Turfgrass Society; Irish Texts Society.

ITT Institute of Travel and Tourism; International Telephone and Telegraph Corporation; insulin tolerance test.

ITTF International Table Tennis Federation.

ITTID International Trust for Terminal and Incurable Diseases.

ITU International Telecommunication Union; International Temperance Union; International Typographical Union; intensive therapy unit.

ITV Independent Television.

IU international unit.

IUA International Union of Advertising.

IUC International Union of Crystallography.

IUCD intrauterine contraceptive device.

IUCW International Union for Child Welfare.

IUD intrauterine death/device.

IUGR intrauterine growth retardation.

IUHHA International Union of Historic House Associations.

IUI International Union of Interpreters.

IUMI International Union of Marine Insurance.

IUP intrauterine pressure.

IUPAC International Union of Pure and Applied Chemistry, an organisation that regulates procedures, such as the nomenclature for naming substances.

IUPLAW International Union for the Protection of Literary and Artistic Works.

IUSA International Underwater Spearfishing Association.

IUSF International Union of Societies of

Foresters; International University Sports Federation.

IUT International Union of Tenants; intrauterine transfusion.

IV Institute of Valuers (South Africa); intravenous; intravenous drip.

iv increased/invoice value.

IVA Invalidity Allowance; individual voluntary arrangement (concerning bankruptcy proceedings).

IVACL International Voluntary Action on Chid Labour.

IVB Invalidity Benefit.

IVBA International Veteran Boxers Association.

IVBF International Volleyball Federation.

IVC International Vacuum Congress; Permanent Committee for the International Veterinary Congresses.

IVF in-vitro fertilization.

IVR International Vehicle Registration.

IVS International Voluntary Service.

IVT International Visual Theatre Research Community; intravenous transfusion.

IVU International Vegetarian Union.

IWA Inland Waterways Association; International Wheat Agreement; International Woodworkers of America; International Workers Aid; Irish Wheelchair Association.

IWB International Waterpolo Board.

IWC Institute for World Concern; Interim Wilderness Committee; International Whaling Commission; International Wildlife Coalition; International Windglider Class; Irish Wildbird Conservancy.

IWCC International Women's Cricket Council; International Wrought Copper Council; International Wood Collectors Council.

IWCT International War Crimes Tribunal.

IWFA International Women's Fishing Association.

IWFS International Wine and Food Society.

IWGA International World Games Association.

IWHC International Wages for Housework Campaign.

IWIBA Irish Women's Indoor Bowling Association.

IWIEF Inventors Workshop International Educational Foundation.

IWLC International Water Lily Club.

IWM Imperial War Museum; Institute of Wastes Management.

IWPR Institute for War and Peace Reporting.

IWRB International Waterfowl and Wetlands Research Bureau.

IWS Industrial Water Society; International Wool Secretariat.

IWTF International Wheelchair Tennis Federation; Intractable Wastes Task Force.

IWW Industrial Workers of the World.

IX *Iesous Christos*, Greek 'Jesus Christ' (the initial letters of the words in Greek capitals).

IYA Irish Yachting Association.

IYAS International Years of the Active Sun.

IYFM International Yoga Fellowship Movement.

IYHF International Youth Hostels Federation.

IYRU International Yacht Racing Union.

Iyswim if you see what I mean.

IZA International Zinc Association.

IZE International Association of Zoo Educators.

IZS insulin zinc suspension.

J

J Journal; Judge; Justice; joule, the SI unit of energy used in physics.

JA Judge Advocate; Justice of Appeal.

JAA Joint Aviation Authorities.

JAAT joint air attack team.

JAC Jewellery Advisory Centre.

JACARI Joint Action Committee Against Racial Interference.

JACNE Joint Advisory Committee on Nutritional Education.

JACT Joint Association of Classical Teachers.

JAF Judge Advocate of the Fleet.

JAG Judge Advocate General.

JAL Japan Air Lines.

j & wo jettison and wash overboard.

JANE Journalists Against Nuclear Extermination.

JANET Joint Academic Network (computer network for scholars).

JANSA Janatorial Supplies Association.

JAS Jamaica Agricultural Society; Japan Association of Shipbuilders; Junior Astronomical Society.

JATCC Joint Aviation Telecommunications Coordination Committee.

JATO jet-assisted take-off.

JAWC Joint Animal Welfare Council.

JAWG Joint Airmiss Working Group.

JB junction box.

JBCNS Joint Board of Clinical Nursing Studies.

JBCSA Joint British Committee for Stress Analysis.

JBES Jodrell Bank Experimental Station.

JBIA Jewish Braille Institute of America.

JC Jesus Christ; Jockey Club; Juvenile Court.

JCAR Joint Commission on Applied Radioactivity.

JCB Joint Coal Board; Joseph Cyril Bamford (trademark), manufacturer of earthmoving machines.

JCBMI Joint Committee for the British Memorial Industry.

JCC Joint Consultants' Committee; Joint Consultative Committee.

JCCBI Joint Committee for the Conservation of British Insects.

JCCMI Joint Committee for Church Music in Ireland.

JCHMT Joint Committee on Higher Medical Training.

JCHST Joint Committee on Higher Surgical Training.

JCL job-control language.

JCLI Joint Council for Landscape Industries.

JCMC Joint Conference on Medical Conventions.

JCMD Joint Committee on Mobility for the Disabled.

JCPBI Joint Commission for the Preservation of British Insects.

JCR junior common room (Oxford colleges); junior combination room (Cambridge colleges).

JCS James Connolly Society; Jersey Cattle Society of the United Kingdom; Joint Chiefs of Staff; Justices' Clerks' Society.

JCSTR Joint Commission on Solar and Terrestrial Relationships.

jct. *or* **jctn** junction.

JCWA Japan Clock and Watch Association.

JD juvenile deliquent.

JDC Jewish Documentation Centre.

JDM juvenile diabetes mellitus.

jds job data sheet.

JEB Joint Examining Board.

JECFI Joint Expert Committee on Food Irradiation.

JESSI Joint European Submicron Silicon Initiative.

JET Joint European Torus.

JFET junction field-effect transistor.

JFK John Fitzgerald Kennedy (US President)

JFTC Joint Fur Trade Committee.

JG junior grade.

JGOFS Joint Global Ocean Flux Study.

jha job hazard analysis.

JHDA Junior Hospital Doctors Association.

JIA Jute Importers Association.

JIB Joint Intelligence Bureau.

JIC joint industrial council.

Jicnars Joint Industry Committee for National Readership Surveys.

JICRAR Joint Industry Committee for Radio Audience Research.

JICTAR Joint Industry Committee for Television Advertising Research.

JII John Innes Institute.

JIT just-in-time (stock control system).

JIU Joint Inspection Unit.

JJ jaw jerk.

JMB Joint Matriculation Board.

JMC Joint Mathematical Council of the United Kingdom.

JMPR Joint Meeting on Pesticide Residues.

JNC Joint Negotiating Committee.

JND just noticeable difference.

JNF Jewish National Fund.

JNR Japanese National Railways.

JOD juvenile onset diabetes.

JONAH Jews Organised for a Nuclear Arms Halt.

JONSIS Joint North Sea Information System.

JOVIAL Jules' Own Version of International Algorithmic Language.

JP Justice of the Peace.

jp jet propelled/propulsion.

JPMO Jersey Potato Marketing Organisation.

jps jet propulsion system.

jpto jet propelled take-off.

JR *Jacobus Rex*, Latin 'King James'.

JRA Japanese Red Army.

JRC Junior Red Cross.

JRCT Joseph Rowntree Charitable Trust.

JS judicial separation.

JSA Japan Silk Association.

JSAWC Joint Services Amphibious Warfare Centre.

JSC Joint Sites Committee.

JSE Johannesburg Stock Exchange.

JSF Japan Skating Federation.

JSP Jackson Structure Programming.

JSS Jacob Sheep Society; Japan Society of Scotland.

JSSC Joint Services Staff College.

jt joint tenancy.

JTC Joint Test of Competence of the Society of Surveying Technicians.

JTIDS Joint Tactical Information Distribution Systems.

JTO jump take-off.

JTSMA Jennifer Trust for Spinal Muscular Atrophy.

JTUAC Joint Trade Union Advisory Committee.

JUD *Juris Utriusque Doctor*, Latin 'Doctor of Both Laws' – canon and civil.

JV jugular vein.

JVC Jorvik Viking Centre.

JVI Joint Vienna Institute.

JVS Jewish Vegetarian and Natural Health Society.

JW Jehovah's Witness.

JWB Jewish Welfare Board.

JWEF Joinery and Woodwork Employers' Federation.

JWG Joint Working Group (between World Council of Churches and the Roman Catholic Church).

JWPAC Joint Waste Paper Advisory Council.

K

K *kalium*, Latin 'potassium' (chemical element); Kelvin; King; Kirkpatrick (enumeration of Scarlatti's works); Köchel (enumeration of Mozart's works); capacity (electrical); carat; constant (mathematics); kaon (physics); king (chess, cards); kitchen; knight (chess); knit; thousand.

k kilo; kilogram; kingdom.

KA King of Arms.

K/A Knights of the Altar International.

KAF Kenya Air Force.

K & B kitchen and bathroom.

KAPWA Kite Aerial Photography Worldwide Association.

KAS Kentucky Academy of Science.

KB King's Bench; Knight of the Order of the Bath; kilobyte; king's bishop (chess); knight bachelor; knowledge base.

KBD King's Bench Division.

KBE Knight (Commander of the Order) of the British Empire.

KBP king's bishop's pawn (chess).

KBS knowledge-based system.

KC Kennel Club; King's College; King's Counsel.

kc kilocycle.

Kcal kilocalorie.

KCB Knight Commander of the Order of the Bath.

KCC Kurdish Cultural Centre.

K cell killer cell.

KCMG Knight Commander of the Order of St Michael and St George.

KCN Kids Club Network.

kc/s kilocycles per second.

KCSJ Knight Commander of the Order of St John or St Jerusalem.

KCVC Knight Commander of the Royal Victorian Order.

KCVO Knight Commander of the Royal Victorian Order.

K-Door Keep Death Off Our Roads.

kd knocked down (disassembled).

KE kinetic energy.

keas knots equivalent airspeed.

keV kiloelectronvolt.

KEY keep extending yourself.

KFA Keep Fit Association.

kg kilogram.

KG Knight of the Order of the Garter.

kg kilogram.

KGB *Komitet Gosudarstvennoi Bezopasnosti*, Russian 'Committee of State Security'.

kgf kilogram-force.

kHz kilohertz.

KIA killed in action.

kias knots indicated airspeed.

KIF Knitting Industries Federation.

KIND Scotland Kids in Need and Distress.

KIO Kenya Information Office.

KJ knee-jerk.

kJ kilojoule.

KJV King James Version (of the Bible).

KKK Ku Klux Klan (USA).

KKt king's knight (chess).

KKtP king's knight's pawn (chess).

kl kilolitre.

KLM *Koninklijke Luchtvaart Maatschappij*, Dutch for Royal Dutch Airlines.

KLNITE Knitting, Lace and Net Industry Training Board.

KLS kidney, liver spleen.

KM Knight of Malta.

km kilometre.

KN king's knight (chess).

KNP king's knight's pawn.

KO kick-off; knockout; knock out.

KOC Kuwait Oil Company.

Komintern *Kommunisticheskii Internatsional*, Russian 'Communist International'.

Komsomol *Kommunisticheskii Soyuz Molodezhi*, Russian 'Communist Union of Youth'.

KP Knight of the Order of St Patrick; king's pawn (chess).

KPD *Kommunistische Partei Deutschland*, German 'German Communist Party'.

kpg kilometres per gallon.

kph *or* **km/h** kilometres per hour.

KPM King's Police Medal.

KPP Keeper of the Privy Purse.

KQC London University's King's College.

KR King's Regulations; king's rook (chess).

Kr krypton (chemical element).

KRL knowledge representation language.

KRP king's rook's pawn.

KS Karposi's sarcoma; King's Scholar; King's School.

KSA Kitchen Specialists Association; Klinefelter's Syndrome Association.

KSF Kashmiri Students Federation.

KT Kingston-upon-Thames; Knight of the Order of the Thistle; Knight Templar.

KTL Keep the Link.

Ku kurchatovium (chemical element).

KUB kidney, ureter, bladder.

kV kilovolt.

kVA kilovolt-ampere.

kW kilowatt.

kwac keyword and context.

kWh kilowatt-hour.

kwic keyword in context.

kwoc keyword out of context.

KZ killing zone.

L

L 50 in Roman numerals; Lake; Latin; Liberal; Licentiate; Loch; Lough; inductance (electrical); large (size in clothing); learner driver; longitude.

l laevorotatory; large; late; latitude; league; leasehold; left; length; line; litre; low.

l. *liber*, Latin 'book'; *libra*, Latin 'pound' (obsolete); line; low.

LA Lard Association; Latin America/n; Lebanese Army; Legislative Assembly; Library Association; Licensing Act; Literate in Arts; Los Angeles; left atrium; local anaesthetic; local authority.

La lanthanum (chemical element).

la low altitude.

LAA light anti-aircraft.

LAB Laboratory Animals Bureau; Latin America Board; Legal Aid Board; low-altitude bombing.

LABAC Licentiate Member of the Association of Business and Administrative Computing.

LABBS Ladies' Association of British Barbershop Singers.

LAC Landscape Advisory Committee; Library Association of China; Licentiate of the Apothecaries' Company.

LACES London Airport Cargo Electronic Processing Scheme.

LACMA Latin American and Caribbean Movers Association.

LACS League Against Cruel Sports.

LACW Leading Aircraftswoman.

LAD language acquisition device.

ladar laser detection and ranging.

LAdv Lord Advocate.

LAFU Ladies Amateur Fencing Union.

LAG Legal Action Group.

LAGB Linguistics Association of Great Britain.

LAIA Latin American Integration Association.

LAM London Academy of Music.

LAMAS London and Middlesex Archaeological Society.

LAMC Livestock Auctioneers Market Committee for England and Wales.

LAMDA London Academy of Music and Dramatic Art.

LAMRTPI Legal Associate Member of the Royal Town Planning Institute.

LAN local area network.

l & d loans and discounts; loss and damage.

l & w living and well.

Lantirn low-altitude navigation and targeting infrared system.

LAP Labour Action for Peace.

LAPES low-altitude parachute extraction system.

LAR limit address register.

LARA Land Access Rights Association.

LARAC Local Authority Recycling Advisory Council.

LAS Legal Aid Society; League of Arab States.

LASER London and South East Advisory Council.

LASI Licentiate of the Ambulance Service Institute.

LASI Licentiate of the Architects and Surveyors Institute.

LASMO London and Scottish Marine Oil.

LASSA Licensed Animal Slaughterers and Salvage Association.

LATA London Amenity and Transport Association.

LATCC London Air Traffic Control Centre.

LATS long-acting thyroid stimulator.

LAUTRO Life Assurance and Unit Trust Regulatory Organisation.

LAUK Library Association of the United Kingdom.

LAUTRO Life Assurance and Unit Trust Regulatory Organization.

LAV light-armoured vehicle.

LAW Land Authority for Wales; Legal Action for Women; Loyalist Association of Workers.

LB late bottled (wine).

lb left back (football); leg bye (cricket); *libra*, Latin 'pound' (an Imperial measure of weight approximating to 454 g).

LBA London Boroughs Association.

LBC London Broadcasting Company.

LBdr Lance Bombardier.

LBES Lifeboat Enthusiasts Society.

LBF liver blood flow.

lbf pound force.

lb-ft pound foot.

LBH length, breadth, height.

LBL lymphoblastic lymphoma.

LBO leveraged buy-out.

LBS London Business School.

LBSG Letter Box Study Group.

lbw leg before wicket (term in cricket).

LBEI Licentiate of the Institution of Body Engineers.

LBIPP Licentiate of the British Institute of Professional Photography.

LBIST Licentiate of the British Institute of Surgical Technologists.

LC Lance Corporal; Library of Congress; Locomotive & Carriage Institute; Lord Chamberlain/Chancellor; Lutheran Council of Great Britain; landing craft; letter of credit.

lc *loco citato*, Latin 'in the place cited'; lower case (printing); left centre.

L/C letter of credit.

LCA Lead Contractors Association; Liverpool Cotton Association.

LCA-GB Lightweight Cycle Association of Great Britain.

LCB Lord Chief Baron.

LCC Labour Co-ordinating Committee; Legalize Cannabis Campaign; London County Council; London Cycling Campaign; life-cycle costing.

LCCC Library of Congress Catalogue Card.

LCCI London Chamber of Commerce and Industry.

LC&TPA Lighting Column and Transmission Pole Association.

LCD Lord Chamberlain's Department; Lord Chancellor's Department; liquid crystal display; lowest common denominator.

LCDT London Contemporary Dance Theatre.

LCE Licentiate in Civil Engineering; London Commodity Exchange.

LCEA Licentiate of the Association of Cost and Executive Accountants.

LCF Law Centres Federation.

LCFI Licentiate of CFI International (Clothing and Footwear Institute).

LCGB Locomotive Club of Great Britain.

LCH London Clearing House.

LCh Licentiate in Chiropody of the Institute of Chiropodists; *Licentiatus Chirurgiae*, Latin 'Licentiate in Surgery'; Lord Chancellor.

LChir *Licentiatus Chirurgiae*, Latin 'Licentiate in Surgery'.

LCIBSE Licentiate of the Chartered Institution of Building Services Engineers.

LCJ Lord Chief Justice.

LCM London College of Music; lowest common multiple.

LCP Licentiate of the College of Preceptors; London College of Printing; last complete programme.

LCpl Lance Corporal.

LCPS Licentiate of the College of Physicians and Surgeons.

LCS London Co-operative Society.

LCSP(BTH) Diploma in Body Massage and Physical Culture.

LCSP(BTH) Diploma in Health and Beauty Therapy.

LCSP(Phys) Diploma in Swedish Massage.

LCST Licentiate of the College of Speech Therapists.

LD Laud Deso, Latin 'praise be to God'; Lady Day; Liberal Democrat; lethal dosage; low density.

L/D letter of deposit.

LDA Lead Development Association; Lithuanian Dental Association.

LDC less developed country.

ldc long-distance call.

LDDC London Docklands Development Corporation.

LDentSc Licentiate in Dental Science.

LDL low-density lipoprotein.

LDN less developed nation.

LDOS Lord's Day Observance Society.

LDP long-distance path.

LDPAS Long Distance Paths Advisory Service.

LDR Liberal, Democratic and Reform Group.

LDS *laus Deo semper*, Latin 'praise be to God always'; Latter-Day Saints; Licentiate in Dental Surgery.

LDSc Licentiate in Dental Science.

LDSRCPSGlas Licentiate in Dental Surgery of the Royal College of Physicians and Surgeons of Glasgow.

LDSRCSEd Licentiate in Dental Surgery of the Royal College of Surgeons of Edinburgh.

LDSRCSEng Licentiate in Dental Surgery of the Royal College of Surgeons of England.

LDTA Large Diameter Tube Association.

LDV Local Defence Volunteers.

LDWA Long Distance Walkers' Association.

LE London Electricity.

LEA Local Education Authority.

LEAD Linking Education and Disability.

LEAP Life Education for the Autistic Person.

LEC Launceston Environment Centre.

LED light-emitting diode.

LEEA Lifting Equipment Engineers' Association.

leg. *legato*, Italian 'smooth' or 'joined' (music).

legg. *leggiero*, Italian 'light' (music).

Leicester. *Leicesteriensis*, Latin 'of Leicester'.

LEM lunar excursion module.

Lenta London Enterprise Agency.

LEO Lyons Electronic Office.

Lepra Leprosy Relief Association.

LESS least-cost estimating and scheduling.

LEU London Ecology Unit.

LEV lunar excursion vehicle.

LF low frequency; line feed.

LFA Licentiate of the Institute of Financial Accountants; less favoured area.

LFAN Lesbian Feminist Action Network.

LFC London Food Commission; Lutheran Free Church.

lfc low-frequency current.

LFCI Licentiate of the Faculty of Commerce and Industry.

LFCS Licentiate of the Faculty of Secretaries.

LFD least fatal dose; low fat diet.

LFG London Freshwater Group.

LFNSA Low Frequency Noise Sufferers Association.

LFS Licentiate of the Faculty of Architects and Surveyors (Surveyors).

LG Life Guards; Low German.

LGA Leek Growers' Association; Local Government Agency.

LGBC Local Government Boundary Commission for England.

LGCL Licentiate of the Guild of Cleaners and Launderers.

LGCM Lesbian and Gay Christian Movement.

LGEB Local Government Examinations Board.

LGFA Lattice Girder Floor Association.

LGIC Laminated Glass Information Centre.

LGPA Lesbian and Gay Police Association.

LGR leasehold ground rent.

LGSM Licentiate of the Guildhall School of Music and Drama.

LGU Ladies' Golf Union.

LH luteinizing hormone.

lh left hand; left-half.

L/H leasehold.

LHA Lord High Admiral; local authority.

lhb left half-back.

lhd left hand drive.

LHCIMA Licentiate of the Hotel, Catering and Institutional Management Association.

LHG Licentiate of the Institute of Heraldic and Genealogical Studies.

LHI Lefthanders International (USA).

LHMC London Hospital Medical College.

LHS left-hand side.

LHU London Housing Unit.

LI Landscape Institute; Liberty International; Lincoln's Inn; light infantry.

Li lithium (chemical element).

LIA Life Insurance Association.

Libid London Inter-Bank Bid Rate.

Libor London Inter-Bank Offered Rate.

LicAc Licentiate of Acupuncture.

LicIQA Licentiate of the Institute of Quality Assurance.

Lidar light detection and ranging.

LIAP Licentiate of the Institution of Analysts and Programmers.

LICW Licentiate of the Institute of Clerks of Works of Great Britain Incorporated.

LIDPM Licentiate of the Institute of Data Processing Management.

LIE loss of independent existence.

LIFFE London International Financial Futures Exchange.

LIFMA Leather Importers, Factors and Merchants Association.

LIFO last in, first out.

LIIST Licentiate of the International Institute of Sports Therapy.

LILAM Licentiate of the Institute of Leisure and Amenity Management.

LILO last in, last out.

LIM Licentiate of the Institute of Metals.

LIMA Licentiate of the Institute of Mathematics and its Applications.

LIMF Licentiate of the Institute of Metal Finishing.

Linac linear accelerator.

Lincoln. *Lincolniensis*, Latin 'of Lincoln'.

LINK Let's Increase Neurofibromatosis Knowledge.

LInstBA Licentiate of the Institute of Business Administration.

LInstBB Licentiate of the Institute of British Bakers.

LInstBCA Licentiate of the Institute of Burial and Cremation Administration.

LInstP Licentiate of the Institute of Physics.

LIP life insurance policy.

LIPS logical inferences per second.

LIPT Ladies' International Polo Tournament.

LIR Licentiate of the Institute of population Registration.

LIS Lesbian Information Service; List and Index Society.

LISC Library and Information Services Council.

LISM Licentiate of the Incorporated Society of Musicians.

Lisp List Processing (computer programming language).

LISTD Licentiate of the Imperial Society of Teachers of Dancing.

Lit. *lire Italiane*, Italian 'Italian lire'.

lit. hum. *litterae humaniores*, Latin 'more humane letters' (Oxford honours degree in Ancient History, Philosophy, Latin and Greek).

LittB *Litterarum Baccalaureus*, Latin 'Bachelor of Letters'.

LittD *Litterarum Doctor*, Latin 'Doctor of Letters'.

LJ Lord Justice.

LJA Lady Jockeys Association; London Jute Association.

LL Lord Lieutenant.

LLB *Legum Baccalaureus*, Latin 'Bachelor of Law'.

LLCM Licentiate of the London College of Music.

LLCM(TD) Licentiate of the London College of Music (Teacher's Diploma).

LLD *Legum Doctor*, Latin 'Doctor of Law'.

LLG Labour Life Group; Landcare Liaison Group.

lli latitude and longitude indicator.

LLL Labour Left Liaison; low-level logic.

LLM *Legum Magister*, Latin 'Master of Law'.

LLNW low level nuclear waste.

LLRW low level radioactive waste.

LLSPT Licentiateship of the London School of Polymer Technology.

LLW low level waste.

LM Licentiate in Midwifery; Lord Mayor.

lm lumen (physics).

LMC London Mennonite Centre.

LMCA Long-Term Medical Conditions Alliance; Lorry Mounted Crane Association.

LME London Metal Exchange.

LMN Live Music Now!.

LMP last menstrual period.

LMPA Qualified Member of the Master Photographers Association.

LMRCP Licentiate in Midwifery of the Royal College of Physicians.

LMRTPI Legal Member of the Royal Town Planning Institute.

LMS Latin Mass Society; London Medieval Society; London Missionary Society; local management of schools.

LMSR London, Midland and Scottish Railway.

LMSSA Licentiate in Medicine and Surgery of the Society of Apothecaries.

LMSSALond Licentiate in Medicine, Surgery and Midwifery of the Society of Apothecaries of London.

LMT local mean time; length, mass, time.

LMX London Market Excess of Loss (insurance).

LMusLCM Licentiate in Music of the London College of Music.

LMusTCL Licentiate in Music, Trinity College of Music, London.

ln *logarithmus naturalis*, Latin 'natural logarithm'.

LNCP Licentiate Member of the National Council of Psychotherapists.

LNER London and North-Eastern Railway.

LNG liquefied natural gas.

LNHS London Natural History Society.

LNLC Ladies' Naval Luncheon Club.

LNS land navigation system.

LO liaison officer.

LOA leave of absence.

loa length overall.

LOAS Loyal Order of Ancient Shepherds.

LOB Location of Offices Bureau.

loc lines of communication.

loc. cit. *loco citato*, Latin 'at the place cited' and used in reference citation.

LOCIG Limited Overs Cricket Information Group.

LOFA Leisure and Outdoor Furniture Asociation.

L of C Library of Congress.

LOFIT London's Organised Fraud Investigation Team

L of N League of Nations.

Loft low-frequency radio telescope.

log logarithm, used in mathematics.

LOI Loyal Orange Institution.

Lola library on-line acquisition.

Londin. *Londiniensis*, Latin 'of London'.

Lonrho London and Rhodesian Mining and Land Company Limited.

loq. *loquitor*, Latin 'he/she speaks'.

LOS line of sight; loss of signal.

LP Labour Party; Lady/Lord Provost; Liberal Party; London Philharmonia; long playing (record); life policy; low pressure.

LPA Leather Producers Association; Liberal Party of Australia; Loyalist Prisoners Aid.

LPAC London Parallel Applications Centre; London Planning Advisory Committee.

LPC Lord President of the Council.

LPG liquefied petroleum gas.

LPGA Ladies Professional Golf Association.

lpi lines per inch.

lpm lines per millimetre/minute.

LPO London Philharmonic Orchestra.

LPRA Low Power Radio Association.

LPRI Licentiate of the Plastics and Rubber Institute.

LPS Lord Privy Seal.

LPU Low Pay Unit.

LQ letter quality.

LR Land Registry; Lloyd's Register.

Lr lawrencium (chemical element).

LRA Lace Research Association.

LRAD Licentiate of the Royal Academy of Dancing.

LRAM Licentiate of the Royal Academy of Music.

LRB London Residuary Body.

LRBM long range ballistic missile.

LRC London Rowing Club.

LRCM Licentiate of the Royal College of Music.

LRCP Licentiate of the Royal College of Physicians.

LRCPEdin, LRCSEdin conjoint diplomas of Licentiate of the Royal College of Physicians of Edinburgh and the Royal College of Surgeons of Edinburgh.

LRCPSGlasg Royal College of Physicians and Surgeons of Glasgow.

LRCPLond, MRCSEng conjoint diplomas of Licentiate of the Royal College of Physicians of London and Member of the Royal College of Surgeons of England.

LRCS League of Red Cross Societies and Red Crescent Societies; Licentiate of the Royal College of Surgeons; Lincoln Red Cattle Society.

LRCVS Licentiate of the Royal College of Veterinary Surgeons.

LRPS Licentiate of the Royal Photographic Society.

LRS Land Registry Stamp; Lloyd's Register of Shipping.

LRSC Licentiate of the Royal Society of Chemistry.

LRSM Licentiate Diploma of the Royal Schools of Music.

LRT London Regional Transport.

LRTA Light Rail Transit Association.

LRTMA London Rubber Terminal Market Association.

LS Law Society; Leading Seaman; Linnaean Society; London Sinfonietta; *loco sigilli*, Latin 'in place of a seal'; long shot; loudspeaker.

ls left side; lump sum.

LSA Land Settlement Association; Lead Sheet Association; Learning Support Assistant; Legal Services Agency; Leisure Studies Association; Licentiate of the Society of Apothecaries; London Sisal Association; Lowe's Syndrome Association; Lute Society of America.

LSB least significant bit.

LSBP Licentiate of the Society of Business Practitioners.

lsc *loco supra citato*, Latin 'in the place cited above'.

LSCP(Assoc) Associate of the London and Counties Society of Physiologists.

LSCS lower segment Caesarian section.

LSD *librae, solidi, denarii*, Latin 'pounds, shillings, pence'; lysergic acid diethylamide.

lsd least significant digit.

LSE London School of Economics and Political Science; London Stock Exchange.

LSG League of St George.

LSgt Lance Sergeant.

LSHTM London School of Hygiene and Tropical Medicine.

LSI Labour and Socialist International; large-scale integration.

LSJ London School of Journalism.

LSO London Symphony Orchestra.

LSS Law Society of Scotland; life support system.

LT London Transport; locum tenens; low tension.

lt local time.

LTA Lawn Tennis Association; Livestock Traders Association of Great Britain; lighter than air.

LTB London Tourist Board.

LTBT Limited Test Ban Treaty.

LTC Lawn Tennis Club.

LTCL Licentiate of Trinity College of Music, London.

LTE London Transport Executive.

LTG Little Theatre Guild of Great Britain.

LTH luteotropic hormone.

LTh Licentiate in Theology.

LTI Licentiate of the Textile Institute.

LTM Licentiate in Tropical Medicine; long-term memory.

LTO Leading Torpedo Operator.

LTOM London Traded Options Market.

LtRN Lieutenant, Royal Navy.

LTSC Licentiate in the Technology of Surface Coatings.

LTUA Lawn Tennis Umpires Association.

Lu lutetium (chemical element).

LUM lunar excursion model.

LURS London Underground Railway Society.

LUV Land Use Volunteer Service.

LV left ventricle; luncheon voucher.

lv low voltage.

LVA Licensed Victuallers' Association.

LVECC Light Vehicles Energy Consumption Committee.

LVS Licentiate in Veterinary Science.

LW lightweight; long wave (radio wavelength of over 1000m/3300 ft); low water.

LWA London Weighting Allowance; London Welsh Association.

lwb long wheel base.

LWC London Women's Centre.

LWL length at waterline; load waterline.

LWM low water mark.

LWR light-water reactor.

LWT London Weekend Television; London Wildlife Trust.

LX electrical; electrics; technical staff working on sound and lighting.

lx lux (physics).

lxxx love and kisses (prior to signature on a letter).

M

M 1000 in Roman numerals; Monday; Monsieur (French 'Mr'); Member; motorway; medium (garment size); metronome (with pulse value); million.

m male; maiden over (cricket); metre; married; masculine; mass; medium; mile; million; minute; month; minim (liquid measure); morning.

3M Minnesota Mining and Manfacturing Company.

MA Master of Arts; Mathematical Association; Microwave Association; Military Academy; Miscarriage Association; Museums Association; menstrual age; mental age.

mA milliampere.

m/a my account.

MAA Manufacturers Agents Association of Great Britain and Ireland; Master at Arms; Money Advice Association; Motor Agents' Association.

MAAC Mastic Asphalt Advisory Council.

MA(Architectural Studies) Master of Arts (Architectural Studies).

MAAT Member of the Association of Accounting Technicians.

MAB Memorial Advisory Bureau; monoclonal antibody.

MABAC Member of the Association of Business and Administrative Computing.

MABE Member of the Association of Business Executives.

MABIC Movement Against Bats in Churches.

MABP mean arterial blood pressure.

MAC Martial Arts Commission; Mobile Advice Centre; Museums Association of Canada; maximum allowable concentration; multiplex analogue components.

MAcA Master of the Acupuncture Association and Register.

MACC military aid to the civilian community.

MAcc Master of Accountancy.

MACE Member of the Association of Conference Executives.

MACP Member of the Association of Computer Professionals.

MAD major affective disorder; mutual assured destruction, this is the basis of the theory that to possess nuclear weapons is a deterrent; magnetic anomaly destruction.

mad maintenance, assembly and disassembly.

MADO Member of the Association of Dispensing Opticians.

MAE Manchester Association of Engineers; Maritime Advisory Exchange.

MA(Econ) Master of Arts in Economic and Social Studies.

MA(Ed) Master of Arts in Education.

maest. *maestoso*, Italian 'majestic' (music).

MAF Missionary Aviation Fellowship.

MAFF Ministry of Agriculture, Fisheries and Food.

MAG Motorcycle Action Group.

maglev magnetically levitated; magnetic levitation.

MAgr Master of Agriculture.

MAgrSc Master of Agricultural Science.

MAI Medical Aid for Iraq; Music Association of Ireland.

MAIB Marine Accident Investigation Board.

MAIE Member of the British Association of Industrial Editors.

MAInstCF Master Fitter of the National Institute of Carpet Fitters.

MAIU Marine Accident Investigation Unit.

MA(LD) Master of Arts (Landscape Design).

MAM Medical Association of Malta.

MAMA Meet-a-Mum Association.

MAMAA Mothers Against Murder and Aggression.

MAMS Member of the Association of Medical Secretaries, Practice Administrators and Receptionists.

MA(MUS) Master of Arts (Music).

MANA Musicians Against Nuclear Arms.

M & B May and Baker; Mills and Boon.

mand. *mandamus*, Latin 'we send' (type of writ).

M & E music and effects.

M & G Mercantile and General.

m & r maintenance and repairs.

M & S Marks and Spencer PLC.

m & s maintenance and supply.

MAnimSc Master of Animal Science.

man. pr. *mane primo*, Latin 'first thing in the morning'.

MAO Master of Arts, Obstetrics; monoamine oxidase.

MAP mean arterial pressure; medical aid post.

MAppArts Master in Applied Arts.

MAppSc Master in Applied Science.

MAPSAS Member of the Association of Public Service Administrative Staff.

MAR memory address register.

MArAd Master of Archive Administration.

MA(RCA) Master of Arts, Royal College of Art (Photography).

MArb Master of Arboriculture.

marc machine-readable cataloguing.

MArch Master of Architecture.

MArchE Master of Architectural Engineering.

MArt/RCA Master of Arts, Royal College of Art.

marv manoeuvrable re-entry vehicle.

MAS Manchester Astronomical Society; Medical Advisory Service; Microbeam Analysis Society; Money Advice Scotland.

MASc Master of Agricultural Science; Master of Applied Scienc.

masc. masculine (used in grammar).

maser microwave amplification by stimulated emission of radiation.

MASH Mobile Army Surgical Hospital.

MASI Member of the Architects and Surveyors Institute.

MA(SocSci) Master of Arts (Social Science).

MASP Member of the Association of Sales Personnel.

MASTA Medical Advisory Service for Travellers Abroad.

MATCH Mothers Apart from their Children.

MA(Theol) Master of Arts in Theology.

matts multiple airborne target trajectory system.

MATV master antenna television.

MAW medium assault weapon.

MAYC Methodist Association of Youth Clubs.

MB *Medicinae Baccalaureus*, Latin 'Bachelor of Medicine'; Maternity Benefit; megabyte.

mb millibar.

MBA Master of Business Administration.

MBAE Member of the British Academy of Experts.

MBAE Member of the British Association of Electrolysis.

MB, BCh *or* **MB, BChir** *or* **MB, BS** conjoint degree of Bachelor of Medicine, Bachelor of Surgery.

MBC Mediterranean Burns Club; Mountain Bike Club.

mbc maximum breathing capacity.

MB, ChB conjoint degree of Bachelor of Medicine, Bachelor of Surgery.

MBCO Member of the British College of Ophthalmic Opticians.

MBCS Member of the British Computer Society.

MBD minimal brain dysfunction.

MBE Member of the Order of the British Empire.

MBF Multiple Births Foundation; Musicians' Benevolent Fund.

MBFR Mutual Balanced Force Recution.

MBEI Member of the Institute of Body Engineers.

MBEng Member of the Association of Building Engineers.

MBHA Member of the British Hypnotherapy Association.

MBHI Member of the British Horological Institute.

MBI management buy-in.

MBID Member of the British institute of Interior Design.

MBIE Member of the British Institute of Embalmers.

MBIFD Member of the British Institute of Funeral Directors.

MBII Member of the British Institute of Innkeeping.

MBIM Member of the British Institute of Management.

MBK missing, believed killed.

MBL menstrual blood loss.

MBO management buy-out; management by objectives.

MBP mean blood pressure.

MBR memory buffer register.

MBS Manchester Business School.

MBSc Master of Business Science.

MBSI Musical Box Society International.

MBSSG Master Glassblower, British Society of Scientific Glassblowers.

MBT Member of the Association of Beauty Teachers; main battle tank.

MC *Magister Chirurgiae*, Latin 'Master of Surgery'; Master of Ceremonies; Medical Corps; Member of Congress; Member of Council; Military Cross; Morse Code; magistrates' court.

MCA Master Carvers Association; Meat Carriers Association; Milling Cutter and Toolbit Association; Motor Cycle Association; Mug Collectors Association; monetary compensatory amounts.

MCANW Medical Campaign Against Nuclear Weapons.

MCB Mastership in Clinical Biochemistry; Metric Conversion Board; memory control block.

mcb miniature circuit breaker.

MCC Marylebone Cricket Club; Maxwell Communications Corporation; Motor Caravanners' Club.

MCCA Minor Counties Cricket Association.

MCCC Marie Curie Cancer Care.

MCCN Marine and Coastal Community Network.

MCCU mobile coronary care unit.

MCD Master of Civic Design.

MCDH Master of Community Dental Health.

MCE Master of Chemical Engineering; Master of Civil Engineering.

MCES Member of the Faculty of Executive Secretaries.

MCGA multicolour graphics array.

MCGPIreI Member of the Irish College of General Practitioners.

MCH mean corpuscular haemoglobin.

MCh *Magister Chirurgiae*, Latin 'Master of Surgery'.

MCHC mean corpuscular haemoglobin concentration.

MChD *Magister Chirurgiae Dentalis*, Latin 'Master of Dental Surgery'.

MChE Master of Chemical Engineering.

MChemEng Master of Chemical Engineering.

MChir *Magister Chirurgiae*, Latin 'Master of Surgery'.

MChOrth *Magister Chirurgiae Orthopaedicae*, Latin 'Master of Orthopaedic Surgery'.

MChS Member of the Society of Chiropodists.

MCIBS Member of the Chartered Institute of Bankers in Scotland.

MCIBSE Member of the Chartered Institution of Building Services Engineers.

MCIM Member of the Chartered Institute of Marketing.

MCIOB Member of the Chartered Institute of Building.

MCIPS Member of the Chartered Institute of Purchasing and Supply.

MCIS Member of the Institute of Chartered Secretaries and Administrators.

MCIT Member of the Chartered Institute of Transport.

MCL Master of Civil Law; Movement for Compassionate Living.

MCollP Member of the College of Preceptors.

MCom Master of Commerce.

MCommH Master of Community Health.

MCOphth Member of the College of Ophthalmologists.

MCP Member of the College of Preceptors; male chauvinist pig.

MCPM Member of the Confederation of Professional Management.

MCPO Master Chief Petty Officer.

MCPS Mechanical Copyright Protection Society; Member of the College of Physicians and Surgeons.

MCR Middle Common Room; mobile control room.

MCS Marine Conservation Society; Master of Commercial Science; Military College of Science; missile control system.

Mc/s megacycles per second.

MCSD Member of the Chartered Society of Designers.

MCSP Member of the Chartered Society of Physiotherapy.

MCST Member of the College of Speech Therapists.

MCT Member of the Association of Corporate Treasurers.

MCTHCM Member of the Confederation of Tourism, Hotel and Catering Management.

MCU medium close-up (photography).

MCV mean corpuscular volume.

MCW modulated continuous wave.

MCYW Member of the Community and Youth Work Association.

MD Managing Director; Middle Dutch; *Medicinae Doctor*, Latin 'Doctor of Medicine'; malicious damage; mentally deficient; muscular dystrophy; musical director.

Md mendelevium (chemical element).

MDA Muscular Dystrophy Association.

mda monochrome display adaptor.

MDAS Malt Distillers Association of Scotland.

MDCR Management Diploma of the College of Radiographers.

MDent Master of Dental Science.

MDentSc Master of Dental Science.

MDes Master of Design.

MDes(RCA) Master of Design, Royal College of Art.

MDF Manic Depression Fellowship; medium density fibreboard.

MDMA methylene-dioxymethamphetamine (the drug Ecstasy).

MDR memory data register; minimum daily requirement.

MDS Master of Dental Surgery.

MDSc Master of Dental Science.

MDU Medical defence Union.

ME Master of Engineering; Methodist Episcopal; Middle East; Middle English, the English language from 1050 to 1550; Most Excellent; mechanical engineer; mining engineer; myalgic encephalomyelitis.

Me methyl, an organic chemical group of carbon and hydrogen (CH_3).

MEC Member of the Executive Council; Methodist Episcopal Church; minimum effective concentration.

MEc Master of Economics.

MECI Member of the Institute of Employment Consultants.

MEcon Master of Economics.

MED minimum effective dose.

MEd Master of Education.

Med(EdPsych) Master of Education (Educational Psychology).

Medlars Medical Literature Analysis and Retrieval System.

MEdStud Master of Educational Studies.

MEE Master of Electrical Engineering.

MEMA Marine Engine and Equipment Manufacturers' Association.

Mencap Royal Society for Mentally Handicapped Children and Adults.

MEng Master of Engineering.

MEP Member of the European Parliament.

mep mean effective pressure.

MERLIN Multi-Element Radio-Linked Interferometer Network.

MERU Maharishi European Research University.

MESc Master of Engineering Science.

Messrs messieurs, French 'sirs' or 'gentlemen' used when writing formally to a group of people or organisation).

m et n *mane et nocte*, Latin 'morning and night'.

metsat meteorological satellite.

MeV mega-electron-volt; million electron-volts.

MEW microwave early warning system.

MF medium frequency.

mf *mezzo-forte*, Italian 'moderately loud' (music).

MFA Master of Fine Arts; Metal Finishing Association; Multi-Fibre Arrangement.

MFARCS Member of the Faculty of Anaesthetists of the Royal College of Surgeons.

MFBA Member of the Faculty of Business Administrators.

MFC Mastership in Food Control.

MFCM Member of the Faculty of Community Medicine.

MFD minimum fatal dose.

MFDO Member of the Faculty of Dispensing Opticians.

MFH Master of Foxhounds; mobile field hospital.

MFHom Member of the Faculty of Homoeopathy.

MFlem Middle Flemish.

mflops million floating-point operations per second.

MFM modified frequency modulation.

MFMI Men for Missions International (USA).

MFN most favoured nation.

MFP Mothers for Peace.

MFPA Mouth and Foot Painting Artists.

MFPC Man-made Fibres Producers' Committee.

MFPHM Member of the Faculty of Public Health Medicine.

MFPHMIrel Member of the Faculty of Public Health Medicine.

MFr Middle French.

mft *mistura fiat*, Latin 'let a mixture be made'.

MFTCom Member of the Faculty of Teachers in Commerce.

mfv motor fleet vehicle.

MG Major-General; Morris Garages; machine gun.

Mg magnesium (chemical element); megagram.

mg milligram.

MGAGB Mounted Games Association of Great Britain.

mgawd make good all works disturbed.

MGC Marriage Guidance Council; Museums and Galleries Commission.

mgd million gallons per day.

MGDSRCSEd Membership in General Dental Surgery, Royal College of Surgeons of Edinburgh.

MGDSRCSEng Membership in General Dental Surgery, Royal College of Surgeons of England.

MGM Metro Goldwyn Meyer; mobile guided missile.

MGN Mirror Group Newspapers.

Mgr Monsignor, as used in the Roman Catholic Church.

MH Master of Horse; Master of Hounds; marital history.

mH millihenry.

MHA Member of the House of Assembly; Methodist Homes for the Aged.

MHC major histocompatibility.

MHD magnetic hydrodynamic.

MHE Master of Home Economics.

MHF medium high frequency.

MHG Middle High German.

MHK Member of the House of Keys.

MHLG Ministry of Housing and Local Government.

MHM Mental Health Media.

MHort(RHS) National Diploma in Horticulture, Royal Horticultural Society.

MHortSc Master of Horticultural Science.

MHFS Member of the Council of Health Fitness & Sports Therapists.

MHR Member of the House of Representatives.

MHRA Modern Humanities Research Association.

MHS Malta Heraldic Society; Meat Hygiene Service; Military Historical Society.

mhs medical history sheet; message handling system.

MHTGR modular high-temperature gas-cooled reactor.

MHW mean high water.

MHz megahertz.

MI Military Intelligence (state security and anti-espionage service in the UK); medical inspection; myocardial infarction.

mi mile.

MI5 Military Intelligence 5 (UK anti-espionage and state security service, officially ceased since 1964).

MI6 Military Intelligence 6 (UK anti-espionage and state security service, officially ceased since 1964).

MIA Maldive International Airlines; Malleable Ironfounders' Association; Music Industries Association; missing in action.

MIAA & S Member of the Incorporated Institute of Auctioneers and Surveyors.

MIAB Member of the International Association of Book-keepers.

MIAEA Member of the Institute of Automotive Engineer Assessors.

MIAgrE Member of the Institution of Agricultural Engineers.

MIAP Member of the Institution of Analysts and Programmers.

MIAT Member of the Institute of Asphalt Technology.

MIAT Member of the Institute of Animal Technology.

MIB Metal Information Bureau; Motor Insurers' Bureau; Mustard Information Bureau (USA).

MIBC Member of the Institute of Building Control.

MIBCM Member of the Institute of British Carriage and Automobile Manufacturers.

MIBCO Member of the Institution of Building Control Officers.

MIBF Member of the Institute of British Foundrymen.

MIBiol Member of the Institute of Biology.

MIC Magnesium Industry Council; Millinery Information Centre.

MICE Member of the Institution of Civil Engineers.

MIChemE Member of the Institution of Chemical Engineers.

MICM Associate Member of the Institute of Credit Management.

MICO Member of the Institute of Careers Officers.

MICorr Member of the Institute of Corrosion.

MICR magnetic ink character recognition.

Micro Multinational Initiative for the Use of Computers in Research Organizations.

MICS Member of the Institute of Chartered Shipbrokers.

MICU mobile intensive care unit.

MICW Member of the Institute of Clerks of Works of Great Britain Incorporated.

MID minimum infective dose.

Midas Missile Defence Alarm System.

MIDI musical instrument digital interface (manufacturer's standard permitting different digital musical equipment to be freely connected when composing or recording).

MIDIRS Midwives Information and Resource Service.

MIDPM Member of the Institute of Data Processing Management.

MIDTA Member of the International Dance Teachers' Association.

MIED Member of the Institution of Engineering Designers.

MIEE Member of the Institution of Electrical Engineers.

MIEIE Corporate Member of the Institution of Electrical and Electronics Incorporated Engineers.

MIEM Master Member of the Institute of Executives and Managers.

MIEx Member of the Institute of Export.

MIEx(Grad) Graduate Member of the Institute of Export.

MIExpE Member of the Institute of Explosives Engineers.

MIF Miners' International Federation; migration inhibition factor.

MIFA Member of the Institute of Field Archaeologists.

MIFF Member of the Institute of Freight Forwarders Ltd.

MIFireE Member of the Institution of Fire Engineers.

MIFST Member of the Institute of Food Science and Technology.

MIG mortgage indemnity guarantee.

MiG Mikoyan and Gurevich (designers of Soviet warplane).

MIGasE Member of the Institution of Gas Engineers.

MIGD Member of the Institute of Grocery Distribution.

MIGeol Member of the Institute of Geologists.

MIH Member of the Institute of Housing.

MIHEC Member of the Institute of Home Economics.

MIHIE Member of the institute of Highway Incorporated Engineers.

MIHT Member of the Institution of Highways and Transportation.

MII Maritime Institute of Ireland.

MIIA Member of the Institute of Internal Auditors.

MIIExE Member of the Institution of Incorporated Executive Engineers.

MIIM Member of the Institution of Industrial Managers.

MIInfSc Member of the Institute of Information Scientists.

MIIRSM Member of the International Institute of Risk and Safety Management.

MIISE Member of the International Institute of Social Economics.

MIISec Member of the Institute of Industrial Security.

MIL Member of the Institute of Linguists.

MILAM Member of the Institute of Leisure and Amenity Management.

MIM Professional Member of the Institute of Materials.

MIManf Member of the Institute of Manufacturing.

MIMarE Member of the Institute of Marine Engineers.

MIMatM Member of the Institute of Materials Management.

MIMBM Member of the Institute of Maintenance and Building Management.

MIMC Member of the Institute of Management Consultants.

MIMechE Member of the Institution of Mechanical Engineers.

MIMechIE Member of the Institution of Mechanical Incorporated Engineers.

MIMF Member of the Institute of Metal Finishing.

MIMgt Member of the Institute of Management.

MIMI Member of the Institute of the Motor Industry.

MIMinE Member of the Institution of Mining Engineers.

MIMM Member of the Institute of Massage and Movement; Member of the Institution of Mining and Metallurgy.

MIMS Member of the Institute of Management Specialists.

min. minute, as used in time; minimum.

MInstAEA Member of the Institute of Automotive Engineer Assessors.

MInstAM(Dip) Member of the Institute of Administrative Management.

MInstBB Member of the Institute of British Bakers.

MInstBCA Member of the Institute of Burial and Cremation Administration.

MInstBE Member of the Institute of British Engineers.

MInstBRM Member of the Institute of Baths and Recreation Management.

MInstBRMDip Diploma Member of the Institute of Baths and Recreation Management.

MInstCh Member of the Institute of Chiropodists.

MInstD Member of the Institute of Directors.

MInstE Member of the Institute of Energy.

MInstMC Member of the Institute of Measurement and Control.

MInstNDT Member of the British Institute of Non-Destructive Testing.

MInstP Member of the Institute of Physics.

MInstPet Member of the Institute of Petroleum.

MInstPkg Member of the Institute of Packaging.

MInstPM Full Member of the Institute of Professional Managers.

MInstPS Corporate Member of the Institute of Purchasing and Supply.

MInstR Member of the Institute of Refrigeration.

MInstSMM Member of the Institute of Sales and Marketing Management.

MInstTA Member of the Institute of Transport Administration.

MInstWM Member of the Institute of Wastes Management.

MIOC Member of the Institute of Carpenters.

MIOFMS Member of the Institute of Financial and Management Studies.

MIOP Member of the Institute of Printing.

MIOSH Member of the Institution of Occupational Safety and Health.

MIMIT Member of the Institute of Musical Instrument Technology.

MIP Member of the Institute of Plumbing; marine insurance policy; monthly investment plan.

mip mean indicated pressure.

MIPA Member of the Institute of Practitioners of Advertising.

MIPC Member of the Institute of Production Control.

MIPHE Member of the Institute of Public Health Engineers.

MIPI Member of the Institute of Professional Investigators.

MIPlantE Member of the Institution of Plant Engineers.

MIPM Member of the Institute of Personnel Management.

MIPR Member of the Institute of Public Relations.

mips millions of instructions per second.

MIPSA Moscow Institute of Painting, Sculpture and Architecture.

MIPTC Men's International Professional Tennis Council.

MIQ Member of the Institute of Quarrying.

MIQA Member of the Institute of Quality Assurance.

MIR mortgage interest relief.

MIRAS mortgage interest relief at source.

MIRRV Member of the Institute of Revenue, Rating and Valuation.

MIRSE Member of the Institution of Railway Signal Engineers.

MIRSO Member of the Institute of Road Safety Officers.

MIRTE Member of the Institute of Road Transport Engineering.

MIRV multiple independently targeted re-entry vehicle, as used in nuclear warfare.

MIS Management Information System; Member of the Institute of Statisticians; Mining Institute of Scotland; Mobility Information Service.

MISD multiple instruction, single data stream.

MISM Member of the Institute of Supervisory Management.

MISOB Member of the Incorporated Society of Organ Builders.

MIST Music in Scotland Trust.

mist. *mistura*, Latin 'mixture'.

MIStructE Member of the Institution of Structural Engineers.

MISW Member of the Institute of Social Welfare.

MIT Massachusetts Institute of Technology.

MITD Member of the Institute of Training and Development.

MITSA Member of the Institute of Trading Standards Administration.

mitts minutes of telecommunications traffic.

MIU Maharishi International University.

MIWEM Member of the Institution of Water and Environmental Management.

MIWPC Member of the Institute of Water Pollution Control.

MJ megajoule.

MJI Member of the Institute of Journalists.

MJQ Modern Jazz Quartet.

MJur Master of Jurisprudence.

MK mark (numbering of car design variants).

mks metre-kilogram-second.

mksa metre-kilogram-second-ampere.

ML Licentiate in Midwifery; medieval Latin.

ml millilitre.

MLA Malta Library Association; Master Locksmiths Association; Member of the Legislative Assembly; Modern Language Association; Music Library Association (USA).

MLAGB Muzzle Loaders Association of Great Britain.

MLC Maori Language Commission; Meat and Livestock Commission; mixed lymphocyte culture.

MLCOM Member of the London College of Osteopathic Medicine.

MLD Master of Landscape Design; mean/minimum lethal dose.

MLF multilateral force.

MLG Middle Low German; Midwifery Legislation Group.

MLibSc Master of Library Science.

MLing Master of Languages.

MLitt *Magister Litterarum*, Latin 'Master of Letters'.

MLP Militant Labour Party.

MLR minimum lending rate; mixed lymphocyte reaction.

MLRS multiple launch rocket system.

MLS Master of Library Science; Member of the Linnean Society.

MLSO Medical Laboratory Scientific Officer.

MLURI Macaulay Land Use Research Institute.

MLV murine leukaemia virus.

MM Maelzel's metronome; Military Medal; mucous membrane.

mm millimetre.

MMA Master of Management and Administration; Meat Manufacturers Association; Medical Missionary Association; Meter Manufacturers Association; Music Masters and Mistresses Association.

MMath Master of Mathematics.

MMB Milk Marketing Board.

MMC Monopolies and Mergers Commission.

MME Master of Mechanical Engineering.

MMed Master of Medicine.

MMedSci Master of Medical Science.

MMeT Master of Metallurgy.

MMetE Master of Metallurgical Engineering.

mmf magnetomotive force.

MMG medium machine gun.

mmHg millimetre of mercury.

MMI man-machine interface.

MMM International Association of Margaret Morris Method; Medical Missionaries of Mary.

MMMA Metalforming Machinery Makers Association; Milking Machine Manufacturers Association.

mmol millimole.

MMP International Organisation of Masters, Mates and Pilots; Military Mounted Police.

MMQ minimum manufacturing quantity.

MMR measles, mumps and rubella; mass miniature radiography.

MMS Massachusetts Medical Society; Member of the Institute of Management Services; Methodist Missionary Society.

MMSE Master of Medical Sciences.

MMTA Minor Metals Traders Association.

MMU memory management unit.

MMus Master of Music.

MMusArt Master of Musical Arts.

Mmus, RCM Degree of Master of Music, Royal College of Music.

MN Master of Nursing; Merchant Navy.

Mn manganese (chemical element).

MNA Multiple Newsagents Association.

MNAD Multinational Airborne Division (NATO).

MNAEA Member of the National Association of Estate Agents.

MNC multinational company.

MNCP Full Member of the National Council of Psychotherapists.

MND motor neurone disease.

MNDA Missionary Sisters of Our Lady of the Angels; Motor Neurone Disease Association.

MNI Member of the Nautical Institute.

MNIMH Member of the National Institute of Medical Herbalists.

MNR marine nature reserve.

MNSc Master of Nursing Science.

MNurs Master of Nursing.

MO Medical Officer; Meteorological Office; mass observation; *modus operandi*, Latin 'way of working'; money order.

Mo molybdenum (chemical element).

MOA Microwave Oven Association; memorandum of agreement.

MOBS multiple orbit bombardment system.

MObstG Master of Obstetrics and Gynaecology.

MOD Ministry of Defence; mail order department.

mod. *moderato*, Italian 'moderate' (music).

modem modulator-demodulator.

MOH Medical Officer of Health; Master of Otter Hounds.

MOLARA Motoring Organizations Land Access & Rights Association.

MOMA Museum of Modern Art.

MOMI Museum of the Moving Image.

MOMIMTS Military & Orchestral Musical Instrument Makers' Trade Society.

MOPA Mail Order Publishers' Authority.

MOR middle-of-the-road (of music that is broadcast).

mor. *morendo*, Italian 'dying' (music).

MORI Market and Opinion Research Institute.

mor. sol. *more solito*, Latin 'in the usual way'.

MOrthRCSEng Membership in Orthodontics, Royal College of Surgeons of England.

MOS metal oxide semiconductor.

MOT Ministry of Transport.

MOTT Men of the Trees.

MOU memorandum of understanding.

MOUS multiple occurrence of unexplained symptoms.

MOUSE minimum orbital unmanned satellite of the earth.

mov. *movimento*, Italian 'motion' (music).

Move Men over Violence (counselling, etc, for wife-beaters).

MOW Movement for the Ordination of Women.

MP Member of Parliament; Metropolitan/ Military Police; Mounted Police.

mp melting point (used in chemistry); *mezzo piano*, Italian 'moderately quiet' (music).

MPA Major Projects Association; Master of Public Administration; Modern Poetry Association; Mortar Producers Association.

MPAA Motion Picture Association of America.

MPAGB Modern Pentathlon Association of Great Britain.

MPAS Mobile Projects Association Scotland.

MPB male pattern baldness.

MPBA Model Power Boat Association.

MPC Metropolitan Police Commissioner.

MPD maximum permissible dose.

MPE Master of Physical Education; maximum permissible exposure (to radiation); maximum possible error.

mpg miles per gallon.

MPH Master of Public Health.

MPh Master of Philosophy.

mph miles per hour.

MPharm Master of Pharmacy.

MPhil Master of Philosophy.

MPhil(Eng) Master of Philosophy in Engineering.

MPhys Master of Physics.

MPI Max Planck Institute; maximum permissible intake.

MPL maximum permissible level.

mpm metres per minute.

MPPS Master of Public Policy Studies.

MPRI Member of the Plastics and Rubber Institute.

MProfBTM Member of Professional Business and Technical Management.

MPS Member of the Pharmaceutical Society; Member of the Philological Society; Mervyn Peake Society; Society for Mucopolysaccharide Diseases.

mps metres per second.

MPsych Master of Psychology.

MPsychMed Master of Psychological Medicine.

MPsychol Master of Psychology.

MPU Medical Practitioners Union.

mpu microprocessor unit.

MPV multipurpose vehicle.

MR Master of the Rolls; magnetic resonance; map reference; mental retardation; metabolic rate; motivational research.

Mr Mister (the title used before a name if the person is male, formerly Master).

MRA moral rearmament.

MRad MRad(D) Master of Radiology (Radiodiagnosis) or (Radiotherapy).

MRAeS Member of the Royal Aeronautical Society.

MRAF Marshal of the Royal Air Force.

MRAS Member of the Royal Astronomical Society; Member of the Royal Asiatic Society.

MRBM medium-range ballistic missile.

MRC Medical Research Council.

MRCA multirole combat aircraft.

MRCGP Member of the Royal College of General Practitioners.

MRCOG Member of the Royal College of Obstetricians and Gynaecologists.

MRCP Member of the Royal College of Physicians.

MRCPath Member of the Royal College of Pathologists.

MRCPIrel Member of the Royal College of Physicians of Ireland.

MRCPsych Member of the Royal College of Psychiatrists.

MRCP(UK) Member of the Royal College of Physicians of the United Kingdom.

MRCSEng Member of the Royal College of Surgeons of England.

MRCVS Member of the Royal College of Veterinary Surgeons.

MRD minimal residual disease.

MRE Master of Religious Education; Microbiological Research Establishment; meals ready to eat.

MREHIS Member of the Royal Environmental Health Institute of Scotland.

MRF Meningitis Research Foundation.

MRG Minority Rights Group.

MRGS Member of the Royal Geographical Society.

MRI magnetic resonance imaging.

MRICS Member of the Royal Institution of Chartered Surveyors.

MRIN Member of the Royal Institute of Navigation.

MRINA Member of the Royal Institution of Naval Architects.

MRIPHH Member of the Royal Institute of Public Health and Hygiene.

MRM mechanically-recovered meat.

mRNA messenger ribonucleic acid.

MRO Member of the Register of Osteopaths.

mrp manufacturer's recommended price.

mrrp manufacturer's recommended retail price.

MRPharms Member of the Royal Pharmaceutical Society of Great Britain.

Mrs mistress, the title used before a married woman's name. The title Ms can also be used but it does not denote marital status.

MRSC Member of the Royal Society of Chemistry.

MRSH Member of the Royal Society of Health.

MRSM Member of the Royal Society of Medicine.

MRTPI Member of the Royal Town Planning Institute.

MRUA Mobile Radio Users Association.

MRV multiple re-entry vehicle.

MS Mammal Society; Manpower Society; Master of Surgery; Master of Science; Media Society; Movement for Survival; Multiple Sclerosis Society of Great Britain and Northern Ireland; *mano sinistra*, Italian 'left hand'; manuscript, mass spectrometry; multiple sclerosis.

Ms the title used before a woman's name, which can be used for either married or single women. It was introduced in the 1970s as an equivalent to Mr.

ms millisecond.

m/s metres per second.

MSA Marine Safety Agency; Master of Agricultural Science; Modern Studies Association; Motor Schools Association of Great Britain; motorway service area.

MSAgr Master of Science in Agriculture.

MSAPP Member of the Society of Advanced Psychotherapy Practitioners.

MSArch Master of Science in Architecture.

MSB most significant bit.

MSBA Master of Science in Business Administration.

MSBP Member of the Society of Business Practitioners.

MSBT Member of the Society of Business Teachers.

MSBTH Member of the Society of Health and Beauty Therapists.

MSBus Master of Science in Business.

MSC Manpower Services Commission.

MSc Master of Science.

msc moved, seconded and carried.

MScAg Master of Science in Agriculture.

MSCD Master of Dental Science.

MSCE Master of Science in Civil Engineering.

MScChemE Master of Science in Chemical Engineering.

MSeEcon Master in Faculty of Economic and Social Studies.

MSc(Econ) Master of Science in Economics.

MSc(Ed) Master of Science in Education.

MSc(Eng) Master of Science in Engineering.

MSCI Index Morgan Stanley Capital International World Index.

MScMed Master of Medical Science.

MSc(Mgt) Master of Science in Management.

MSCT Member of the Society of Cardiological Technicians.

MScTech Master of Technical Science.

MS-DOS MicroSoft Disk-Operating System.

MSE Member of the Society of Engineers.

MSF Manufacturing, Science and Finance Union; Master of Science in Forestry; Médécins sans Frontières; Multiple Shops Federation; medium standard frequency.

MSG monosodium glutamate.

MSGB Manorial Society of Great Britain.

MSH Master of Stag Hounds.

MSHR Missionary Sisters of the Holy Rosary.

MSI Marie Stopes Interrnational; medium-scale integration.

MSIAD Member of the Society of Industrial Artists and Designers.

MSIE Master of Science in Industrial Engineering.

MSL mean sea level.

MSM Meritorious Service Medal.

MSN Master of Science in Nursing.

MSocSc Master of Social Science.

MSRA Multiple Shoe Retailers' Association.

MSRG Mediaeval Settlement Research Group; Moated Site Research Group.

MSS Master of Social Science; mass storage system.

MSSCH Member of the School of Surgical Chiropody.

MSSc Master of Social Science.

MSSc Master of Surgical Science.

MSSF Member of the Society of Shoe Fitters.

MSST Member of the Society of Surveying Technicians.

MST Mountain Standard Time; mean survival time.

MSt Master of Studies.

MSTA Member of the Swimming Teachers' Association.

MSU Migrant Support Unit; mid-stream specimen of urine.

msv millisievert.

MSW Master in Social Work; Medical Social Worker; magnetic surface wave.

MSY maximum sustainable yield.

MT Mechanical Transport; Middle Temple; machine translation; mean time.

Mt meitnerium (chemical element).

mt megaton; metric ton.

MTA Master Tanners Association; Mica Trades Association.

MTB motor torpedo-boat.

MTBF mean time between failures.

MTD Master of Transport Design; maximum tolerated dose; moving target detector.

MTech Master of Technology.

MTFCI Model T Ford Club International.

MTh Master of Theology.

MTheol Master of Theology.

MTI moving target indicator.

MTM methods time measurement.

MTTR mean time to repair.

MTP Master of Town and Country Planning.

MTPI Master of Town Planning.

Mt. Rev. Most Reverend.

MTropMed Master of Tropical Medicine.

MU Mothers' Union; Musicians' Union.

MUA Machinery Users Association; Mail Users Association.

MUF maximum usable frequency.

MUFTI minimum use of force tactical intervention.

MUniv Master of the University (Honorary).

MusB *Musicae Baccalaureus*, Latin 'Bachelor of Music'.

MusD Doctor of Music.

MusM Master of Music.

MusM(Comp) Master of Music (Composition).

MusMPerf Master of Music (Performance).

mV millivolt.

mv market value; merchant/motor vessel; *mezzo voce*, Italian 'half the power of voice' (music); muzzle velocity.

MVDA Motor Vehicle Dismantlers Association of Great Britain.

MVM Master of Veterinary Medicine.

MVO Member of the Royal Victorian Order.

MVRG Mediaeval Villages Research Group.

MVSc Master of Veterinary Science.

MVT Military Vehicle Trust.

MVWGS Multi-Vintage Wine Growers Society.

MW medium wave; megawatt.

mW milliwatt.

MWA Married Women's Association; Mystery Writers of America.

MWC Mental Welfare Commission.

MWeldI Member of the Welding Institute.

MWF Medical Women's Federation.

MWES Member of the Women's Engineering Society.

MWGM Most Worshipful Grand Master (freemasonry).

MWh megawatt hour.

MY motor yacht.

MYA Model Yachting Association.

MYD Member of the Youth Development Association.

my million years.

myob mind your own business.

MX missile experimental.

N

N nitrogen (chemical element); Norse; knight (chess); national; navy; neutral (electrical wiring); newton; north.

n indefinite number; name; nano-; *natus*, Latin 'born'; neuter; new; nominative; noon; note; noun.

NA Napoleonic Association; Narcotics Anonymous; North America.

Na *natrium*, Latin 'sodium' (chemical element).

n/a no account; not applicable; not available.

NAA National Artists Association; Neckware Association of America; North Atlantic Assembly.

NAAFI Navy, Army and Air Force Institutes.

NAAS National Agricultural Advisory Scheme.

NAAW National Association of Amateur Winemakers.

NABBA National Amateur Body Building Association.

NABC National Association of Boys' Clubs.

NABD National Association of Blood Donors.

NABISCO National Biscuit Company.

NAC National Amusements Council; National Anglers Council; National Association for the Childless; National Association of Choirs; National Asthma Campaign; New Assembly of Churches.

NACA National Athletic and Cycling Association.

NACAB National Association of Citizens' Advice Bureaux.

NACAM National Association of Corn and Agricultural Merchants.

NACLE National Association of Chimney Lining Engineers.

NACM National Association of Charcoal Manufacturers; National Association of Cider Makers; National Association of Colliery Manufacturers.

NACODS National Association of Colliery Overmen, Deputies and Shotfirers.

NACRO National Association for the Care and Resettlement of Offenders.

NACT National Association of Clinical Tutors; National Association of Cycle Traders.

NAD National Association of the Deaf (Eire); no abnormality detected; no appreciable difference; not on active duty.

NADECT National Association for Drama in Education and Children's Theatre.

NADJ National Association of Disc Jockeys.

NADW National Association of Disabled Writers.

NAEA National Association of Estate Agents.

NAEW Nato Airborne Early Warning.

NAFB & AE National Association of Farriers, Blacksmiths & Agricultural Engineers.

NAFBRC National Association of Family Based Respite Care.

NAFD National Association of Funeral Directors.

NAFO National Association of Fire Officers; Northwest Atlantic Fisheries Organization.

NAFSCA National Automatic Sprinkler and Fire Control Association.

NAFSO National Association of Field Study Officers.

NAG National Acquisitions Group; National Association of Goldsmiths of Great Britain and Ireland; National Association of Groundsmen; Nystagmus Action Group.

nag net annual gain.

NAGC National Association of Gifted Children.

NAGCS National Association for Gifted Children in Scotland.

NAGS National Allotments and Gardens Society.

NAHT National Association of Head Teachers.

NAI non-accidental injury.

NAIBD National Association of Industries for the Blind and Disabled.

NAIRU non-accelerating inflation rate of unemployment.

NAITA National Association of Independent Travel Agents.

NAIWC National Association of Inland Waterway Carriers.

NALC National Association of Ladies Circles of Great Britain and Ireland; National Association of Laryngectomee Clubs; National Association of Lawyers for Children.

NALGO National and Local Government Officers' Association.

NALHF National Association of League of Hospital Friends.

NALI National Association of the Launderette Industry.

NALM National Association of Lift Makers.

NALSAT National Association of Land Settlement Association Tenants.

NAMB National Association of Master Bakers, Confectioners and Caterers.

NAMCW National Association for Maternal and Child Welfare.

NAME National Association of Marine Enginebuilders; New American Music in Europe.

NAMG National Association of Multiple Grocers.

NAMHO National Association of Mining History Oranisations.

NAMM National Association of Master Masons.

N & Q notes and queries.

n & v nausea and vomiting.

NAO National Audit Office.

NAPGC National Association of Public Golf Courses.

NAP National Association of the Paralysed.

NAPF National Association of Pension Funds.

NAPO National Association of Probation Officers.

NAPP National Association for Patient Participation; National Association for the Protection of Punters.

NAPR National Association of Pram Retailers.

NAPS National Association for Premenstrual Syndrome; National Association of Personal Secretaries; National Auricula and Primula Society; Nationwide Association of Preserving Specialists.

NAPT National Association of Percussion Teachers.

NAPV National Association of Prison Visitors.

NARO Naval Aircraft Repair Organisation.

NARPS National Association of UK River Protection Societies.

NARSIS National Association for Road Safety Instruction in Schools.

NAS National Adoption Society; National Association of Shopfitters; Nautical Archaeology Society; Noise Abatement Society.

NASA National Aeronautics and Space Administration (US government agency founded in 1958 with its main offices at the Kennedy Space Centre).

NASC National Association of Scaffolding Contractors; National Aviation Security Committee.

NASH National Association of Specimen Hunters.

NASPM National Association of Seed Potato Merchants.

NASS National Ankylosing Spondylitis Society; National Association of Semen Suppliers; National Association of Steel Stockholders.

NAS/UWT National Association of Schoolmasters/Union of Women Teachers.

nat. *natus*, Latin 'born'.

NATCOL Natural Food Colours Association.

NATD National Association of Teachers of Dancing; National Association of Tool Dealers; National Association of Tripe Dressers.

NATFHE National Association of Teachers in Further and Higher Education.

Natlas National Testing Laboratory Accreditation Scheme.

NATO National Association of Temperance Officials; National Association of Tenants Organisations (Eire); North Atlantic Treaty Organization.

Natsopa National Society of Operative Printers, Graphical and Media Personnel (previously Printers and Assistants).

NATT National Association of Teachers of Travellers.

NATTKE National Association of Television, Theatrical and Kinematographic Employees.

NatVALA National Viewers & Listeners Association.

NatWest National Westminster Bank PLC.

NAV net asset value.

NAVA National Audio-Visual Association.

NAVGRA Navy and Vickers Gearing Research Association.

NAVH National Association of Voluntary Hostels.

NAVL National Anti-Vaccination League.

NAVM Nurses Anti-Vivisection Movement.

NAVS National Anti-Vivisection Society.

navsat navigational satellite.

NAW National Assembly of Women; National Association of Widows.

NAWB National Association of Wine and Beermakers; National Association of Workshops for the Blind.

NAWPU National Association of Water Power Users.

NAYC Youth Clubs UK (previously National Association of Youth Clubs).

NAYPIC National Association of Young People in Care.

NAYT National Association of Youth Theatres.

Nazi *Nationalsozialist*, German 'National Socialist' (the party led by Hitler 1920–45).

NB *nota bene*, Latin 'note well'.

Nb niobium (chemical element).

nb no ball.

NBA National Blood Authority; National Braille Association; National Brassfoundry Association; Net Book Agreement.

NBC National Broadcasting Corporation (USA); nuclear, biological and chemical (as in warfare).

nbg no bloody good.

NBI National Benevolent Institution.

NBL National Book League.

NBPA National Back Pain Association.

NBPS National Backgammon Players Society of Great Britain.

NBR National Buildings Record.

NBRI National Building Research Institute.

NBS National Bureau of Standards (US organisation that regulates the standards on weights and measures).

NBSS National Bible Society of Scotland; National British Softball Society.

NBTA National Baton Twirling Association.

NBTS National Blood Transfusion Service.

nbv net book value.

NC National Certificate; National Curriculum; Nature Conservancy.

nc numerical/ly control/led.

n/c no charge.

NCA National Certificate in Agriculture; National Caving Association; National Childminding Association; National Coffee Association of the USA; National Council of Aviculture; National Cricket Association; Nordic Concrete Association.

nca no copies available.

NCB National Children's Bureau; National Coal Board; no-claims bonus.

NCBA National Cattle Breeders' Association.

NCBW nuclear, chemical and biological warfare.

NCC National Caravan Council; National Cavy Club; National Computing Centre Limited; National Consumer Council; National Curriculum Council; Nature Conservancy Council.

NCCA National Carpet Cleaners Association; National Club Cricket Association; National Cotton Council of America.

NCCL National Council for Civil Liberties.

NCCPG National Council for the Preservation of Plants and Gardens.

ncd no can do.

NCDL National Canine Defence League.

NCF National Clayware Federation; National Coaching Foundation; National Cooperage Federation.

NCFE Northern Council for Further Education.

NCH National Children's Home.

NCL National Carriers Limited.

NCO non-commissioned officer.

NCP National Car Parks Limited; National Conference of Priests; National Council of Psychotherapists; New Communist Party.

NCPS non-contributory pension scheme.

NCR National Cash Register Company Limited.

ncr no carbon required.

NCS National Chrysanthemum Society; National Corrosion Service.

NCSS National Council for School Sports.

NCT National Centre for Tribology; National Chamber of Trade; National Childbirth Trust.

NCTU Northern Carpet Trades Union.

NCU National Communications Union; National Cyclists' Union.

NCUMC National Council for the Unmarried Mother and her Child.

ncup no commission until paid.

ncv no commercial value.

NCVO National Council for Voluntary Organizations.

NCVQ National Council for Vocational Qualifications.

ND Diploma in Naturopathy; National Debt; National Diploma.

Nd neodymium (chemical element).

nd no date; not dated/drawn; nothing doing.

NDA National Dairymen's Association; National Development Association.

NDBL National Deaf Blind League.

NDD National Diploma in Design.

NDE near-death experience.

NDF National Diploma in Forestry.

NDFS National Deposit Friendly Society.

NDH National Diploma in Horticulture.

NDP net domestic product.

NDSF National Diploma of the Society of Floristry.

NDT National Diploma in the Science and Practice of Turf Culture and Sports Ground Management; non-destructive testing.

NE northeast.

Ne neon (chemical element).

ne not essential; not exceeding.

n/e new edition; not entered; no effects (no funds).

NEA National Energy Authority of Iceland; National Exhibitors Association; Neighbourhood Energy Action; Northern Examination Association.

NEAC New English Art Club.

NEB New English Bible; National Enterprise Board.

NEC National Executive Committee; National Exhibition Centre.

nec not elsewhere classified.

NECSR North East Coast Ship Repairers.

NEDC National Economic Development Council.

Neddy National Economic Development Council.

NEDL National Equine Defence League.

NEDO National Economic Development Office.

NEF National Energy Foundation.

NEFA North East Forest Alliance.

NEH National Endowment for the Humanities.

NEL National Engineering Laboratory.

NEMA National Early Music Association.

nem. con. *nemine contradicente*, Latin 'with no one opposing'.

nem. diss. *nemine dissentiente*, Latin 'with no one dissenting'.

NEMS North of England Museums Service.

NEMSA North of England Mule Sheep Association.

NEPRA National Egg Producers Retail Association.

NERC Natural Environment Research Council; National English Rabbit Club.

NERCSPS North of England Rose, Carnation and Sweet Pea Society.

NERIS National Educational Resources Information Service.

NES National Eczema Society; Numerical Engineering Society Limited.

nes not elsewhere specified.

net not earlier than.

n et m *nocte et mane*, Latin 'night and morning'.

NF National Front; Norman/Northern French; no funds; noise factor.

NFA National Federation of Anglers; National Film Archive; National Food Authority; National Foremen's Association; Not Forgotten Association.

nfa no further action.

NFAC National Federation of Aerial Contractors.

NFAS National Field Archery Society.

NFBPM National Federation of Builders' and Plumbers' Merchants.

NFC National Fireplace Council; National Freight Consortium; Northern Fisheries Committee.

nfc not favourably considered.

NFCA National Foster Care Association.

NFCF National Federation of Cemetery Friends; National Federation of City Farms.

NFER National Foundation for Educational Research.

NFF Narrow Fabrics Federation; National Farers' Federation; National Federation of Fishmongers.

NFFC National Film Finance Corporation.

NFFPOW National Federation of Far-Eastern Prisoners of War Clubs.

NFFPT National Federation of Fruit and Potato Trades.

NFFQO National Federation of Freestone Quarry Owners.

NFMS National Federation of Music Societies.

NFPA National Foster Parents Association.

NFPS Norse Film & Pageant Society.

nfr no further requirements.

NFRC National Freight Rail Corporation.

NFRS National Fancy Rat Society.

NFS National Federation of Shopmobility.

nfs not for sale.

NFS & MC National Federation of Sailing and Motor Cruising Schools.

NFSC National Federation of Football Supporters' Clubs.

NFSE National Federation of Self-Employed and Small Businesses.

NFSS National Federation of Sea Schools.

NFT National Film Threatre.

NFTS National Film and Television School.

NFU National Farmers' Union.

NFWI National Federation of Women's Institutes.

NFYFC National Federation of Young Farmers' Clubs.

NG National Gallery.

ng no good; not given.

NGA National Graphical Association.

NGAC National Greenhouse Advisory Committee.

NGBF National Grocers' Benevolent Fund.

NGC National Gypsy Council; New General Catalogue (an astronomical listing known in 1888).

NGCAA National Golf Clubs Advisory Association.

NGNP nominal gross national product.

NGO non-governmental organization.

NGRC National Greyhound Racing Club.

NGS National Gardens Scheme; National Geographic Society (USA).

NGU non-gonococcal urethritis.

NGVA Natural Gas Vehicle Association.

NH National Heritage: the Museums' Action Movement; National Hunt.

NHA National Horse Association of Great Britain; National Housewives Association.

NHBRC National House-Builders' Registration Certificate/Council.

NHBS National Horse Brass Society.

NHC National Hyperbaric Centre.

NHF National Hairdressers' Federation.

NHI National Health Insurance.

NHLS National Hedge-Laying Society.

NHM Natural History Museum.

NHMF National Heritage Memorial Fund.

nhp nominal horsepower.

NHR National Hunt Rules.

NHS National Health Service.

NI National Insurance; Nautical Institute; Northern Ireland.

Ni nickel (chemical element).

NIAS Northern Ireland Archery Society.

NIC National Insurance Contributions.

nic newly industrialised country; not in contract.

NICEC National Institute for Careers, Education and Counselling.

NICEIC National Inspection Council for Electrical Installation Contracting.

NICSA Northern Ireland Countryside Staff Association.

NICU neonatal intensive care unit.

NIDFA National Independent Drama Festivals Association.

NIESR National Institute of Economic and Social Research.

NII Nuclear Installations Inspectorate.

nimby not in my back yard.

NIMH National Institute of Medical Herbalists; National Institute of Mental Health.

NIMR National Institute for Medical Research.

NIR Northern Ireland Railways.

NIRC National Industrial Relations Court.

Nirex Nuclear Industry Radioactive Waste Executive.

nis not in stock.

NIT negative income tax.

NJ New Jersey.

NJA National Jewellers' Association; National Jogging Association; Nepal Journalists Association.

NJAC National Joint Council.

NJCC National Joint Consultative Committee of Architects, Quantity Surveyors and Builders.

NJFA National Jazz Foundation Archive.

NJNC National Joint Negotiating Committee.

NLB National Library for the Blind; Northern Lighthouse Board.

NLB & D National League of the Blind and Disabled.

NLCB National Lottery Charities Board.

NLF National Liberation Front.

NLL National Land League (Eire).

nln no longer needed.

NLP natural language processing.

NLQ near letter quality (printer characters).

nlt not later/less than.

NLW National Library of Wales.

nm nanometre; nautical.mile.

n/m not married.

NMA National Museum of Australia; Needlemakers Association; Nordic Midwives Association.

NMC National Motorcycle Council; National Mouse Club; National Museum of Canada; National Music Council of Great Britain.

nmc no more credit.

NMHRA National Mobile Homes Residents Association.

NMR nuclear magnetic resonance.

NMS National Museums of Scotland; Natural Medicines Society; Norwegian Dairies Sales Centre.

nmt not more than.

NMTF National Market Traders' Federation.

nnd neonatal death.

NNE north-northeast.

NNEB National Nursery Examination Board.

NNHT Nuffield Nursing Homes Trust.

NNI Noise and Number Index (aircraft noise).

NNT nuclear non-proliferation treaty.

NNW north-northwest.

NO natural order.

No nobelium (chemical element).

no not out, as in cricket.

no. *or* **No.** number.

NOAH National Office of Animal Health Limited.

NOC National Olympic Committee.

NOD Naval Ordnance Department.

nohp not otherwise herein provided.

NOIL Naval Ordnance Inspection Laboratory.

nok next of kin.

nol. pros. *nolle prosequi*, Latin 'do not continue'.

nom. nominative, as used in grammar.

non rep. *non repetatur*, Latin 'let it not be repeated'.

non seq. *non sequitur*, Latin 'it does not follow logically'.

NOP National Opinion Poll.

nop not otherwise provided.

NOPWC National Old People's Welfare Council.

NOR nucleolar-organizing region.

NORMAC Northern Prawn Fishery Management Committee.

Norvic. *Norvicensis*, Latin 'of Norwich'.

NOS National Osteoporosis Society.

NOTB National Ophthalmic Treatment Board.

NP National Park; National Power PLC; Notary Public.

Np neptunium (chemical element).

np net profit; new paragraph; *nisi prius*, Latin 'unless previously'; *nomen proprium*, Latin 'its own name' (labelling instruction to pharmacists).

NPA National Parks Association; National Pasta Association (USA); National Pawnbrokers' Association; National Pigeon Association; National Pistol Association; National Playbus Association; Newspaper Publishers' Association; Nordic Planetarium Association.

NPBA National Pig Breeders' Association; National Prefabricated Building Association.

NPC National Packaging Confederation; National Peace Council; National Peach Council (USA); National Population Council; National Postcode Centre.

NPF National Poetry Foundation.

npf not provided for.

NPFA National Playing Fields Association.

NPG National Portrait Gallery.

NPHT Nuffield Provincial Hospitals Trust.

NPIS National Poisons Information Service.

NPL National Physical Laboratory.

npo *nil per os*, Latin 'nothing by mouth'.

NPPS National Plants Preservation Society.

NPPTB National Pig Progeny Testing Board.

NPS National Philatelic Society; National Pony Society; Nature Photographic Society.

NPT normal pressure and temperature.

NPTC National Proficiency Tests Council.

NPWA National Pure Water Association.

npv net present value.

NQA National Quoits Association.

NR North Riding (former division of Yorkshire).

NRA National Retreat Association; National Rifle Association; National Rivers Authority; National Rounders Association; National Rustproofers Association.

nra never refuse anything.

NRC Nuclear Research Council.

NRDC National Research Development Corporation.

NRDS neonatal respiratory distress syndrome.

NREM non-rapid eye movement.

NRPB National Radiological Protection Board.

NRS National Rose Society; Navy Records Society.

nrv net realizable value.

NS National Society of Paints, Sculptors and Printmakers; New Style; Nova Scotia; Nutrition Society; new series.

ns nanosecond; near side; non-smoker; not significant/specified.

n/s news sheet; not sufficient.

NSA National Sawmilling Association; National Sheep Association; National Skating Association; National Sprint Association Limited; Nuclear Stock Association.

NSAFF National Society Against Factory Farming.

NSAID non-steroidal anti-inflammatory drug.

NSAS National Smoke Abatement Society.

NSB National Savings Bank.

NSBA National School Band Association; National Silica Brickmakers' Association.

NSBC North Sea Bird Club.

NSC National Safety Council; National Snorkellers Club; National Stone Centre.

NSCA National Society for Clean Air; Natural Sausage Casing Association.

NSCR National Society for Cancer Relief.

NSD nominal standard dose; normal spontaneous delivery.

NSESG North Sea Environmental Study Group.

NSF National Science Foundation; National Squash Federation.

nsf not sufficient funds.

NSFGB National Ski Federation of Great Britain.

NSG nonstatutory guidelines (concerning the National Curriculum).

NSGT Non-Self-Governing Territory.

NSL National Sporting League.

NSNS National Society of Non-Smokers.

NSPCA National Society for the Prevention of Cruelty to Animals.

NSPCC National Society for the Prevention of Cruelty to Children.

nspf not specifically provided for.

NSPS National Sweet Pea Society.

NSQA Natural Slate Quarries Association.

NSRA National Scooter Riders Association; National Small-Bore Rifle Association; National Society for Research into Allergy.

NSS National Secular Society Limited; Noonan Syndrome Society.

NSSA National School Sailing Association; National Scooter Sport Association; National Sensitive Sites Alliance.

NSTP Nuffield Science Teaching Project.

NSU non-specific urethritis.

NSW New South Wales.

NSWA National Small Woods Association.

NT National Theatre; National Trust; New Testament; Northern Territory; no trumps (cards).

NTA National Training Award; New Towns Association.

NTETA National Traction Engine and Tractor Association.

NTF National Television Fund; National Trainers Federation.

NTFMFS National Tile Faience and Mosaic Fixers' Society.

ntp normal temperature and pressure; no title page.

NTPS National Turf Protection Society.

NTS National Trust for Scotland.

NTVLRO National Television Licence Records Office.

NU name unknown; number unobtainable.

NUAAW National Union of Agricultural and Allied Workers.

NUCPS National Union of Civil and Public Servants.

NUGMW National Union of General and Municipal Workers.

NUI National University of Ireland.

NUIW National Union of Insurance Workers.

NUJ National Union of Journalists.

NUJMB Northern Universities Joint Matriculation Board.

NUM National Union of Mineworkers.

Numast National Union of Marine, Aviation and Shipping.

NUPE National Union of Public Employees.

NUR National Union of Railwaymen.

NUS National Union of Seamen; National Union of Students.

NUT National Union of Teachers.

NUTG National Union of Townswomen's Guilds.

NUTS National Union of Tract Statisticians.

NUWW National Union of Women Workers.

NV New Version (of Bible); non-vintage.

nv non-voting.

n/v non-vintage.

NVALA National Viewers' and Listeners' Association.

nvd no value declared.

NVQ National Vocational Qualification.

NW northwest.

NWAF National Womens Aid Federation.

NWCAF North West Councils Against Fluoridation.

NWEB North Western Electricity Board.

NWF Native Woodland Forum.

NWML National Weights and Measures Laboratory.

NWRAC North Western Regional Advisory Council for Further Education.

NWT Northwest Territories.

NWTA National Waterways Transport Association.

NWW New Ways to Work.

NY New York.

NYA National Youth Agency.

NYAM New York Academy of Music.

NYC New York City.

NYD not yet diagnosed.

NYHA National Yacht Harbour Association.

NYLC National Young Life Campaign.

Nymex New York Mercantile Exchange.

NYO National Youth Orchestra.

NZ New Zealand.

NZAA New Zealand Archaeological Association.

NZGA New Zealand Grassland Association.

NZRFU New Zealand Rugby Football Union.

O Office; Order (of nuns, etc); oxygen (chemical element); ordinary.

o *ottava*, Italian 'octave' (music).

OA Officers Association; Overeaters Anonymous; office automation; operations analysis; osteoarthritis.

oa overall.

o/a on account of.

OAA Obstetric Anaesthetists Association; Opticians Association of America; Outdoor Advertising Association of Great Britain.

OAC Oceanic Affairs Committee.

OAD obstructive airways disease.

O & C Oxford and Cambridge.

o & c onset and course.

O & G obstetrics and gynaecology.

O & M organization and methods.

oao off and on; one and only.

OAP old age pensioner.

OAPEC Organization of Arab Petroleum Exporting Countries.

OAS Secret Army Organisation (Algeria); on active service.

OAT outside air temperature.

OATG outside air temperature gauge.

OAU Organization of African Unity.

OB obstetrics; old boy; outside broadcast.

ob. *obiit*, Latin 'he/she died'; oboe.

o/b on or before.

obb. *obbligato*, Italian 'essential'.

OBC Old Bottle Club of Great Britain; on-board computer.

OBD organic brain disease.

OBE Officer of the Order of the British Empire; out-of-the-body experience.

OC Officer Commanding; Officer in Charge; oral contraceptive; original cover (in stamp collecting).

oc office copy; only child.

o/c overcharge.

OCB Offshore Certification Bureau.

OCC Offshore Construction Council.

OCD obsessive compulsive disorder.

OCF Officiating Chaplain to the Forces.

OCIMF Oil Companies International Marine Forum.

OCR optical character recognition.

OCS Office of the Chief Scientist; Oriental Ceramic Society.

OCSC Office of the Civil Service Commissioners.

OCTU Officer Cadet Training Unit.

OD Officer of the Day; Old Dutch; Ordnance Datum; overdose; overdraft; overdrawn.

od outer diameter.

o/d on demand.

ODA Offa's Dyke Association; Overseas Development Administration.

ODC Order of Discalced Carmelites.

ODI Open Door International for the Economic Emancipation of the Woman Worker.

ODSBA Oxford Down Sheep Breeders Association.

OE Old English; Old Etonian.

Oe oersted (unit of magnetic field strength).

oe omissions excepted.

OECD Organization for Economic Co-operation and Development.

OED Oxford English Dictionary.

OEDA Occupational and Environmental Diseases Association.

OEM original equipment manufacturer.

OF Oddfellow; Old French; Operation Friendship; oil-fired.

OFC Overseas Food Corporation.

Offer Office of Electricity Regulation.

OFG Organic Farmers and Growers Limited.

Ofgas Office of Gas Supply.

OFM *Ordo Fratrum Minorum*, Latin 'Order of Minor Friars' (Franciscans).

OFris Old Friesian.

OFS Orange Free State.

Ofsted Office for Standards in Education.

OFT Office of Fair Trading.

Oftel Office of Telecommunications.

OFW Opportunities For Women.

Ofwat Office of Water Services.

OG Openly Gay.

og original gravity (strength of beer); original gum (philately); own goal.

OGA Organic Growers Association.

OGM Ordinary General Meeting.

oh office hours; *omni hora*, Latin 'every hour'.

OHMS On Her/His Majesty's Service.

ohp overhead projector.

OHS Occupational Health Service.

OIC Optical Information Council.

OIEO offers in excess of.

OILC Offshore Industry Liaison Committee.

OIRO offers in the region of.

Ojocs overnight declaration of jockeys (horse-racing).

OK satisfactory.

OL on-line; outside left.

OLA Organic Living Association.

OLG Office of Local Government.

OLML Our Lady's Missionary League.

OLRT on-line real time.

OM Order of Merit.

om *omni mane*, Latin 'every morning'.

OMA Overall Manufacturers Association of Great Britain.

omc operation and maintenance costs.

OMIG Opencast Mining Intelligence Group.

omo one-man operation (buses).

OMR optical mark reader.

OMRS Orders and Medals Research Society.

OMS Oriental Missionary Society International.

oms output per man shift.

on *omni nocte*, Latin 'every night'.

ONA Office of National Assessments.

ONC Ordinary National Certificate.

OND Ordinary National Diploma; other neurological disorders.

ono or near/est offer.

ONS Offshore North Sea Technology Conference; Oriental Numismatic Society.

ONTR orders not to resuscitate.

o/o on order; offers over.

oop out of pocket (expenses, etc).

oot out of town.

OP *Ordo Praedicatorum*, Latin 'Order of Preachers'; observation point/post; opposite prompt (an actor's position on stage); outpatient.

op open-plan; out of print; over proof.

OPA Oil and Pipelines Agency.

OPB Occupational Pensions Board.

op. cit. *opere citato*, Latin 'in the work cited'.

OPCA Ornamental Plant Collections Association (Australia).

OPCS Office of Population, Censuses and Surveys.

OPD Outpatient Department.

OPEC Organization of Petroleum-Exporting Countries.

OPFS One Parent Families Scotland.

OPKA Original Pearly Kings and Queens Association.

OPMA Overseas Press and Media Association.

OPPS Oxford Project for Peace Studies.

OPS Ophthalmic Photographers Society.

OPSIS National Association for the Education, Training and Support of Blind and Partially Sighted People.

opt. optative; optic/al; optimal; *optime*, Latin 'excellently'; optimum; optional.

OPV oral poliomyelitis vaccine.

OR Odinic Rite; Official Receiver; Order of the Road; operating room; operational research; other ranks.

or owner's risk.

ORACLE optional reception of announcements by coded line electronics.

ord owner's risk of damage.

orf owner's risk of fire.

ORG Oxford Research Group.

ORL otorhinolarynology (treatment of the ear, nose and throat).

ORRA Oriental Rug Retailers of America.

ORT oral rehydration therapy.

ORTPA Oven-Ready Turkey Producers Association.

OS Oceanography Society; Old Saxon; Old Style; Omnibus Society; operating system; Ordinary Seaman; Ordnance Survey; outsize.

Os osmium (chemical element).

os only son.

o/s out of stock; outstanding.

OSA Official Secrets Act; *Ordo Sancti Augustini*, Latin 'Order of St Augustine'.

OSB *Ordo Sancti Benedicti*, Latin 'Order of St Benedict'.

OSCAR Organization for Sickle Cell Anaemia Research.

OSCH off-peak storage central heating.

OSF *Ordo Sancti Francisci*, Latin 'Order of St Francis'.

OSFC *Ordo Sancti Francisci Cappuchinorum*, Latin 'Cappuchin Order of St Francis'.

OSGB Orchid Society of Great Britain.

OSI Open Systems Interconnection.

OSIC Overseas Spinning Investment Company.

OSM *Ordo Servorum Beatae Virginis Mariae*, Latin 'Order of the Servants of the Blessed Virgin Mary'.

osp *obiit sine prole*, Latin 'died without issue'; off-street parking.

OSSC Oil Spill Service Centre.

OST Office of Science and Technology.

OstJ Officer of the Order of St John of Jerusalem.

OT Old Testament; occupational therapy; operating theatre; overtime.

OTC Officers' Training Corps; over the counter.

OTDOGS Opposition to Destruction of Open Green Space.

OTE on-target earnings; or the equivalent.

OTG outside temperature gauge.

OTT over the top.

OTU operational training unit.

OU Open/Oxford University.

OUDS Oxford University Dramatic Society.

OUP Oxford University Press.

OVAC Overseas Visual Aids Centre.

ovc other valuable consideration.

ovno or very near offer.

OWA One World Action.

OWC Order of Woodcraft Chivalry.

OWTC Orkney Water Test Centre.

Oxbridge Oxford and Cambridge.

OXFAM Oxford Committee for Famine Relief.

Oxon. *Oxonia*, Latin 'Oxford' (as used in the county abbreviation); *Oxoniensis*, Latin 'of Oxford' (used with bishop's signature and in degrees).

OYC Ocean Youth Club.

oz. av. avoirdupois ounce.

oz T troy ounce.

P

P phosphorus (chemical element); President; parking; pawn (chess).

p *piano*, Italian 'softly' (music).

p. page; paragraph; part; passive; past; penny; per; piano, Italian 'softly' (music); pico; pint; positive; *post*, Latin 'after'; power; *pro*, Latin 'in favour of'; proton; purl.

PA Paintmakers Association of Great Britain; Patients' Association; Pedestrians Association; Personal Assistant; Pizza Association; Politics Association; Postcard Association; Press Agent; Press Association; Prisoners Abroad; Protestant Alliance; Psoriasis Association; Public Address system; Publishers' Association.

Pa protactinium (chemical element); pascal (unit of pressure).

p.a. *per annum*, Latin 'yearly'; participial adjective; per annum.

p/a private account.

PAA Paper Agents Association; Population Association of America.

PAAI Poster Advertising Association of Ireland.

PABIAC Paper and Board Industry Advisory Committee.

PABLA problem analysis by logical approach.

PABX private automatic branch exchange.

PAC Permanent Agricultural Committee; Public Accounts Committee.

PACA Public Art Commissions Agency.

PACC Pesticides and Agricultural Cchemicals Committee; Prestwick Airport Consultative Committee.

PACE Parental Alliance for Choice in Education; Police and Criminal Evidence Act; Polytechnic Association for Continuing Education; Protestant and Catholic Encounter; Performance and cost evaluation.

PACSA People Against Child Sex Abuse.

PAD packet assembler/disassembler; payable after death.

PADI Professional Association of Diving Instructors.

PADT Public Art Development Trust.

PAF Public Art Forum.

PAGB Poultry and Egg Producers' Association of Great Britain.

PAIN Parents Against Injustice; Prisoners Advice and Information Network.

PAL Parents Anonymous London; Planning Aid for London; phase alternation line (colour TV system).

PAM pulse-amplitude modulation.

PAMR Public Access Mobile Radio.

PAN Pesticides Action Network.

Panaftel Pan-African Telecommunications Network.

PanAm Pan-American World Airways Incorporated.

PanCan Panama Canal.

P & G Procter and Gamble.

P & GWA Pottery and Glass Wholesalers Association.

p & l profit and loss.

P & O Peninsular and Oriental Steamship Navigation Company.

p & p postage and packing.

P & S Pike & Shot Society.

PANN Professional Association of Nursery Nurses.

PAP Profesional Association of Partners.

PAPA Pizza and Pasta Association.

PAR precision approach radar.

par planed all round (wood).

par. aff. *pars affecta*, Latin 'the injured part'.

PARC Parallel Algorithm Research Centre.

part. aeq. *partes aequales*, Latin 'equal portions'.

PARU post-anaesthetic recovery unit.

PARVO Professional and Academic Regional Visits Organisation.

PAS Poetry Association of Scotland; Prisoners' Advice Service; public address system.

pas power assisted steering.

pass. *passim*, Latin 'here and there'.

PAT Professional Association of Teachers; planned actvities time.

PAU Pan American Union.

PAX private automatic exchange.

pax per annum, exclusive (of rent net of Council Tax, water rates, etc).

PAYE pay as you earn/enter.

PAYP pay as you play (of golf clubs, etc, membership).

PAYV pay as you view.

PB Pharmacopoeia Brittanica; Plymouth Brethren; Prayer Book; passbook.

Pb *plumbum*, Latin 'lead' (chemical element).

pb paperback.

p/b purpose-built; push-button.

PBFA Provincial Booksellers Fairs Association.

PBI Peace Brigades International; poor bloody infantry.

PBM permanent benchmark.

PBMA Plastic Bath Manufacturers' Association.

pbr payment by results.

PBS Prayer Book Society.

PBT President of the Board of Trade.

pbt profit before tax.

PBX private branch exchange.

PC Panama Canal; Parish Council; Peace Corps; *Plaid Cymru*, Welsh 'Party of Wales'; Police Constable; Press Council; Printmakers' Council; Privy Council/lor; personal computer; political correctness; politically correct; postcard.

pc parsec; per cent; postcard; *post cibum* Latin 'after meals'.

p/c petty cash; prices current.

PCA Paperweight Collectors' Association; Parliamentary Commissioner for Administration (the official title of the Ombudsman); Parochial Clergy Association; Permanent Court of Arbitration (Netherlands); Police Complaints Authority; Prestressed Concrete Association; Printed Circuit Association; Professional Cycling Association; Proprietary Crematoria Association.

PCAS Polytechnics Central Admissions System.

PCB polychlorinated biphenyl; post-coital bleeding; printed circuit board.

pcb petty cash book; printed circuit board.

PCC Pacific Conference of Churches; Panama Canal Commission; Press Complaints Commission; Print Collectors Club; Professional Conduct Committee (of British Medical Association).

PCCS Primate Captive Care Society.

pcf pounds per cubic foot.

PCFC Polytechnics and Colleges Funding Council.

PCFRE Professional Council for Religious Education.

PCG Period Costume Group; Plant Charter Group.

PCGG Primary Care Group in Gynaecology.

PCI Pax Christi International.

pci pounds per cubic inch.

PCID Pontifical Council for Inter-Religious Dialogue.

PCIFC Permanent Commission of the International Fisheries Convention.

PCIJ Permanent Court of International Justice.

PCIS Period Cottage Improvement Society.

PCJ Sisters of the Poor Child Jesus.

PCL printer control language.

pcm per calendar month; pulse code modulation.

PCMA Plastic Crate Manufacturers' Association; Potato Chip Manufacturers' Association; Precision Chain Manufacturers' Association.

PCN personal communications network.

PCOCA Parti-Colour Oriental Cat Association.

PCOD polycystic ovary disease.

PCP Pneumocystis carinii pneumonia; pentachlorophenol; phencyclidine (angel dust).

PCPCU Pontifical Council for Promoting Christian Unity.

PCPI Parent Co-operative Preschools International; Permanent Committee on Patent Information.

PCR politically correct retailing; polymerase chain reaction.

PCS Principal Clerk of Session.

PCTE portable common tool environment.

PCV passenger-carrying vehicle.

PCWPC Permanent Committee of the World Petroleum Congress.

PCZ Panama Canal Zone.

PD preventive detention; public domain.

Pd palladium (chemical element).

pd *per diem*, Latin 'each day'; postage due; post-dated.

p/d price dividend.

PDA Association of Management & Professional Staff Divers Section; Packaging Distributors Association; Photographic Dealers Association; Pump Distributors Association of Great Britain.

pdi pre-delivery inspection.

PDL page description language.

PDN public data network.

pdq pretty damn quick.

PDRA postdoctoral research assistant.

PDS Parkinson's Disease Society of the United Kingdom.

PDSA People's Dispensary for Sick Animals.

PE Protestant Episcopal; phase-encoded; physical education.

pe personal estate; plastic explosive.

p/e price earnings.

PEA Physical Education Association of Great Britain and Northern Ireland.

PEAB Professional Engineers' Appointments Bureau.

PEC Plain English Campaign; Protestant Episcopal Church.

pec photoelectric cell.

PED Emergency Preparedness and Disaster Relief Co-ordination Office.

PEF European Pentecostal Fellowship.

PEFC Paper Exporters Freight Committee.

PEI Prince Edward Island.

PEL Priests' Eucharistic League.

PEN Poets, Playwrights, Editors, Essayists, Novelists. A literary association founded in 1921 by C.A. Dawson Scott to further international understanding among writers.

PEP personal equity plan; political and economic planning.

PER Professional and Executive Recruitment; Professional Employment Register.

PERA Production Engineering Research Association of Great Britain.

perd. *perdendosi*, Italian 'vanishing' (music).

PERME Propellants, Explosives and Rocket Motor Establishment.

per pro *per procurationem*, Latin 'by the agency of'.

PERT programme evaluation and review technique.

PESD Private and Executive Secretary's Diploma, London Chamber of Commerce and Industry.

PESGB Petroleum Exploration Society of Great Britain.

PEST Pressure for Economic and Social Toryism.

PET polyethylene terephthalate; pre-eclamptic toxaemia.

PETA People for the Ethical Treatment of Animals; Postal Equipment Trade Association.

Petras Polytechnic Educational Resources Advisory Service.

Petriburg. *Petriburgensis*, Latin 'of Peterborough'.

PF Pagan Federation; Patriotic Front (Zimbabwe); Police Federation; Procurator Fiscal.

pF picofarad.

pf *piano e forte*, Italian 'soft and then loud' (music); *più forte*, Italian 'louder' (music); public funding.

PFA Popular Flying Association; Power Fastenings Association; Professional Footballers' Association.

PFAS President of the Faculty of Architects and Surveyors.

PFB preformed beam.

PFBC Polled Friesian Breeders Club.

PFC polychlorinated fluorocarbon.

pfc passed flying college.

PFE Platform 'Fortress Europe'.

PFM pulse frequency modulation.

PFMA Pet Food Manufacturers Association; Phenolic Foam Manufacturers Association; Pressed Felt Manufacturers Association.

PFP Partnership For Peace; personal financial planning.

PFPA Pitch Fibre Pipe Association of Great Britain.

PFPUT Pension Fund Property Unit Trust.

PFR prototype fast reactor.

PFS Palmerston Forts Society.

PFSF Parents For Safe Food.

PFSS Pet Fostering Service Scotland.

PG Parental Guidance (film classification); paying guest; postgraduate.

PGA Power Generation Association; Prison Governors' Association; Professional Golfers' Association.

PGAH Pineapple Growers Association of Hawaii.

PGC Patent Glazing Conference.

PGCE Postgraduate Certificate in Education.

PGDipLCM Postgraduate Diploma of the London College of Music.

PGDRS psychogeriatric dependency rating scale.

PGF polypeptide growth factor.

PGG Professional Gardeners' Guild.

PGL persistent generalised lymphadenopathy.

PGM Past Grand Master; precision guided missile.

pgt per gross ton.

pH potential of hydrogen ions (in an aqueous solution, a measure of acidity).

PHA Promotional Handling Association; Public Heatlh Alliance; Pullet Hatcheries Association.

PHAB Physically Handicapped and Able Bodied.

PharB or **PharmB** *Pharmaciae Baccalaureus*, Latin 'Bachelor of Pharmacy'.

PharD or **PharmD** *Pharmaciae Doctor*, Latin 'Doctor of Pharmacy'.

PharM or **PharmM** *Pharmaciae Magister*, Latin 'Master of Pharmacy'.

PhB *Philosophiae Baccalaureus*, Latin 'Bachelor of Philosophy'.

PHC pharmaceutical chemist; primary health care.

PHCA Pig Health Control Association; Private Hire Car Association.

PhD *Philosophiae Doctor*, Latin 'Doctor of Philosophy'.

PHD(RCA) Doctor of Philosophy (Royal College of Art).

PHI Public Health Inspector; permanent health insurance.

PHJC Poor Handmaids of Jesus Christ.

PhL Licentiate in Philosophy.

PHLS Public Health Laboratory Service.

PHLSB Public Health Laboratory Service Board.

PhM *Philosophiae Magister*, Latin 'Master of Philosophy'.

php pounds per horsepower.

PHRG Parliamentary Human Rights Group.

PHS Philosophical Society of England; Plastics Historical Society; Police History Society; Presbyterian Historical Society.

PHSA Provincial Hospital Services Association.

PHWR pressurised heavy water reactor.

PI Parents Initiative; Performers and Artists for Nuclear Disarmament International; Philippine Islands; Privacy International; parainfluenza virus; programmed instruction.

PIA Personal Investment Authority; Photographic Importers Association; Pilots International Association.

PIAC Petroleum Industry Advisory Council.

PIB Petroleum Information Bureau; Piers Information Bureau; Prices and Incomes Board.

Pibor Paris Interbank Offered Rate.

PIBS permanent interest-bearing share.

PIC Poultry Industry Conference; programmable interrupt controller.

PICAGB Police Insignia Collectors Association of Great Britain.

PICC Provisional International Computation Centre.

PICUTPC Permanent and International Committee of Underground Town Planning and Construction.

PICV Permanent International Commission of Viticulture.

PID pelvic inflammatory disease; personal identification device; prolapsed intervertebral disc (slipped disc).

PIDS primary immune deficiency syndrome.

PIFA Packaging and Industrial Films Association; Practitioner of the Institute of Field Archaeologists.

PIH Paintings in Hospitals; pregnancy-induced hypertension.

pik payment in kind.

PIL Pest Infestation Laboratory.

pil payment in lieu.

pil. *pilula*, Latin 'pill'.

PILL programmed instruction language learning.

PIM personal information manager.

PIME *Pontificium Institutum pro Missionibus Externis*, Latin 'Pontifical Institute for Foreign Missions'.

PIMS profit impact of market strategy.

PIN personal identification number.

Pinc property income certificate.

pinx. *pinxit*, Latin 'painted it'.

PIRA Paper and Board, Printing and Packaging Industries Research Association.

PITB Petroleum Industry Training Board.

pizza. *pizzicato*, Italian 'plucking string with fingers' (music).

PJ Presiding/Probate Judge.

pk psychokinesis.

PKTF Printing and Kindred Trades Federation.

PKU phenylketonuria.

PL Poet Laureate; Primrose League; Public Library; patrol leader (scouting).

P/L profit and loss.

PL/I Programming Language 1.

PLA Para Legal Association; Port of London Authority; Private Libraries Association; programmable logic array.

PLATO Programmed Logic for Automatic Teaching Operation.

PLC *or* **plc** public limited company.

PLCW & TWU Power Loom Carpet Weavers' and Textile Workers' Union.

PLO Palestine Liberation Organization.

PLP Parliamentary Labour Party.

PLR public lending right.

Pl. Sgt platoon sergeant.

PLSS portable life-support system.

PLWA People Living With AIDS (Canada).

PM Past Master; Paymaster; Postmaster; Prime Minister; Provost-Marshal; post mortem.

pm or PM *post meridiem*, Latin 'after noon'; premolar.

Pm promethium (chemical element).

PMA Pacific Maritime Association; Personal Managers Association; Polystyrene Moulders' Association (Eire); Property Managers Association; paramethoxyamphetamine (an hallucinogenic drug).

PMB Potato Marketing Board.

PMBX private manual branch exchange.

PMC Philatelic Music Circle; Planning Ministers Council.

PMDA Pianoforte Manufacturers' and Distributors' Association.

PMG Paymaster/Postmaster-General.

PMH previous medical history.

pmh per man-hour.

PMI Pensions Management Institute.

PMInstPM Provisional Member of the Institute of Professional Managers.

PML Plymouth Marine Library.

PMMS Plainsong and Mediaeval Music Society.

PMO Principal Medical Officer.

PMRAFNS Princes Mary's Royal Air Force Nursing Service.

PMS premenstrual syndrome.

PMT photomechanical transfer; premenstrual tension.

PMU Pontifical Missionary Union.

PN postnatal.

pn promissory note.

PNA Psychiatric Nurses' Association.

PND postnatal depression.

PNdb perceived noise decibel.

PNEU Parents' National Education Union.

png *persona non grata*, Latin 'unacceptable person' (a diplomat not accepted by government of host country).

pnr prior notice required.

PNS parasympathetic nervous system.

PO Personnel Officer; Petty/Pilot Officer; Postal Order; Post Office.

Po polonium (chemical element).

po *per os*, Latin 'through the mouth'.

POA Prison Officers' Association.

POD pay on delivery; point of debarkation.

POE port of embarkation; port of entry.

POEU Post Office Engineering Union.

PofB Ponies of Britain.

POL Patent Office Library; petrol, oil and lubricants.

pol problem-oriented language.

POLIS Parliamentary On-Line Information Service.

POLITE Preserve Our Local Independent Traders.

POM prescription-only medicine.

POP Post Office preferred (size of envelope); point of purchase.

pop plaster of Paris.

POPA Property Owners' Protection Association.

Popin Population Information Network.

Poplab International Programme of Laboratories for Population Statistics.

POPS Partners of Prisoners and Families Support Group.

por pay on receipt/return.

POS point of sale.

POSAS Patent Office Search and Advisory Service.

POST Parliamentary Office of Science and Technology; point-of-sale terminal.

POUNC Post Office Users' National Council.

pov point of view; privately owned vehicle.

POW Prince of Wales; Prisoner of War.

POWAGOD Prince of Wales' Advisory Group on Disability.

PP Phonographic Performance; parish priest; past president.

pp past participle; *per procurationem*, Latin 'on behalf of'; *pianissimo*, Italian 'very soft' (music); planning permission; post paid; *post prandium*, Latin 'after meals'; privately printed.

pp. pages.

PPA Peat Producers Association of Great Britain and Ireland; Piano Publicity Association; Pipeline Protection Association; Potato Processors Association; Pre-School Playgroups Association.

PPARC Particle Physics and Astronomy Research Council.

ppb paper, printing and binding; parts per billion.

ppc progressive patient care; prospective parliamentary candidate.

PPE Philosophy, Politics and Economics.

PPFAS Past President of the Faculty of Architects and Surveyors.

PPG Player Piano Group.

PPH post-partum haemorrhage.

PPI Pensioners for Peace International.

ppi plan-position indicator (radar).

PPITB Printing and Publishing Industry Training Board.

PPL Private Pilot's Licence.

PPM peak programme meter.

ppm pages per minute; parts per million.

PPMA Petrol Pump Manufacturers Association; Plastic Pipe Manufacturers Association; Produce Packagaing and Marketing Association.

PPN public packet network.

PPP personal pension plan; Point to Point Protocol (computing); Private Patients' Plan; Psychology, Philosophy and Physiology.

ppp *pianississimo*, Italian 'extremely quietly' (music).

pppm per person per month.

pppn per person per night.

PPR printed paper rate.

PPRA Past President of the Royal Academy.

PPRNCM Professional Performance of the Royal Northern College of Music.

PPS Parliamentary/Principal Private Secretary; pelvic pain syndrome; *post postscriptum*, Latin 'additional postscript'.

PPSG Protein and Peptide Science Group.

PPU Peace Pledge Union.

PQ parliamentary question.

pq previous question.

PR Pipe Roll; press release; prize ring; proportional representation; public relations.

Pr praseodymium (chemical element).

pr *per rectum*, Latin 'by way of the rectum'.

PRA Paint Research Association; Petrol Retailers Association; Prairie Rail Authority (Canada); President of the Royal Academy; Psychiatric Rehabilitation Association.

PRB Pre-Raphaelite Brotherhood.

PRC *post Romam conditam*, Latin 'after the foundation of Rome'.

Precis preserved context index system.

PREP post-registration education and practice (nursing).

PSC Private Secretary's Certificate, London Chamber of Commerce and Industry.

PR public relations or proportional representation.

Pr praseodymium (chemical element).

PRC People's Republic of China.

PRF Pain Relief Foundation; pulse repetition frequency.

PRG Producer Responsibility Group.

PRI Penal Reform International; Plastics and Rubber Institute.

PRIBA President of the Royal Institute of British Architects.

primip. *primipara*, Latin 'first-time mother'.

prm personal radiation monitor.

prn *pro re nata*, Latin 'as the situation may require'.

PRO Public Records Office; public relations officer.

pro-am professional-amateur.

Prolog Programming in Logic (programming langauge).

PROM programmable read-only memory.

PROP Preservation of the Rights of Prisoners.

pro tem. *pro tempore*, Latin 'for the time being'.

prox. *proximo*, Latin 'next month'.

prox. acc. *proxime accessit*, Latin 'came closest' (to the winner in a competition, etc).

prox. luc. *proxima luce*, Latin 'on the preceding day'.

PRP performance related pay.

PRR pulse repetition rate.

PRS Pattern Recognition Society (USA); Performing Rights Society; Pre-Raphaelite Society; President of the Royal Society; Protestant Reformation Society.

PRT Prison Reform Trust.

PRTC Princess Royal Trust for Carers.

PS Parliamentary/Private Secretary; Pastel Society; Permanent Secretary; Pharmaceutical Society of Great Britain; Philological Society; Physical Society; Planetary Society; Police Sergeant; Polite Society; Privy Seal; *post scriptum*, Latin 'after writing'; private secretary; prompt side (actor's place on stage).

PSA Pakistan Sociological Association; Passenger Shipping Association; Peace Studies Association; Pickles and Sauces Association; Poultry Science Association; Prices Surveillance Authority; Property Services Authority; Public Services Authority.

PSAC Production Statistics Advisory Committee.

PSBR Public Sector Borrowing Requirement.

PSC Pipe Smokers' Council.

psc passed staff college.

PSDA Paper Sack Development Association.

PSDR Public Sector Debt Repayment.

PSE psychological stress evaluator (similar to a lie detector).

psf per square foot.

PSGB Pharmaceutical Society of Great Britain.

PSI Policy Studies Institute.

psi pounds per square inch.

PSIF Prison Service Industries and Farms.

PSIS Permanent Secretaries' Committee on the Intelligence Services.

psk phase shift keying.

PSL Polish Peasant Party; private sector liquidity; public sector loan.

PSM product sales manager.

PSMA Pressure Sensitive Manufacturers Association.

PSN Poor Sisters of Nazareth; packet switching network.

PSO principal scientific officer.

PSPS Paddle Steamer Preservation Society.

PSS Partially Sighted Society; packet switching system.

PST Pacific Standard Time.

pstn public switched telephone network.

PSU Public Service Union; power supply unit.

PSV public service vehicle.

PSW Public Service Watch; psychiatric social worker.

PT Pacific Time; part time; physical training; physiotherapist; postal telegraph; post town; pupil teacher; purchase tax.

Pt platinum (chemical element).

pt past tense; *pro tempore*, Latin 'for the moment'.

PTA Parent-Teacher Association; Passenger Transport Authority; Piano Tuners' Association; Postcard Traders Association; Property Transfer Association; prior to admission.

PTBT partial test-ban treaty.

PTC Pacific Telecommunications Council; Peace Tax Campaign.

PTD permanent total disability.

PTE Passenger Transport Executive.

PTES People's Trust for Endangered Species.

PTFE polytetrafluoroethylene.

PTH parathyroid hormone.

PTI public tool interface.

PTIA Pet Trade and Industry Association.

PTIU Public Transport Information Unit.

PTM pulse-time modulation.

PTN public telephone network.

PTO Public Telecommunications Operator; Public Trustee Office; please turn over.

PTS Philatelic Traders' Society; Protestant Truth Society.

PTSD post-traumatic stress disorder.

PTU Plumbing Trades Union.

PTUF Professional Tennis Umpires' Federation.

ptw per thousand words.

PTx parathyroidectomy.

PU passed urine; peptic ulcer; polyurethane; processing unit.

Pu plutonium (chemical element).

PUA Pacific Union Association.

pud pick-up and delivery.

PUFA polyunsaturated fatty acids.

pulv. *pulvis*, Latin 'powder'.

pums permanently unfit for military service.

PUO pyrexia of uncertain/unknown origin.

PUS Parliamentary/Permanent Under Secretary.

pus permanently unfit for service.

PUVA psoralen plus ultra-violet A (treatment for psoriasis).

pv *per vaginam*, Latin 'by way of the vagina'.

PVA polyvinyl acetate.

PVC polyvinyl chloride.

PVD peripheral vascular disease.

PVFS post-viral fatigue syndrome.

PVM Prisons Video Magazine Trust.

PVOA Passenger Vehicle Operators' Association.

PVS persistent vegetative state; post-viral syndrome.

pvt pressure, volume, temperature.

PW Policewoman; Positively Women.

pw per week.

PWC Pakistani Workers' Association; People's World Convention; Postwar Credits.

PWD Public Works Department.

PWFS Prisoners Wives & Families Society.

PWG Permanent Working Group of European Junior Hospital Doctors.

PWI Permanet Way Institution.

PWLB Public Works Loan Board.

PWM pulse with modulation.

PWPS Pure Water Preservation Society.

PWR pressurised water reactor.

PWSWA Processed Woodchip, Sawdust and Woodfloor Association.

PX physical examination; private exchange.

px part exchange.

PYBT Prince's Youth Business Trust.

PYO pick your own.

Q

Q Quarto (early Shakespeare text); Quebec; Queen; Queensland; quality; quantity; quartermaster; queen (cards, etc); question.

q quark; quart/er; query; quintal; quire.

QA quality assurance, quarters allowance.

qa quick assembly.

QAA Quality Ash Association.

QAB Queen Anne's Bounty.

QADS quality asurance data system.

QAIMNS Queen Alexandra's Imperial Military Nursing Serivce.

QALY quality-adjusted life year (concerned

with the cost:benefit assessment of possible treatment).

Q & A question and answer.

Qantas Queensland and Northern Territory Aerial Service (Australian airline).

QARANC Queen Alexandra's Royal Army Nursing Corps.

QARNNS Queen Alexandra's Royal Naval Nursing Service.

QB Queen's Bench; queen's bishop (chess).

QBC Quality British Celery Association.

QBD Queen's Bench Division.

Q-boat query-boat (ship with hidden guns and so of uncertain status).

QBP queen's bishop's pawn (chess).

QC Queen's Counsel.

qc quality control.

QCA Quaker Concern for Animals.

QCD quantum chromodynamics.

QCE quality control engineering.

QCGA Queensland Cane Growers' Association (Australia).

QCT quality control technology.

qds *quater die sumendus*, Latin 'to be taken four times a day'.

qe *quod est*, Latin 'which is'.

QE2 Queen Elizabeth the Second (ship).

QED quantum electrodynamics; *quod erat demonstrandum*, Latin 'which was to be proved'.

QEF *quod erat faciendum*, Latin 'which was to be done'.

QEH Queen Elizabeth Hall.

QEI *quod erat inveniendum*, Latin 'which was to be found'.

QF quick-firing.

QFD quantum flavour dynamics.

QFSM Queen's Fire Service Medal.

QG Quartermaster General.

QGM Queen's Gallantry Medal.

qh *quaque hora*, Latin 'every hour'.

QI quartz-iodine.

QIB Qatar Islamic Bank.

qid *quater in die*, Latin 'four times a day'.

QISAM queued indexed sequential access method.

QKOA Quarantine Kennel Owners' Association.

QKt queen's knight (chess).

QL query language.

ql *quantum libet*, Latin 'as much as you please'.

QLA Quantum Leap Society.

QM Quartermaster; quantum mechanics.

qm *quaque mane*, Latin 'each morning'.

Qmess Queen's Messenger.

QMG Quartermaster-General.

QMP Quality Milk Producers.

QMS Quartermaster-Sergeant.

QMW Queen Mary and Westfield College, University of London.

QN queen's knight (chess).

qn *quaque nocte*, Latin 'each night'.

QNI Queen's Nursing Institute.

QNP queen's knight's pawn (chess).

qns quantity not sufficient.

QP queen's pawn (chess).

qp *quantum placet*, Latin 'as much as you wish'.

QPM Queen's Police Medal.

QPR Queen's Park Rangers.

QPS Quaker Peace and Service.

qq. hor. *quaque hora*, Latin 'each hour'.

QR queen's rook (chess).

QRA quick reaction alert.

QRP queen's rook's pawn (chess).

QRPG Quebec Rubber and Plastic Group (Canada).

QS Queen's Scholar; quarter sessions.

qs quadrophonic stereo; *quantum sufficit*, Latin 'enough'.

QSO quasi-stellar object.

QSS quasi-stellar radio source.

QST Quality Scottish Trout.

QSTOL quiet short take-off and landing.

QT quiet (such as 'on the QT').

QTOL quiet take-off and landing.

qualgo quasi-autonomous local government organisation.

quango quasi-autonomous non-governmental organisation.

quasar quasi-stellar object.

QUB Queen's University of Belfast.

QUNG Quaker United Nations Group.

quotid. *quotidie*, Latin 'daily'.

qv *quantum vis*, Latin 'as much as you wish'; *quod vide*, Latin 'which see'.

qwerty standard keyboard layout of typewriter, etc (from order of top-row keys from the left).

qwl quality of working life.

R

R Rabbi; Réaumur (temperature scale); Rector; *Regina*, Latin 'the Queen'; Republican; *Rex*, Latin 'King'; River; Röntgen; Royal; railway; *recipe*, Latin 'take'; reply; return (train ticket, etc); reverse; right.

r radius; rear, recto, right; rises (of the Sun); run.

R18 Restricted 18 (film classification in which it can be shown or distributed only from premises where no one under that age is allowed).

RA Racecourse Association; Ramblers' Association; Rear Admiral; Referees' Association; Refugee Action; Religious of the Assumption; Rice Association; Royal Academician; Royal Academy of Art, London; Royal Artillery; Rural Action; rheumatoid arthritis; right atrium.

Ra radium (chemical element).

RAA Regional Arts Association; Rice Growers' Association of Australia; Royal Academy of Arts.

RAAF Royal Australian Air Force; Royal Auxiliary Air Force.

RAAS Racial Adjustment Action Society; Royal Amateur Arts Society.

RABDF Royal Association of British Dairy Farmers.

RABI Royal Agricultural Benevolent Institution.

RAC Royal Agricultural College; Royal Armoured Corps; Royal Automobile Club; Rubber Association of Canada.

RACE rapid automatic checkout equipment.

RAD Royal Academy of Dancing; Royal Association in Aid of Deaf People; reflex anal dilatation.

RADA Royal Academy of Dramatic Art.

RADAR Royal Association for Disability and Rehabilitation.

RADC Royal Army Dental Corps.

RADD Royal Association in Aid of the Deaf and Dumb.

RAdm Rear Admiral.

radmon radiological monitoring.

RAE Royal Aerospace Establishment.

RAEC Royal Army Educational Corps.

RAeC Royal Aero Club of the United Kingdom.

RAeS Royal Aeronautical Society.

RAF Royal Air Force.

RAFA Royal Air Forces Association.

RAFBF Royal Air Force Benevolent Fund.

RAFES Royal Air Force Educational Service.

RAFGSA Royal Air Force Gliding and Soaring Association.

RAFMS Royal Air Force Medical Services.

RAFR Royal Air Force Regiment.

RAFRO Royal Air Force Reserve Officers.

RAFT Restoration of Appearance and Function Trust.

RAFSC Royal Air Force Staff College; Royal Air Force Strike Command.

RAFVR Royal Air Force Volunteer Service.

RAG Rainforest Action Group.

RAGE Radiotherapy Action Group Exposure.

RAGS Recycling Advisory Group Scotland.

RAH Royal Albert Hall.

RAI Reading Association of Ireland; Restaurants Association of Ireland; Royal Anthropological Institute; Royal Archaeological Institute.

RAIS Royal Air International Service.

Rajar Radio Joint Audience Research.

rall. *rallentando*, Italian 'slowing' (music).

RAM Royal Academy of Music; random access memory.

ram relative atomic mass.

RAMC Royal Army Medical Corps.

RAN Royal Australian Navy.

RANA Royal Animal Nursing Auxiliary.

R & A Royal and Ancient (Scottish golf club).

R & B rhythm and blues.

r & cc riot and civil commotion.

R & D research and development.

R&DSoc Research and Development Society.

R & E research and engineering.

R & I *Regina et Imperatrix*, Latin 'Queen

and Empress'; *Rex et Imperator*, Latin 'King and Emperor'.

r & m reliability and marketing; reports and memoranda.

R & R rescue and resuscitation; rest and recreation; rock and roll.

R & VA Rating and Valuation Association.

RAOB Royal Antediluvian Order of Buffaloes.

RAOC Royal Army Ordnance Corps.

RAP Radical Alternatives to Prison; Refugee Arrival Project.

RAPC Royal Army Pay Corps.

RAPID Register for the Ascertainment and Prevention of Inherited Diseases.

RARDE Royal Armament Research and Development.

RARO Regular Army Reserve of Officers.

RAS Recruitment and Assessment Services; Royal Agricultural Society; Royal Aeronautical Society; Royal Asiatic Society; Royal Astronomical Society.

RASC Royal Army Service Corps.

RATD Register of Apparel and Textile Designers.

RATO rocket-assisted take-off.

RAVC Royal Army Veterinary Corps.

RAW Reality at Work Scotland.

RAWC Radioactive Waste Co-ordinating Committee.

RAX rural automatic exchange.

RB Rifle Brigade; Royal Ballet; reconnaissance bomber.

Rb rubidium (chemical element).

rb right back.

RBA Refined Bitumen Association; Retail Book, Stationery and Allied Trades Employees Association; Royal Bhutanese Army; Royal Society of British Artists.

RBC red blood cell.

RBE relative biological effectiveness (concerning radiation treatment).

RBG Royal Botanic Gardens (Kew).

RBL Royal British Legion.

RBLS Royal British Legion Scotland.

RBNA Royal British Nurses' Association.

RBOA Residential Boat Owners Association.

RBPF Royal Bahamas Police Force.

RBS Rare Breeds Society; Royal Ballet School; Royal Botanical Society; Royal Society of British Sculptors.

RBST Rare Breeds Survival Trust.

RBT random breath-testing.

RC Red Cross, Rifle Club; Roman Catholic; Royal Commission; red cell; red corpuscle; reversed charge (telephone).

rc reinforced concrete.

RCA Race Course Association; Radio Corporation of America; Reinforced Concrete Association; Residential Care Association; Royal Choral Society; Royal College of Art; Royal Company of Archerts; Rural Crafts Association.

RCC Revolutionary Conservative Caucus; Roman Catholic Church.

RCCC Royal Caledonian Curling Club.

RCD residual current device.

RCDS Royal College of Defence Studies.

RCF Redundant Churches Fund.

RCGP Royal College of General Practitioners.

RCHM Royal Commission on Historical Manuscripts/Monuments.

RCI Radiochemical Inspectorate.

rci radar coverage indicator.

RCJ Royal Courts of Justice.

RCM Regimental Court Martial; Royal College of Midwives; Royal College of Music; radar countermeasures.

RCMP Royal Canadian Mounted Police.

RCN Royal Canadian Navy; Royal College of Nursing.

RCO Royal College of Organists.

RCOG Royal College of Obstetricians and Gynaecologists.

RCP Revolutionary Communist Party; Royal College of Physicians; Royal College of Preceptors.

RCPath Royal College of Pathologists.

RCPB Revolutionary Communist Party of Great Britain.

RCPsych Royal College of Psychiatrists.

RCR Royal College of Radiologists.

RCRP Rape Counselling and Research Project.

RCS Rainforest Conservation Society; Royal Choral Society; Royal College of Science; Royal College of Surgeons; Royal Commonwealth Society; Royal Corps of Signals; Rural Counselling Service.

RCSEd Royal College of Surgeons of Edinburgh.

RCSC Royal College of Surgeons of England.

RCSC Radio Components Standardization Committee.

RCT Royal Corps of Transport; randomised clinical trial; regimental combat team; remote-control transmitter.

RCU remote control unit.

RCVS Royal College of Veterinary Surgeons.

RD Reserve Decoration; Rural Dean; refer to drawer.

RDA Revolving Doors Agency; Riding for the Disabled Association; recommended daily/dietary allowance.

rd & d research, development and demonstration.

rd & e research, development and engineering.

RDAT rotary-head digital audio tape.

RDBMS relational database management system.

RDC Red Deer Commission (Scotland); Rural Development Commission; Rural District Council.

RDCC Royal Dutch Cattle Company.

rdd required delivery date.

RDF radio direction-finding; rapid deployment force; refuse-derived fuel.

rDNA recombinant deoxyribonucleic acid.

RDS Railway Development Society; Research Defence Society; Royal Drawing Society; Royal Dublin Society (Eire); radio data system; respiratory distress syndrome.

rdt & e research, development, testing and engineering.

RDX Research Department Explosive (cyclonite).

RDZ radiation danger zone.

RE Reformed Episcopal; Royal Engineers; Royal Exchange; Royal Society of Painter-Printmakers (previously Royal Society of Painter-Etchers and Engravers); religious education.

Re rhenium (chemical element).

re with regard to.

REACH Retired Executives Action Clearing House.

REAL Road Emulsion Association Limited.

React Research, Education and Aid for Children with Potentially Terminal Illness.

REC regional electricity company.

REconS Royal Economic Society.

REE rare earth elements.

REF Railway Engineers Forum.

REHIS Royal Environmental Health Institute of Scotland.

REHVA Representatives of European Heating and Ventilating Associations.

REInstCF Registered Fitter of the National Institute of Carpet Fitters.

REM rapid eye movement.

REMC Radio and Electronics Measurements Committee.

REME Royal Electrical and Mechanical Engineers.

RES Royal Economic Society; Royal Entomological Society.

RESCARE National Society for Mentally Handicapped People in Residential Care.

RESCUE Rescue Trust for British Archaeology.

Ret'dFBID Retired Fellow of the British Institute of Interior Design.

Ret'dMBID Retired Member of the British Institute of Interior Design.

Ret'dABID Retired Associate of the British Institute of Interior Design.

R et I *Regina et Imperatrix*, Latin 'Queen and Empress'; *Rex et Imperator*, Latin 'King and Emperor'.

RETRA Radio, Electrical and Television Retailers Association.

Rev Revelation; Reverend.

REVOLT Rural England Versus Overhead Live Transmissions.

rev/s revolutions per second.

RF Rural Forum; radio frequency; rugby football.

Rf rutherfordium (chemical element).

rf radio frequency; range finder; rapid fire.

rf. *rinforzando*, Italian 'reinforcing' (music).

RFA Royal Fleet Auxiliary; Rugby Fives Association.

RFAC Royal Fine Art Commission.

RFBPA Raw Fat and Bone Processors Association.

RFC request for comment (Internet); Royal Flying Corps; Rugby Football Club.

RFD radio frequency device; reporting for duty.

RFL Rugby Football League.

RFH Royal Festival Hall.

RFI radio-frequency interference.

RRQ request for quotation.

RFR Royal Fleet Reserve.

RFS Registry of Friendly Societies; Royal Forestry Society.

RFSU Rugby Football Schools Union.

RFTF Retail Fruit Trade Federation.

RFU Rugby Football Union.

RGB red-green-blue (colour transmission system).

RGG Royal Grenadier Guards.

RGN Registered General Nurse.

RGNP real gross national product.

RGO Royal Greenwich Observatory.

RGOF Royal Gardeners' Orphan Fund.

RGS Royal Geographical Society.

Rgt Regiment.

RGV remote guidance vehicle.

RH Royal Highness.

Rh rhesus (blood group); rhodium (chemical element).

rh right half (football); right-hand.

RHA Regional Health Authority; Road Haulage Association; Royal Horse Artillery.

RHACT Red Hot AIDS Charitable Trust.

RHAS Rider Haggard Appreciation Society.

RHB Regional Hospital Board.

RHD right-hand drive.

RHEL Rutherford High Energy Laboratory.

RHF Royal Highland Fusiliers.

RHG Royal Horse Guards.

RHHI Royal Hospital and Home for Incurables.

RHistS Royal Historical Society.

RHM Rank Hovis McDougall.

rhp rate horsepower.

RHQ regimental headquarters.

RHR Royal Highland Regiment.

RHS Robin Hood Society; Royal Highland Show; Royal Historical Society; Royal Horticultural Society; Royal Humane Society; Russian Heraldry Society.

rhs right-hand side; round headed screw.

RHT Railway Heritage Trust; Rural Housing Trust.

RHV Registered Health Visitor.

RI Railway Inspectorate; *Regina et Imperatrix*, Latin 'Queen and Empress'; Religious Instruction; *Rex et Imperator*, Latin 'King and Emperor'; Rhode Island; Rotary International; Royal Institute of Painters in Water Colours; Royal Institution.

ri refractive index.

RIA Royal Irish Academy.

RIB Racing Information Bureau.

RIBA Royal Institute of British Architects.

RIC Radio Industry Council; Railway Industry Council; Rice Improvement Conference; Royal Institute of Chemistry; Royal Institution of Cornwall; Royal Irish Constabulary.

RICA Research Institute for Consumer Affairs.

RICE Research Institute for the Care of the Elderly.

RICS Royal Institution of Chartered Surveyors.

RICSS Royal Institution of Chartered Surveyors in Scotland.

RIE recognised investment exchange.

RIF reduction in force.

RIGS regionally important geological site.

RILC Racing Industry Liaison Committee.

RILKO Research into Lost Knowledge Organization.

RIIA Royal Institute of International Affairs.

Rimnet Radioactive Incident Monitoring Network.

RIOP Royal Institute of Oil Painters.

RIP *requiescat in pace*, Latin 'may he/she rest in peace'.

rip. *ripieno*, Italian 'filled up' (music for extra players).

RIPA Royal Institute of Public Administration.

RIPHH Royal Institute of Public Health and Hygiene.

RIPS Radiotherapy Injured Patients Support.

RIR Royal Irish Regiment.

RIS Research Information Service.

RISC reduced instruction set computer.

RIT Rorschach Inkblot Test.

rit. *ritardando*, Italian 'slowing down' (music).

riten. *ritenuto*, Italian 'held back' (music).

RJDip Diploma for Retail Jewellers.

RJE remote job entry.

RJET remote job entry terminal.

RK religious knowledge.

RL Rugby League; reference library.

RLAF Right Livelihood Awards Foundation.

RLC Refugee Legal Centre; Royal Logistic Corps.

RLF Royal Literary Fund.

RLLMA Red Lead and Litharge Manufacturers' Association.

RLO Returned Letter Office.

RLPS Royal Liverpool Philharmonic Society.

RLSS Royal Life Saving Society.

RM Registered Midwife; Resident Magistrate; Royal Mail; Royal Marines.

RMA Royal Military Academy; Royal Musical Association.

RMAG Rocky Mountain Association of Geologists (USA).

RMCM Royal Manchester College of Music.

RMCS Royal Medical and Chirurgical Society; Royal Military College of Science.

RMetS Royal Meteorological Society.

RMFVR Royal Marine Forces Volunteer Reserves.

RMN Registered Mental Nurse.

RMO Resident Medical Officer.

RMP Royal Marine Police; Royal Military Police.

RMR Royal Marines Reserve.

RMS Records Management Society; Royal Medical Society; Royal Microscopical Society; Royal Society of Miniature Painters, Sculptors and Gravers.

rms root-mean-square.

RMSchMus Royal Military School of Music.

RMT National Union of Rail, Maritime and Transport Workers.

RN Registered Nurse; Royal Navy.

Rn radon (chemical element).

rn reception nil.

RNA Romantic Novelists' Association; Royal Naval Association; ribonucleic acid.

RNAA Royal Norfolk Agricultural Association.

RNAS Royal Naval Air Service.

r'n'b rhythm and blues.

RNBS Royal Naval Benevolent Society.

RNBT Royal Naval Benevolent Trust.

RNBWS Royal Naval Bird Watching Society.

RNC Royal Naval College.

RNCC Royal Northern & Clyde Yacht Club.

RNCM Royal Naval College of Music.

RNEC Royal Naval Engineering College.

RNHA Registered Nursing Home Association.

RNHU Royal National Homing Union.

RNIB Royal National Institute for the Blind.

RNID Royal National Institute for the Deaf.

RNLI Royal National Lifeboat Institution.

RNMDSF Royal National Mission to Deep Sea Fishermen.

RNMH Registered Nurse for the Mentally Handicapped.

RNMS Royal Naval Medical School.

RNR Royal Naval Reserve.

r'n'r rock and roll.

RNRS Royal National Rose Society.

RNS Royal Numismatic Society.

RNSA Royal Naval Sailing Association.

RNSC Royal Naval Staff College.

RNSR Royal Naval Special Reserve.

RNSS Royal Naval Scientific Service.

RNZAS Royal Astronomical Society of New Zealand.

RNT Royal National Theatre.

RNTE Royal Naval Training Establishment.

RNTU Royal Naval Training Unit.

RNVR Royal Naval Volunteer Reserve.

RNXS Royal Naval Auxiliary Service.

RO Returning Officer; Royal Observatory.

ro run out (cricket).

ROA Racehorse Owners' Association; Record of Achievement; return on assets.

ROAR right of admission reserved.

ROC Royal Observer Corps; return on capital.

ROE Royal Observatory, Edinburgh; return on equity.

ROF Royal Ordnance Factory.

Roffen. *Roffensis*, Latin 'of Rochester'.

ROH Royal Opera House (Covent Garden).

ROI Royal Institute of Oil Painters; return on investment.

ROM rupture of membranes; read-only memory.

RORC Royal Ocean Racing Club.

ro-ro roll-on, roll-off (type of ferry).

ROSCO Road Operators' Safety Council.

ROSE Research Open Systems in Europe.

ROSL Royal Overseas League.

RoSPA Royal Society for the Prevention of Accidents.

ROT registered occupational therapist; rule of thumb.

ROV remotely-operated vehicle.

ROW Rights of Women; right of way.

RP Received Pronunciation; Reformed Presbyterian; Registered Plumber; Regius Professor; Royal Society of Portrait Painters; recommended price; reply paid; reprint; retinitis pigmentosa.

rp reception poor.

RPA Radio Paging Association; Rationalist Press Association; Record of Personal Achievement; Registered Plumbers' Association; Rural Pharmacists Association; Rural Preservation Association.

RPB recognised professional body.

RPI retail price index.

rpm revolutions per minute.

RPRA Royal Pigeon Racing Association; Rubber and Plastics Reclamation Association.

RPS Racial Preservation Society; Rare Poultry Society; Royal Philatelic Society; Royal Philharmonic Society; Royal Photographic Society.

rps revolutions per second.

RPT Reptile Protection Trust.

RPV remotely piloted vehicle.

RRA Road Roller Association; Rubber Research Association (Israel).

RRP recommended retail price.

RS Royal Society.

rs right side.

RSA Racket Sports Association; Refined Sugar Association; Relay Services Association of Great Britain; Republic of South Africa; Royal Scottish Academy of Painting,

Sclpture and Architecture; Royal Society of Arts; Royal Society of Australia.

RSABI Royal Scottish Agricultural Benevolent Institution.

RSAI Royal Society of Antiquaries of Ireland.

RSAS Royal Surgical Aid Society.

RSBA Royal Society of British Artists.

RSBEI Registered Student of the Institution of Body Engineers.

RSC Refugee Support Centre; Royal Shakespeare Company; Royal Society of Chemistry.

RSCDS Royal Scottish Country Dance Society.

RSCN Registered Sick Children's Nurse.

RSDA Road Surface Dressing Association.

RSE Royal Society of Edinburgh.

RSFS Royal Scottish Forestry Society.

RSM Regimental Sergeant-Major; Royal School of Mines; Royal Society of Musicians.

RSMG Rubber Stamp Manufacturers Guild.

RSN Royal Society of Needlework.

RSPB Royal Society for the Protection of Birds.

RSPCA Royal Society for the Prevention of Cruelty to Animals.

RSPCC Royal Society for the Prevention of Cruelty to Children.

RSPS Royal Scottish Pipers Society.

RSR Royal Sailors' Rests.

RSRC Rural Studies Research Centre.

RSRIGS Royal Society for the Relief of Indigent Gentlewomen of Scotland.

RSS Remote Sensing Society; Robert Simpson Society; Royal Statistical Society.

RSTM&H Royal Society of Tropical Medicine and Hygiene.

RSV Revised Standard Version, concerning the Bible.

RSVP *répondez s'il vous plaît*, French 'please reply'.

RTA Racehorse Transporters Association; Road Transport Association; Roofing Tile Association; Rose Trade Association.

RTCS Round Tower Churches Society.

Rt Hon Right Honourable, the title used by British members of Parliament.

Rt Rev Right Reverend.

RTI Round Table International; respiratory tract infection.

RTITB Road Transport Industry Training Board.

RTK right to know.

RTL real time language.

RTOL reduced take-off and landing.

RTP room temperature and pressure.

RTPI Royal Town Planning Institute.

RTR Royal Tank Regiment.

RTS Religious Tract Society; Risk Theory Society; River Thames Society; Royal Television Society; Royal Toxophilite Society.

RTSA Retail Standards Association.

RTTC Road Time Trials Council.

rtu returned to unit.

rtw ready to wear.

RTYC Royal Thames Yacht Club.

RTZ Rio Tinto Zinc Corporation Limited.

RU Rugby Union.

Ru ruthenium (chemical element).

RUA Royal Ulster Academy.

RUBSSO Rossendale Union of Boot, Shoe and Slipper Operatives.

RUC Royal Ulster Constabulary.

RUCR Royal Ulster Constabulary Reserve.

RUG restricted users group.

RUKBA Royal United Kingdom Beneficent Association.

RUR Royal Ulster Regiment.

Rural Society for the Responsible Use of Resources in Agriculture and on the Land.

RUSI Royal United Services Institute for Defence Studies.

RUSM Royal United Service Museum.

RV Revised Version (translation of Bible); rateable value; right ventricle.

rv rendezvous.

RVA Returned Volunteer Action.

RVC Royal Veterinary College.

RVSVP *répondez vite, s'il vous plaît*, French 'please reply quickly'.

RW Right Worshipful; Right Worthy; runway.

r/w read/write.

RWA Race Walking Association.

RWAS Royal Welsh Agricultural Society.

RWD radioactive waste disposal.

rwd rear wheel drive.

RWF Royal Welsh Fusiliers.

RWFCS Red and White Friesian Cattle Society.

RWIC Rioja Wine Information Centre.

RWM radioactive waste management.

RWMAC Radioactive Waste Management Advisory Committee.

RWS Royal Society of Painters in Water Colours.

RYA Royal Yachting Association.

RYS Royal Yacht Squadron.

RZS Royal Zoological Society.

S

S Sabbath; Saint; Saturday; September; Signor, Italian 'Mr'; Society; sulphur (chemical element); Sunday; school; *segno*, Italian 'sign' (music); siemens; slow; small (clothing size); soprano; south; spades (cards); square; summer; sun.

s second; section; semi-; series; sets (of the sun); shilling (former UK monetary unit); singular; sister; son; suit.

SA Salvation Army; Saudi Arabia; Society of Antiquaries; Society of Arts; Soil Association; South Africa; South America; South Australia; Superintendents' Association; sex appeal; small arms; subsistence allowance.

sa *secundum artem*, Latin 'in the standard way'; semi-annual.

s/a subject to acceptance/approval.

SAA Scottish Aeromodellers Association; Scottish Archery Association; Scottish Assessors' Association; Society of American Archivists; Society of Archer-Antiquaries; South African Airways; Sub-Aqua Association; Systems Application Architecture (software operating system); small arms ammunition.

SAAA Scottish Agricultural Arbiters Association; Scottish Amateur Athletic Association.

Saab *Svensk Aeroplan Aktiebolag*, Swedish 'Swedish Aeroplane Company' (car and aircraft manufacturer).

SAABS Scottish Action Against Blood Sports.

SAAD small arms ammunition depot.

SAAPE Scottish Association of Advisers in Physical Education.

SAAS Scottish Adoption Advice Service; South African Archaeological Society.

SAB Scientific Advisory Board; soprano, alto, bass.

SABA Scottish Amateur Boxing Association; South African Brick Association.

SABC Scottish Association of Boys' Clubs; South African Broadcasting Corporation.

Sabena *Société Anonyme Belge d'Exploitation de la Navigation Aérienne*, French 'Belgian Company for the Development of Air Travel'.

SABHATA Sand and Ballast Hauliers and Allied Trades Alliance.

SABIC Society for the Advancement of Brain-Injured Children.

SAC Post Office Stamp Advisory Committee; Salmon Advisory Committee; Scottish Agricultural College; Scottish Arts Council; Scottish Automobile Club; Senior Aircraftman; Strategic Air Command (US); Sugar Association of the Caribbean.

SACA South African Cricket Association.

SACAB Scottish Association of Citizens' Advice Bureaux.

SACC Society of All Cargo Correspondents; South African Council of Churches.

SACGB Shark Angling Club.

SACHR Standing Advisory Commission on Human Rights.

SACP Scottish Agricultural Consultative Panel; South African Communist Party.

SACRO Scottish Association for the Care and Resettlement of Offenders.

SACTRA Standing Advisory Committee on Trunk Road Assessment.

SACU Scottish Auto-Cycle Union; Society for the Promotion of Anglo-Chinese Understanding.

SACS Senior Aircraftwoman.

SAD Scottish Action on Dementia; Scottish Association for the Deaf; seasonal affective disorder.

SADI Society of Approved Driving Instructors.

sae stamped addressed envelope; self-addressed envelope.

SAEF Stock Exchange Automatic Execution Facility.

SAEMA Suspended Access Equipment Manufacturers Association.

SAF Scottish Athletic Federation; Singapore Air Force; Society of American Florists; South African Foundation; Sports Aid Foundation.

SAFA Scottish Amateur Football Association.

SAFE Struggle Against Financial Exploitation; Sustainable Agriculture, Food and Environment.

SAFrD South African Dutch (Afrikaans).

SAFU Scottish Amateur Fencing Union.

SAG Scandinavian Society of Geneticists; Steroid Action Group.

SAGA Scottish Amateur Gymnastics Association; Society of American Graphic Artists.

SAGB Schizophrenia Association of Great Britain; Shellfish Association of Great Britain; Skibob Association of Great Britain; Spiritualist Association of Great Britain.

SAGGA Scout and Guide Graduate Association.

SAGTA School and Group Travel Association.

SAH Supreme Allied Headquarters; subarachnoid haemorrhage.

SAHC Scottish Association of Health Councils.

SAHGB Society of Architectural Historians of Great Britain.

SAHR Society of Army Historical Research.

SAI Scout Association of Ireland.

SAIC Scottish Agricultural Improvement Council.

SAIF Society of Allied & Independent Funeral Directors; South African Institute of Forestry.

SAISSA Scottish Amateur Ice Speed Skating Association.

SAJ Shipbuilders Association of Japan; Sumo Association of Japan.

SALRC Society for Assistance to Ladies in Reduced Circumstances.

SALT Scottish Association for Language

Teaching; Strategic Arms Limitation Talks/ Treaty.

SAM Scottish Aids Monitor; Scottish Airline Museum; Scottish Association for Metals; South Australian Museum.

SAm South America/n.

sam surface-to-air missile.

SAMA Scottish Agricultural Machinery Association; Scottish Amateur Music Association; Shock Absorber Manufacturers Association; South African Museums Association.

SAMB Scottish Association of Master Bakers; Scottish Association of Master Blacksmiths.

SAMH Scottish Association for Mental Health.

SAMSA Silica and Moulding Sands Association.

SAN Science Association of Nigeria; Society for Ancient Numismatists.

SANA Scottish Anglers' National Association.

s & d search and destroy; song and dance.

s & f stock and fixtures.

s & fa shipping and forwarding agents.

s & h shipping and handling.

S & M *or* **S and M** sadism and masochism.

s & m sausages and mash; stock and machinery.

SAND Scotland Against Nuclear Dumping.

SANDS Stillbirth and Neonatal Death Society.

S and T signalling and telecommunications.

s & t supply and transport.

S & TA Salmon and Trout Association.

SANE Schizophrenia: A National Emergency.

SANFP Scottish Association for Natural Family Planning.

sanrs subject to approval - no risks.

sap soon as possible.

SAPC Scottish Accident Prevention Council.

SAPCT Scottish Association of Painting Craft Teachers.

SAPT Scottish Association for Public Transport.

SAR South African Railways; synthetic aperture radar.

sar search and rescue.

SARA Scottish Amateur Rowing Association; Scottish Anti-Racist Alliance; Society of American Registered Architects.

SARDA Search and Rescue Dog Association.

SARM Scottish Anti-Rascist Movement.

SARS Safety and Reliability Society; Scots Ancestry Research Society.

SARSAT Search and Rescue Satellite (for maritime disasters).

SAS Scottish Australian Society; *Società in accomandita semplice*, Italian 'Limited'; *Societatis Antiquariorum Socius*, Latin 'Fellow of the Society of Antiquaries'; Society for Armenian Studies; Special Air Service; Surfers Against Sewage.

SASA Scottish Amateur Snooker Association; Scottish Amateur Swimming Association; South African Sugar Association.

SASF Salvation Army Students' Fellowship.

SASLI Scottish Association of Sign Language Interpreters for the Deaf.

SASMA Silk and Art Silks Mills Association (India).

SASO Senior Air Staff Officer.

SASR Special Air Service Regiment.

SASS Scottish Agricultural Statistics Service; Sir Arthur Sullivan Society.

SASV Scottish Association for the Speaking of Verse.

SAT Senior Member of the Association of Accounting Technicians; South Australia Time.

SAt South Atlantic.

SAT Standard Assessment Task.

SATB soprano, alto, tenor, bass.

SATCO signal automatic air-traffic control system.

SATIPS Society of Assistant Teachers in Preparatory Schools.

SATRA Shoe and Allied Trades Research Organization.

SATRO Science and Technology Regional Organization.

SAus South Australia/n.

SAV sale at valuation; stock at valuation.

Save Save Britain's Heritage.

SAVS Scottish Anti-Vivisection Society.

SAW Scottish Association of Writers; Society of Architects in Wales; surface acoustic wave.

SAWA Scottish Amateur Wrestling Association; Scottish Asian Women's Association.

SAWGU South African Wattle Growers Union.

SAWJ Scottish Association of Watchmakers and Jewellers.

SAYC Scottish Association of Youth Clubs.

SAYE save as you earn.

SB Savings Bank; Special Branch (police); Sugar Bureau; selection board; sick bay; simultaneous broadcast; smooth bore; stillbirth.

Sb *stibium*, Latin 'antimony' (chemical element).

sb single-breasted.

SBA School of Business Administration; Scottish Basketball Association; Scottish Beekeepers Association; Scottish Bonsai Association; Scottish Bowling Association; Smaller Businesses Association; Society of Botanical Artists; Steam Boat Association of Great Britain; sick bay attendant.

SBAC Society of British Aerospace Companies.

SBBA Scottish Boat Builders Association.

SBBC Shell Better Britain Campaign.

SBBNF Ship and Boat Builders' National Federation.

SBC Stamp Bug Club; Swiss Broadcasting Corporation; single-board computer.

SBGI Society of British Gas Industries.

SBH Scottish Board of Health.

SBL Society of Biblical Literature; Society of Black Lawyers.

SBN Standard Book Number.

SBP systolic blood pressure.

SBPR Society for Back Pain Research.

SBR strict bed rest.

SBS Save British Science Society; Special Boat Service; sick building syndrome.

SBSA Scottish Board Sailing Association; Standard Bank of South Africa.

SBSB Society of British Snuff Blenders.

SBTD Society of British Theatre Designers.

SBU Scottish Badminton Union; strategic business unit.

SC Schools Council; Security Council (UN); Signal Corps; Social Club; Special Constable; Sports Club; Staff College; sailing club; standing committee; structural change; subcutaneous.

Sc scandium (chemical element).

Sc. Scandinavia/n; Scotland; Scottish.

sc small capitals.

s/c self-catering; self-contained.

S4C *Sianel 4 Cymru*, Welsh 'Channel 4 Wales'.

SCA Scottish Canoe Association; Scottish Cashmere Association; Scottish Chess Association; Scottish Council on Alcohol; Scottish Croquet Assocation; Sea Cadet Association; Social Care Association; Specialist Cheesemakers Association; Sprayed Concrete Association; Steel Cladding Association; Suez Canal Authority; sickle-cell anaemia.

SCAARF Scottish Combined Action Against Racism and Fascism.

SCAFA Scottish Child and Family Alliance.

SCAHT Scottish Churches Architectural Heritage Trust.

SCAMP Scottish Association of Magazine Publishers.

SCAN suspected child abuse and neglect.

SCANN South Coast Against Nuclear Navies.

SCAR Scientific Committee on Antarctic Research.

SCARF Sickle Cell Anaemia Research Foundation.

SCAS Society for Companion Animal Studies.

SCB Solicitors' Complaints Bureau; Speedway Control Board (motor-cycle racing).

ScB *Scientiae Baccalaureus*, Latin 'Bachelor of Science'.

SCBU Special Care Baby Unit.

SCC Scandinavian Collectors Club; Science Council of Canada; Scottish Churches Council; Scottish Consumer Council; Sea Cadet Corps; Silhouette Collectors Club; Society of Cheese Connoisseurs; Structural Concrete Consortium; Sylvac Collectors' Club.

scc single column centimetre.

SCCA Scottish Consumer Credit Association; Society of Company and Commercial Accountants.

SCCL Scottish Council for Civil Liberties.

SCD Scottish Council on Disability.

ScD *Scientiae Doctor*, Latin 'Doctor of Science'.

SCDC Schools Curriculum Development Committee.

SCE Scottish Certificate of Education.

SCEC Scottish Community Education Council.

SCF Save the Children Fund; Spanish Cycling Federation; Standing Committee on Fishing.

scf standard cubic feet.

scfh standard cubic feet per hour.

scfd standard cubic feet per day.

SCGB Ski Club of Great Britain.

sci single column inch.

SCIAF Scottish Catholic International Aid Fund.

SCID Scotland's Campaign Against Irresponsible Drivers; severe combined immunodeficiency disease.

SCIVU Scientific Council of the International Vegetarian Union.

SCL Scottish Central Library; Society for Caribbean Linguistics; Society of Construction Law; Society of Civil Law.

SCLC Scottish Child Law Centre.

SCM Society of Coal Merchants; State Certified Midwife; Student Christian Movement.

ScM *Scientiae Magister*, Latin 'Master of Science'.

SCMA Scottish Carpet Manufacturers Association; Scottish Cement Merchants Association; Scottish Childminding Association; Stilton Cheese Manufacturers' Association.

SCMAC Scottish Catholic Marriage Advisory Council.

SCMM Sisters of Charity of Our Lady Mother of Mercy.

SCNI Sports Council for Northern Ireland.

SCO Scottish Committee of Optometrists.

Scobec Scottish Business Education Council.

SCOLAG Scottish Legal Action Group.

SCONUL Standing Conference of National and University Libraries.

SCOPE Scientific Committee on Phosphates in Europe; Scottish Council for Opportunities in Play Experience.

SCOT Scottish Confederation of Tourism.

SCOTTIE Society for the Control of Troublesome and Toxic Industrial Emissions.

Scotvec Scottish Vocational Educational Council.

SCP Scottish Communist Party; Society of Christian Philosophers; single-cell protein.

SCPA Scottish Cashmere Producers Association; Scottish Clay Pigeon Association.

SCPL Senior Commercial Pilot's Licence.

SCPS Scottish Centre for Pollen Studies; Society of Civil and Public Servants.

SCR senor common room (Oxford colleges); senior combination room (Cambridge colleges); sequence control register.

SCRAM Scottish Campaign to Resist the Atomic Menace.

SCRE Scottish Council for Racial Equality; Scottish Council for Research in Education.

Scream Society for the Control and Registration of Estate Agents and Mortgage Brokers.

SCUBA Self-contained Underwater Breathing Apparatus.

SCS Scottish Crime Squad; Singapore Civil Service; Society of Cosmetic Scientists; Swiss Cooks Society.

SCSA Scottish Cold Storage Association; Strip Curtain Suppliers Association.

SCSI small computer systems interface.

SCTA Scottish Clay Target Association.

SCU Scottish Cricket Union; Scottish Crofters' Union; Scottish Cyclists' Union; Special Care Unit.

SCUA Scottish Conservative and Unionist Association; Suez Canal Users' Association.

SCV *Stato della Città del Vaticano*, Italian 'Vatican City State'.

SD senile dementia.

sd semi-detached; *sine die*, Latin 'without a day'; special delivery; stage door.

SD&BBA Soft Drink and Beer Bottlers Association (Eire).

SDA Scottish Darts Association; Scottish Decorators' Association; Scottish Development Agency; Seventh Day Adventists General Conference.

SDASA Scottish Deaf Amateur Sports Association.

S-DAT stationary digital audio tape.

SDAT senile dementia of the Alzheimer type.

SDC Society of Designer-Craftsmen; Society of Dyers and Colourists; Sustainable Development Commission.

SDCGB Square Dance Callers of Great Britain.

SDD Scottish Development Department; subscriber direct dialling.

SDG *soli Deo gloria*, Latin 'glory be to God alone'.

SDHBS South Devon Herd Book Society.

SDI Strategic Defence Initiative.

SDLP Social Democratic and Labour Party (in N. Ireland).

SDMJ September, December, March, June (re quarterly payments).

SDO senior duty officer.

SDP Social Democratic Party; social domestic and pleasure (motor insurance).

SDR special despatch rider; special drawing right.

SDSA Scottish Down's Syndrome Association.

SDT Society of Dairy Technology.

SDTA Scottish Dance Teachers Alliance.

SDTU Sign and Display Trades Union.

SDUK Society for the Diffusion of Useful Knowledge.

SE Scottish Enterprise; Society of Engineers; Stock Exchange; southeast.

Se selenium (chemical element).

se standard error.

SEA Shipbuilding Exports Association; Slag Employers Association; Society for Electronic Access; South-East Asia.

SEAC Schools Examinations and Assessment Council; South-East Asia Command.

SEAL Society of English and American Lawyers; South East Adult Learning.

SEALION Sea Level Instrumentation and Observation Network.

SEAQ Stock Exchange Automated Quotations.

SEATO South-East Asia Treaty Organization.

SEB Society for Experimental Botany.

SEC Scottish Evangelistic Crusade; Secondary Examinations Council.

Secam *Séquentiel Couleur à Mémoire*, French 'colour sequence by memory' (Russian and French colour television system).

SED Scottish Education Department.

SEE Save Eyes Everywhere (British Council for the Prevention of Blindness).

SEF Scottish Environmental Forum; Shipbuilding Employers' Federation.

SEFA South East Forest Alliance.

SEG socioeconomic grade.

SEIS submarine escape immersion suit.

SEM scanning electron microscope.

se(m) standard error (of the mean).

SEMA Spray Equipment Manufacturers Association; Storage Equipment Manufacturers Association.

SEMG Spring Makers' Export Group.

semp. *sempre*, Italian 'always' (music).

SEN Special Educational Needs; State Enrolled Nurse.

SenAWeldI Senior Associate of the Welding Institute.

SenMWeldI Senior Member of the Welding Institute.

SEng, FInstSMM Qualified Sales Engineer of the Institute of Sales and Marketing Management.

SENNAC Special Educational Needs National Advisory Council.

SENSE Scottish Environmental Network for a Sustainable Economy; The National Deafblind and Rubella Association.

SEO Senior Executive Officer; Senior Experimental Officer; Society of Education Officers.

seoo *sauf erreurs ou omissions*, French 'errors and omissions excepted'.

SEPA Scottish Environment Protection Agency.

SEPFA South-East Professional Fishermen's Association.

seq. luce *sequenti luce*, Latin 'on the following day'.

SERC Science and Engineering Research Council.

SERL Services Electronics Research Laboratory.

SERPS State Earnings-Related Pension Scheme.

SES Scientific Exploration Society; Scottish Equipment Suppliers; Solar Energy Society; socioeconomic status.

SET Society for Experimental Therapy; selective employment tax.

SETA Scottish Egg Trade Association.

SETI search for extra-terrestrial intelligence.

SF Sinn Féin; Society of Friends; Stone Federation; science fiction; signal frequency.

sf sinking fund; *sub finem*, Latin 'towards the end'.

SFA Scientific Film Association; Scottish Football Association; Securities and Futures Authority; Shetland Fishermen's Association; Small Farmers' Association; sweet Fanny Adams.

SFBIU Scottish Farm Buildings Investigation Unit.

SFBMS Small Farm Business Management Scheme.

SFC Scottish Film Council; specific fuel consumption.

SFD small for dates.

SFF Scottish Fishermen's Federation; Scottish Flag Fund.

SFHEA Scottish Further and Higher Education Association.

SFInstE Senior Fellow of the Institute of Energy.

SFL Scottish Football League; sequenced flashing lights (on runway).

SFLA Solicitors' Family Law Association.

sfm surface feet per minute.

SFMA Scottish Flour Millers' Association.

SFO Senior Flag Officer; Serious Fraud Office.

SFSA Scottish Federation of Sea Anglers; Scottish Field Studies Association.

SFSR Socialist Federation of Soviet Republics.

SFU suitable for upgrade (on airline tickets).

sfz. *sforzando*, Italian 'strengthening' (music).

SG Seaman Gunner; Secretary General; Showmen's Guild of Great Britain; Siege Group; Society of Genealogists; Solicitor-General; Surgeon General.

Sg seaborgium (chemical element).

sg specific gravity; steel girder.

SGA Sand and Gravel Association; Scottish Games Association; Scottish Glass Association; Society of Graphic Artists; small for gestational age.

SGB Scottish Gas Board.

SGBI Schoolmistresses' and Governesses' Benevolent Institution.

SgC Surgeon Captain.

sgdg *sans garantie du gouvernement*, French 'without government guarantee' (on French patents).

SGF Scottish Grocers' Federation.

SGHWR steam-generating heavy water reactor.

SGlam South Glamorgan.

SgLCr Surgeon Lieutenant-Commander.

SGM Sea Gallantry Medal.

SGMA Soup and Gravy Manufacturers Association.

SGML Standardized Generalized Mark-up Language.

SGPA Stained Glass Professionals Association (USA).

SgRA Surgeon Rear Admiral.

SGT Society of Glass Technology.

SGTS Scottish Gaelic Texts Society.

SGU Scottish Gliding Union; Scottish Golf Union.

SgVA Surgeon Vice-Admiral.

SH sexual harassment; southern hemisphere.

sh scrum half; second-hand.

s/h shorthand.

SHA Scottish Hockey Association; Secondary Heads' Association; Society of Heraldic Arts; Special Health Authority; Swiss Hotel Association.

SHAC Shelter Housing Aid Centre; Society for the History of Alchemy and Chemistry.

SHACT Scottish Housing Associations Charitable Trust.

SHAEF Supreme Headquarters, Allied Expeditionary Forces (World War II).

SHAPE Supreme Headquarters, Allied Powers Europe.

SHARP Self Help Addiction Recovery Programme; Society for the History of Authorship, Reading and Publishing.

S/HE Sundays and holidays excepted.

SHEFC Scottish Higher Education Funding Council.

Sheffield. *Sheffieldensis*, Latin 'of Sheffield'.

SHEx Sundays and holidays excepted.

shf superhigh frequency.

SHGF Scottish Hang-Gliding Federation.

SHHD Scottish Home and Health Department.

SHLTA Skin, Hide & Leather Traders' Association.

shm simple harmonic motion.

SHMIS Society of Headmasters and Headmistresses of Independent Schools.

SHNC Scottish Higher National Certificate.

SHND Scottish Higher National Diploma.

SHO Senior House Officer.

shoran short-range navigation.

shp shaft horsepower; single-flowered hardy perennial (rose).

SHQ supreme headquarters.

SHRG Scottish Homosexual Rights Group.

SHS Scottish History Society; Shire Horse Society; Social History Society; *Societatis Historicae Socius*, Latin 'Fellow of the Historical Society'.

sht single-flowered hybrid tea (rose).

SHU Scottish Hockey Union.

shv *sub hac voce*, Latin 'under this word'.

SHW safety, health and welfare.

SI Smithsonian Institution; Socialist International; Society of Indexers; Survival International; *Système International d'Unités*, French 'International Units System'; seriously ill; statutory instrument.

Si silicon (chemical element).

si sum insured.

SIA Securities Industry Association; Service Innovation Action; Singapore International Airlines; Society of Investment Analysts; Solvents Industry Association; Spinal Injuries Association.

SIAD Society of Industrial Artists and Designers.

SIB Securities and Investments Board; Shipbuilding Industry Board; Society of Independent Businesses; Special Investigations Branch; self-injurious behaviour.

SIBA Scottish Indoor Bowling Association; Services Insurance Brokers Association.

SIBH Society for the Interpretation of Britain's Heritage.

SIBOR Singapore Inter-Bank Offered Rate.

SIC Standard Industrial Classification.

sic. *siccus*, Latin 'dry'.

SICAV *Société d'Investissement à Capital Variable*, French 'unit trust'.

sid sudden ionospheric disturbance.

SIDP Society of Infectious Diseases Pharmacists.

SIDS sudden infant death syndrome.

SIEDip Securities Industry Examination Diploma.

SIF Society for Individual Freedom; Society of Irish Foresters.

SIG special interest group.

Sig. *Signor*, Italian 'Mr'.

SIGBI Soroptomist International of Great Britain and Ireland.

sigint signal intelligence.

sig. nom. pro. *signa nomine proprio*, Latin 'label with the correct title'.

SigO Signals Officer.

SIH Society for Italic Handwriting.

SIM self-inflicted mutilation.

SIMA Scientific Instrument Manufacturers' Association of Great Britain.

Simca *Société Industrielle de Mécanique et Carrosserie Automobiles*, French 'Car Engine and Coachbuilding Company'.

simd single instruction, multiple data.

SIMM single in-line memory module.

SINA Scottish Independent Nurseries Association; Shellfish Institute of North America.

SInstBB Student of the Institute of British Bakers.

SInstPet Student of the Institute of Petroleum.

sio serial input/output.

sipo serial in, parallel out.

SIPS side impact protection system.

SIRP Society of Independent Roundabout Proprietors.

SIS Satellite Information Services; Scientific Instrument Society; Secret Intelligence Service.

SISA Scottish Ice Skating Association; Scottish Industrial Sports Association.

SISD Scottish Information Service for the Disabled.

SISTER Special Institutions for Scientific and Technical Education and Research.

SITC Standard International Trade Classification.

Sitpro Simpler Trade Procedures Board (originally Simplification of International Trade Procedures).

SIW self-inflicted wound.

SIWA Scottish Inland Waterways Association.

SJ Society of Jesus (Jesuits).

sj *sub judice*, Latin 'under trial'.

SJAA St John Ambulance Association.

SJAB St John Ambulance Brigade.

SJBI Scottish Joint Breast-Feeding Initiative.

SJC standing joint committee.

SJCRE Scottish Joint Committee on Religious Education.

SJF Scottish Judo Federation.

SJH Society of Jewellery History.

SJJA Scottish Ju-Jitsu Association.

SK Sealed Knot.

SKA Scottish Knitwear Association.

SKC Scottish Kennel Club; Scottish Knitwear Council.

SKFA Scottish Keep Fit Association.

SL Sergeant-at-Law; Solicitor at Law; Squadron Leader; sea level.

SLA Scaffold Lashings Association; School Libraries Association; Scottish Library Association; Sleep-Learning Association; Small Landowners Association.

SLADE Society of Lithographic Artists, Designers, Engravers and Process Workers.

SLAM stand-off land-attack missile.

SLAR side-looking airborne radar.

SLAS Scottish Law Agents Society; Society for Latin American Studies.

SLASH Scottish Local Authorities Special Housing Group.

SLBM submarine-launched ballistic missile.

SLC Scottish Land Court; Scottish Law Commission; Secretarial Language Certificate; Surgeon Lieutenant-Commander.

SLCM sea-launched cruise missile.

SLD Secretarial Language Diploma; Social and Liberal Democrats; self-locking device.

SLDP Social and Liberal Democratic Party.

SLdr Squadron Leader.

SLE systemic lupus erythematosus.

SLF Scottish Landowners' Federation.

slf straight line frequency.

SLG Socialist Labour Group; Socialist Lesbian Group.

SLGA Scottish Ladies' Golfing Association.

SLLA Scottish Ladies Lacrosse Association.

SLM ship-launched missile.

SLMC Scottish Ladies Mountaineering Club.

SLO senior liaison officer.

SLOA Steam Locomotive Operators' Association.

SLP Scottish Labour Party; Serbian Liberal Party.

slp *sine legima prole*, Latin 'without legitimate issue'.

SLR single-lens reflex; self-loading rifle.

SLRS Sexual Law Reform Society.

SLS Scots Language Society; Society of Landscape Studies; Stephenson Locomotive Society.

SLTA Scottish Lawn Tennis Association; Scottish Licensed Trade Association; Sri Lanka Tourist Association.

SLV Society of Licensed Victuallers; space launch vehicle; standard launch vehicle.

SM *Scientiae Magister*, Latin 'Master of Science'; Sergeant-Major; Surgeon Major; sado-masochist; sales manager; stage manager; stipendiary magistrate; strategic missile; systolic murmur.

Sm samarium (chemical element).

SMA Society of Miniaturists; Salt Manufacturers' Assocation; Sheffield Metallurgical Association; Society for Mediaeval Archaeology; Society of Motor Auctions; Society of Museum Archaeologists; St Mungo Association; Stage Management Association; Survey & Mapping Alliance.

SMAC Standing Medical Advisory Committee.

SMAS St Margaret of Scotland Adoption Society.

SMATV satellite master antenna television.

SMBF Scottish Musicians' Benevolent Fund.

SMBG self-monitoring of blood glucose.

SMC School Meals Campaign; Scottish Mountaineering Club; Scottish Museums Council.

SMD senile macular degeneration; surface-mounted device.

SME *Sancta Mater Ecclesia*, Latin 'Holy Mother Church'.

SMetO Senior Meteorological Officer.

SMG submachine-gun.

SMGC Scottish Marriage Guidance Council.

SML Science Museum Library.

sml small, medium, large (range of sizes).

SMM *Sancta Mater Maria*, Latin 'Holy Mother Mary'.

SMMB Scottish Milk Marketing Board.

SMMT Society of Motor Manufacturers and Traders.

SMO Senior Medical Officer; Society of Museum Officers.

SMP Society of Mural Painters; Statutory Maternity Pay.

smp *sine mascula prole*, Latin 'without male issue'.

SMPA Scottish Master Patternmakers Association.

SMR standard metabolic rate; standard mortality rate.

SMRC Scottish Motor Racing Club; Society of Miniature Rifle Clubs.

SMRE Safety in Mines Research Establishment.

SMS Shipwrecked Mariners' Society; Socialist Movement Scotland; Society of Master Saddlers; Society of Model Shipwrights.

SMSR Society of Master Shoe Repairers.

SMTA Scottish Motor Trade Association.

SMTF Scottish Milk Trade Federation.

SMTWTFS Sunday, Monday, Tuesday, Wednesday, Thursday, Friday, Saturday.

SMWBA Scottish Master Wrights and Builders Association.

SMWS Scottish Malt Whisky Society.

Sn *stannum*, Latin 'tin' (chemical element).

sn *secundum naturam*, Latin 'according to nature'; *sine nomine*, Latin 'without name'; *sub nomine*, Latin 'under the name'.

s/n serial number/service number; signal-to-noise (ratio).

SNA Scottish Netball Association.

SNACMA Snack, Nut and Crisp Manufacturers Association.

SNAP Shelter Neighbourhood Action Project; systems for auxiliary nuclear power.

SNB&RTU Screw, Nut, Bolt & Rivet Trade Union.

SNBTS Scottish National Blood Transfusion Service.

SNC Scottish National Certificate.

SND Scottish National Diploma; Sisters of Notre Dame.

SNF solids, non-fat.

SNFU Scottish National Farmers' Union.

SNG synthetic natural gas.

SNH Scottish Natural Heritage.

snig sustainable noninflationary growth.

SNLA Scottish National Liberation Army.

snlr services no longer required.

SNLV strategic nuclear launch vehicle.

SNMA Scottish Net Manufacturers' Association.

SNNEB Scottish Nursery Nurses Examination Board.

SNO Scottish National Orchestra; Senior Naval/Nursing Officer.

SNP Scottish National Party; Society for Natural Philosophy (USA).

SNR Society for Nautical Research; signal-to-noise ratio.

SNSC Scottish National Ski Council.

SNSPRCS Scottish National Sweet Pea, Rose and Carnation Society.

SNSS School Natural Science Society.

SNU Spiritualists' National Union.

SNUG Scottish Network Users' Group.

SO Scottish Office; Signal/Staff Officer; Stationery Office; special/standing order; sub-office; symphony orchestra.

so seller's option; shipping order.

SOA Scottish Orienteering Association.

SOAPA Scottish Old Age Pensions Association.

SoA Society of Authors.

soa state of the art.

SOAS School of Oriental and African Studies.

SOB shortness of breath.

sob son of a bitch.

SOBHD Scottish Official Board of Highland Dancing.

SOBS Society of Bookbinders.

SOC Scottish Ornithologists' Club; Specialised Oceanographic Centre.

SOCGPA Seed, Oil, Cake and General Produce Association.

SOCO scene of crime officer.

SOE Special Operations Executive (WW II).

SOED Scottish Office Education Department; Shorter Oxford English Dictionary.

SOF Society of Floristry; share of freehold.

S of M Society of Metaphysicians.

S of S Secretary of State; Song of Solomon *or* Song of Songs (book of the Bible).

SOGAT Society of Graphical and Allied Trades.

SOH sense of humour.

SOM Society of Occupational Medicine.

SOMA Sharing of Missionaries Abroad; Society of Medical Authors.

SONRA Society of Newfoundland Radio Amateurs.

SOP significant other person; standard operating procedure; sum of products.

SOR sale or return.

SORG Stratospheric Ozone Review Group.

SOS Save Our Seatrout (Eire); Save Our Shires; Society of Schoolmasters; Stars Organisation for Spastics; save our souls (former international radio distress signal).

SoS Secretary of State.

sos *si opus sit*, Latin 'if necessary'.

SOV subject-object-verb.

sov shut-off valve.

Soweto Southwestern Townships (South Africa).

SP Shining Path; Socialist Party; starting price; submarine patrol.

sp self-propelled; *sine prole*, Latin 'without issue'; stop payment.

SPA Saudi Press Agency; Scottish Pipers' Association; Scottish Pistol Association; Scottish Publishers' Association; Singapore People's Alliance; Society of St Peter Apostle for Native Clergy.

SPAB Society for the Protection of Ancient Buildings.

SPAC Standing Pharmaceutical Advisory Committee.

SPANA Society for the Protection of Animals in North Africa.

sparc scalable processor architecture.

SPBA Scottish Pipe Band Association.

SPBP Society for the Preservation of Birds of Prey.

SPBW Society for the Preservation of Beers from the Wood.

SPC Seed Production Committee; Sherry Producers' Committee; Society of Pension Consultants; Southern Pacific Commission; stored program control.

SPCK Society for Promoting Christian Knowledge.

SPDA single-premium deferred annuity.

SPE Society for Photographic Education; Society for Pure English.

SPEC South Pacific Bureau for Economic Co-operation.

SPECT single photon emission computed tomography.

Speed Scottish Partnership in Electronics for Effective Distribution.

SPES South Place Ethical Society.

SPET single photon emission tomography.

SPF Scottish Pensioners' Forum; Scottish Police Federation; South Pacific Forum; sun protection factor.

SPG Society for the Propagation of the Gospel; Special Patrol Group.

SPGA Scottish Professional Golfers' Association.

SPGB Socialist Party of Great Britain.

SPII Scottish Pig Industry Initiative; Seed and Plant Improvement Institute (Iran).

spirit. *spiritoso*, Italian 'lively' (music).

SPKC Small Pig Keepers' Council.

spl *sine prole legitima*, Latin 'without legitimate issue'.

SPLF Society for the Preservation of Life from Fire.

spm *sine prole mascula*, Latin 'without male issue'.

SPMA Scottish Modern Pentathlon Association; Sewage Plant Manufacturers Association; Shoe Pattern Manufacturers Association (USA).

SPMO Senior Principal Medical Officer.

SPMU Society of Professional Musicians in Ulster.

SPNM Society for the Promotion of New Music.

SPNR Society for the Promotion of Nature Reserves.

SPOA Scottish Plant Owners' Association; Scottish Prison Officers' Association.

SPOOF Society for the Perpetration of Outrageous Farces.

SPORE Society for the Preservation of the Rain-Forest Environment.

SPP Seed Potato Promotions of Northern Ireland; sub-pubic prostatectomy.

SPPA Scottish Pre-School Play Association.

SPQR *Senatus Populusque Romanus*, Latin 'Senate and people of Rome'; small profits and quick returns.

SPR Society for Psychical Research; strategic petroleum reserve.

SPRC Society for the Prevention and Relief of Cancer.

SPRI Scott Polar Research Institute.

sprint solid-propellant rocket-intercept missile.

SPS Scottish Painters' Society; Scottish Prison Society; Society of Portrait Sculptors.

sps *sine prole superstite*, Latin 'without surviving offspring'.

SPSO Senior Principal Scientific Officer.

SPTA Small Potteries Trade Association.

SPTC Scottish Parent Teacher Council; Single Parent Travel Club.

SPUC Society for the Protection of the Unborn Child.

SPVD Society for the Prevention of Venereal Disease.

sq square; stereophonic-quadrophonic.

SQA Scottish Qualifications Authority; software quality assurance.

SQBLA Scotch Quality Beef and Lamb Association.

SQL standard/structured query language.

SQMS Staff Quartermaster Sergeant.

SqnQMS Squadron Sergeant Major.

SqO Squadron Officer.

SQUASH Squatters Action for Secure Homes.

squid superconducting quantum interference device.

SR Saunders Roe; Senior Registrar; Southern Region.

Sr *Señor*, Spanish 'Mr'; Sir; Sister; strontium (chemical element).

sr self-raising.

s/r sale or return.

SRA Snail Racing Association; Squash Rackets Association.

SRAM static random access memory.

sram short-range attack missile.

SRAP Scottish Rent Assessment Panel.

SRBM short-range ballistic missile.

SRC Science Research Council; Scottish Refugee Council; Sheriff Court Rules Council; *Sociedad Regolar Collectiva*, Spanish 'partnership'; Student Representative Council.

srcc strikes, riots and civil commotions.

SRCh State Registered Chiropodist.

SRCN State Registered Children's Nurse.

SRD Safety and Reliability Directorate (UKAEA); State Registered Dietitian.

SRDE Signals Research and Development Establishment.

SRE *Sancta Romana Ecclesia*, Latin 'Holy Roman Church'.

SRG Strategic Research Group.

SRGC Scottish Rock Garden Club.

SRHE Society for Research into Higher Education.

SRIS Science Reference Information Service.

SRI Saudi Arabian riyal.

SRM short-range missile.

SRMN State Registered Mental Nurse.

SRN State Registered Nurse.

SRNA Shipbuilders and Repairers National Association.

sRNA soluble ribonucleic acid.

SRO Scottish Record Office; Society of Registration Officers; self-regulatory organization; single room occupancy; standing room only; statutory rules and orders.

SRP Society for Radiological Protection; Society for Recorder Players; State Registered Physiotherapist; suggested retail price.

SRPA Squash Rackets Professional Association.

SRPS Scottish Railway Preservation Society.

SRR Society for Research in Rehabilitation.

SRS Scottish Record Society; Scottish Reformation Society; Scottish Rhododendron Society; *Societatis Regiae Sodalis*, Latin 'Fellow of the Royal Society'; Surgical Research Society; Swiss Railways Society.

SRU Scottish Research into UFOs; Scottish Rugby Union.

SRWS Scottish Rights of Way Society.

SS Secretary of State; *Schutzstaffel*, German 'protection group' (Nazi special police force); Social Security; Spastics Society; Stereoscopic Society; screw steamer; steamship; surface to surface (missile, etc).

SSA School Secretaries Association; Scottish Schoolmasters' Asssociation; Scottish Skateboard Association; Scottish Sound Archive; Side-Saddle Association; Silver Steel Association; Sisters of St Anne; Society of Scottish Artists; standard spending assessment.

SSAC Scottish Society for Autistic Children; Scottish Sub-Aqua Club; Social Security Advisory Committee.

SSAD Scottish Sports Association for People with Disabilities.

SSAE stamped, self-addressed envelope.

SSAFA Soldiers', Sailors' and Airmen's Families Association.

SSAP Statement of Standard Accounting Practice.

SSC Scottish Schoolboys' Club; Scottish Ski Club; Scottish Society of Composers; Scottish Sports Council; Secretarial Studies Certificate; Surgical Society of China; short service commission.

SSCA Scottish Ship Chandlers Association; Social Science Computing Association.

SSCR Scottish Society for Crop Research.

SSD *Sanctissimus Dominus*, Latin 'the most holy lord' (pope); Social Services Department.

SSE south-southeast.

SSEC Secondary Schools Examinations Council.

SSEES School of Slavonic and East European Studies.

SSEG Scottish Solar Energy Group.

SSF Scottish Surfing Federation; Society for the Study of Fertility; Society of Shoe Fitters; Society of St Francis.

SSFA Scottish Schools' Football Association; Shetland Salmon Farmers' Association.

SSFTA Scottish Soft Fruit Trade Association.

SSGA Scottish Salmon Growers Association; Scottish Shellfish Growers Association.

SSGBP Society of Snuff Grinders, Blenders and Purveyors.

SSHA Scottish Special Housing Association.

SSHC Society to Support Home Confinement.

SSI Sculptors Society of Ireland; Social Services Inspectorate; site of scientific interest.

SSJE Society of St John the Evangelist.

SSLH Society for the Study of Labour History.

SSM Saturday, Sunday, Monday; Staff Sergeant Major; surface-to-surface missile.

SSMH Scottish Society for the Mentally Handicapped.

SSN severely subnormal; standard serial numer.

SSNTA Scottish Seed and Nursery Trade Association.

SSO Senior Supply Officer.

SSP Scottish Socialist Party; Scottish Society of Playwrights; statutory sick pay.

SSPCA Scottish Society for the Prevention of Cruelty to Animals.

SSPS Sheffield Sawmakers' Protection Society.

SSPWB Scottish Society for the Protection of Wild Birds.

SSR Soviet Socialist Republic.

SSRA Scottish Seaweed Research Association; Scottish Squash Rackets Association.

SSRC Social Science Research Council.

SSRI selective seratonin uptake inhibitor (antidepressant drug).

SSS Secretary of State for Scotland; Ship Stamp Society; Simplifield Spelling Society; Sunday Shakespeare Society; sick sinus syndrome; standard scratch score.

SSSA Scottish Salmon Smokers Association; Scottish Schools Swimming Association; Synthetic Sports Surfaces Association.

SSSI Soil Science Society of Ireland; site of special scientific interest.

SSSU Scottish Speed Skating Union.

SST Scottish Scenic Trust; Scottish Sculpture Trust; supersonic transport.

SSTA Scottish Secondary Teachers' Association.

SSTC sold subject to contract.

SSU Sunday School Union.

SSW south-south-west.

SSWA Scottish Solway Wildfowlers' Association.

ST Standard/Summer Time; sanitary towel; septic tank.

st short ton.

STA Sail Training Association; Scottish Textile Association; Scottish Trampoline Association; Solar Trade Association; Supersonic Tunnel Association (Sweden); Swimming Teachers Association.

StAAA St Andrew's Ambulance Association.

stacc. *staccato*, Italian 'detached' (music).

STAGS sterling accruable government securities.

START Strategic Arms Reduction Talks/Treaty.

STAS Scottish Training Advisory Service.

STAUK Seed Trade Association of the United Kingdom.

STB *Sacrae Theologiae Baccalaureus*, Latin 'Bachelor of Sacred Theology'; Scottish Tourist Board; set-top box (for digital TV).

STC Scandinavian rade Centre; Standard Telephones and Cables Limited; Surgical Textiles Conference; short-title catalogue; subject to contract.

STD *Sacrae Theologiae Doctor*, Latin 'Doctor of Sacred Theology'; Society of Teachers of the Deaf; sexually transmitted disease; subscriber trunk dialling.

STE Society of Telecom Executives.

STEM scanning transmission electron microscopy.

STEP Special Temporary Employment Programme.

STGWU Scottish Transprt and General Workers' Union.

STH somatrophic hormone.

STIM scanning transmission ion microscope.

STIR surplus to immediate requirements.

STLO Scientific and Technical Liaison Officer.

STM *Sacrae Theologiae Magister*, Latin 'Master of Sacred Theology'; scanning tunnelling microscope; scientific, technical and medical; short-term memory.

STO Scottish Tenants' Organization; senior technical officer.

STOL short take-off and landing.

STOLVCD short take-off and landing, vertical climb and descent.

STOP suction termination of pregnancy.

STOPP Society of Teachers Opposed to Physical Punishment.

STP *Sacrae Theologiae* Professor; Latin 'Professor of Sacred Theology'; scientifically treated petroleum (colloquial name for a hallucinogenic drug).

stp standard temperature and pressure.

str surplus to requirements.

STRG Scottish Tory Reform Group.

STRIVE Society for the Preservation of Rural Industries and Village Enterprises.

STS Scottish Tartans Society; Scottish Text Society.

STSF Scottish Target Shooting Federation.

STSO Senior Technical Staff Officer.

STT Sacred Trees Trust; Scottish Tree Trust.

STTA Scottish Table Tennis Association.

STUA Scottish Trust for Underwater Archaeology.

STUC Scottish Trades Union Congress.

StudentIEIE Student of the Institution of Electrical and Electronic Incorporated Engineers.

StudentIMechIE Student of the Institution of Mechanical Incorporated Engineers.

StudSElec Student of the Society of Electroscience.

StudIAP Student of the Institution of Analysts and Programmers.

StudIManf Student Member of the Institute of Manufacturing.

StudIMS Student of the Institute of Management Specialists.

StudProfBTM Student of Professional Business and Technical Management.

StudSE Student of the Society of Engineers.

StudWeldI Student of the Welding Institute.

STV Scottish Television; single transferable vote.

SU Scripture Union; Soviet Union; Supporters Union.

sub. *subito*, Italian 'suddenly' (music).

SUBAW Scottish Union of Bakers and Allied Workers.

SUDS sudden unexplained death syndrome.

SUM surface-to-underwater missile.

SUNS sonic underwater navigation system.

SUNY State University of New York.

surf spent unreprocessed fuel.

surv standard underwater research vessel.

SUS Scottish Union of Students.

SUT Society for Underwater Technology.

SV *Sancta Virgo*, Latin 'Holy Virgin'; *Sanctitas Vestra*, Latin 'your Holiness'; simian virus.

sv *sub verbo*, Latin 'under the word'; *sub voce*, Latin 'under the heading'.

s/v surrender value.

SVA Scottish Volleyball Association.

SVC superior vena cava.

SVD swine vesicular disease.

S-VHS Super Video Home System.

SVO subject, verb, object.

SVP *s'il vous plaît*, French 'please'.

svr *spiritus vini rectificatus*, Latin 'rectified spirit of wine'.

SVS Society of Visiting Scientists; still-camera video system.

SW Samaritans Worldwide; short wave; small women's (size of clothing); southwest/ern.

S/W software.

SWA Scotch Whisky Association; Scottish Whitebait Association; Scottish Women's Aid; Society of Women Artists; Sports Writers' Association; Steel Window Association.

SWACS Space Warning and Control System.

swalk sealed with a loving kiss.

SWAP Save Waste and Prosper Limited; Scottish Women Against Pornography.

SWAPO South-West Africa People's Organization.

swb short wheelbase.

SWCL Scottish Wildlife and Countryside Link.

SWE Society of Wood Engravers.

SWET Society of West End Theatres.

SWF single white female.

SWFA Scottish Women's Football Association.

SWG Song Writers' Guild of Great Britain.

swg standard wire gauge.

SWHA Scottish Women's Hockey Association.

SWI Scottish Woollen Industry.

SWIFT Society for Worldwide Interbank Financial Transmission.

swing sterling warrant into gilt-edged stock.

swl safe working load.

SWLA Society of Wildlife Artists.

SWLG Scottish Wild Land Group.

SWM single white male.

SWMF South Wales Miners' Federation.

SWOA Scottish Woodland Owners Association.

swot strengths, weaknesses, opportunities and threats (product marketing analysis).

SWP Socialist Workers' Party.

swp safe working pressure.

SWPF single white professional female.

SWR standing-wave ratio.

SWRI Scottish Women's Rural Institutes.

SWS Society of Wetland Scientists; static water supply.

SWT Scottish Wildlife Trust.

SX Sundays excepted.

SY steam yacht.

SYHA Scottish Youth Hostels Association.

SYP Society of Young Publishers.

T

T Thursday; Tuesday; tablespoon; tenor; tesla; thousand (car mileage).

t tare; temperature; tense; tera-; *tome*, French 'volume'; ton/ne; transitive; troy.

TA Territorial Army; Transactional Analysis; Transport Association; Tricycle Association.

Ta tantalum (chemical element).

ta target area; time and attendance.

TAA Territorial Army Association; Ticket Agents Association; Trans-Antarctic Association; Trans-Australia Airlines; Tropical Agriculture Association.

TA & VRA Territorial, Auxiliary and Volunteer Reserve Association.

TAB typhoid-paratyphoid A and B (vaccine).

TABMAC The All British Martial Arts Council.

TAC Theatres Advisory Council; Tobacco Advisory Council.

TACAC Trans Atlantic Committee on Agricultural Change.

tacan tactical air navigation.

TACT Tories Against Cruise and Trident.

TAFE Technical and Further Education.

TAFF Take-Away and Fast Food Federation.

TAG Towpaths Action Group.

TAH total abdominal hysterectomy.

tal traffic and accident loss.

Talisman Transfer Accounting Lodgement for Investors and Stock Management.

tal. qual. *talis qualis*, Latin 'just as they come'.

TAM Television Audience Measurement; tactical air missile.

TAMBA Twins and Multiple Births Association.

TAN Third Age Network.

TANCA Technical Assistance to Non-Commonwealth Countries.

T & A tonsils and adenoids.

T & AVR Territorial Army Volunteer Reserve.

t & b top and bottom.

t & e test and evaluation; tired and emotional (drunk); travel and entertainment; trial and error.

T & G Transport and General Workers' Union.

t & g tongued and grooved.

t & o taken and offered.

t & p theft and pilferage.

T & RA Tennis and Rackets Association.

t & s toilet and shower.

T & SG Television and Screenwriters' Guild.

T & T taxed and tested (of second-hand cars); Trinidad and Tobago.

TARO Territorial Army Reserve of Officers.

TARS The Arthur Ransome Society.

TAS true air speed.

TASHA Tranquilliser Anxiety Stress Help Association.

TASM tactical air-to-surface missile.

TASS Technical, Administrative and Supervisory Section (AEUEW); *Telegrafnoye Agentsvo Sovietskovo Soyuza*, Russian 'Telegraph Agency of the Soviet Union'.

TAT Tree Advice Trust; thematic apperception test; tired all the time; transatlantic telephone cable.

TATHS Tool and Trades History Society.

TAUN Technical Assistance of the United Nations.

TAURUS Transfer and Automated Registration of Uncertified Stock.

TAVR Territorial and Army Volunteer Reserve.

TAVRA Territorial, Auxiliary and Volunteer Reserve Association.

taw twice a week.

TB torpedo boat; tubercle bacillus; tuberculosis.

Tb terbium (chemical element).

tb trial balance.

TBA Tea Buyers' Association; Teaching Brothers' Association; The Buying Agency (Department of Environment procurement agency); Thoroughbred Breeders Association; Tropical Biology Association.

tba to be advised/agreed/announced; tyres, batteries, accessories.

tb & s top, bottom and sides.

tbcf to be called for.

TBD torpedo-boat destroyer.

tbd to be determined.

TBF Teachers' Benevolent Fund.

TBG Tidy Britain Group.

TBI throttle-body injection; total body irradiation.

tbl through bill of lading.

TBM tactical ballistic missile; tuberculous meningitis.

TBO time between overhauls.

TBOAA Tuna Boat Owners Association of Australia.

TBT tributyl tin.

TC Tandem Club; Technician Certificate; Trusteeship Council (UN); travellers' cheque; *tre corde*, Italian 'three strings' (direction to release left-hand pedal of piano).

Tc technetium (chemical element).

tc time check; true course.

TCA Technician in Costing and Accounting; Tertiary Colleges Association; Textile Converters Association; tricyclic antidepressant.

TCAS Three Counties Agricultural Society.

TCB Thames Conservancy Board; tumour cell burden.

TCBM trans-continental ballistic missile.

TCC Textile Conservation centre; Toxic Chemicals Committee.

TCCB Test and County Cricket Board.

TCD Trinity College, Dublin.

TCDD tetrachlorobenzodioxin (an environmental pollutant).

TCE trichloroethylene (a solvent).

TCert Teacher's Certificate.

TCF Touring Club de France.

tcf trillion cubic feet.

TCGF T-cell growth factor.

TCI Tall Clubs International (USA); Tasmanian Confederation of Industries; Touring Club Italiano; Tree Council of Ireland.

TCJCC Trades Councils Joint Consultative Committee.

TCL Trinity College of Music, London.

T-CLL T-cell chronic lymphatic leukaemia.

TCM Trinity College of Music, London.

TCMB Tomato and Cucumber Marketing Board.

TCP transmission control protocol; trichlorophenylmethyliodisalicyl, an antiseptic.

TCPA Town and Country Planning Association.

TD *Teachda Dála*, Gaelic 'Member of the Dáil'; Teaching Diploma; Technician Diploma; Territorial Decoration; Tunisian Dinar (unit of currency); tardive dyskinesia; technical drawing.

td technical data; test data; time delay.

TD&RA Twist Drill and Reamer Association.

TDA Tableware Distributors' Association; Timber Development Association; Timber Drying Association.

TDCR Teacher's Diploma of the College of Radiographers.

TDD telecommunications device for the deaf.

TDE total digestible energy.

TDDL time-division data link.

TDG Timeshare Developers Group.

TDL tunable diode laser.

TDM time-division multiplexing.

TDMA time-division multiple access.

TDN total digestible nutrients.

TDP technical development plan.

tdr *tous droits réservés*, French 'all rights reserved'.

TDRSS tracking and data-relay satellite system.

tds *ter die sumendus*, Latin 'to be taken thrice daily'.

Te tellurium (chemical element).

te thermal efficiency.

t/e time expired; twin-engined.

TEAC Technical Education Advisory Council.

TEACH Teacher Education Admissions Clearing House.

TEAR The Evangelical Alliance Relief Fund.

TEC Total Environment Centre; Training and Enterprise Council.

Tech(CEI) Technician (Council of Engineering Institutions).

TechRMS Technological Qualification in Microscopy.

TechWeldI Technician of the Welding Institute.

Tedco Thames Estuary Development Company.

TEDIS Trade Electronic Data Interchange System (EC).

TEE Telecommunications Engineering Establishment; Trans-Europe Express; total energy expenditure.

TEF Textile Employers' Federation.

TEFL Teaching English as a Foreign Language.

teg top edges gilt.

TEL tetraethyl lead (petrol additive).

TELO Tamil Elam Liberation Organization.

TEM transmission electron microscopy.

Templar Tactical Expert Mission Planner (military computer).

temp. prim. *tempo primo*, Italian 'original speed' (music).

TENS transcutaenous electrical nerve stimulation.

TEPP tetraethyl pyrophosphate (pesticide).

Tercom terrain contour matching.

TermNet International Network for Terminology.

TES Times Educational Supplement.

TESCO T.E. Stockwell and J. Cohen.

TESL Teaching of English as a Second Language.

TESSA Tax-Exempt Special Savings Account.

TeV tera-electron volt.

tewt tactical exercise without troops.

tf tax-free.

TFA Tenant Farmers' Association; Texas Forestry Association (USA); Textile Finishers' Association; The Freedom Association; total fatty acids.

TFAP Tropical Forestry Action Plan.

TFC Tasmanian Forestry Commission.

TFOF Taxi Fleet Operators' Federation.

TFS testicular feminization syndrome.

TFSC Turkish Federated State of Cyprus.

TFSK Turkish Federated State of Kibris (Cyprus).

TFSR Tools For Self Reliance.

TFTA Traditional Farm-Fresh Turkey Association.

TFU telecommunications flying unit.

TFX tactical fighter, experimental.

TG Tate Gallery; Townswomen's Guild; transformational grammar.

TGA Timber Growers Association; Tropical Growers Association.

TGAT Task Group on Assessment and Testing.

tgb tongued, grooved and beaded.

TGE transmissible gastroenteritis.

TGF transforming growth factor.

TGI Target Group Index; Tory Green Initiative.

TGIA Toy and Giftware Importers' Association.

TGUK Timber Growers United Kingdom Limited.

TGV *Train à Grande Vitesse*, French 'High Speed Train'.

TGWU Transport and General Workers' Union.

Th thorium (chemical element).

ThB *Theologiae Baccalaureus*, Latin 'Bachelor of Theology'.

THB Traditional Housing Bureau.

THC tetrahydrocannabinol (component of cannabis).

THD total harmonic distortion.

ThD *Theologiae Doctor*, Latin 'Doctor of Theology'.

THE Technical Help to Exporters.

THES Times Higher Education Supplement.

THF Trust House Forte.

THG Telecommunications Heritage Group.

THI temperature-humidity index.

ThM *Theologiae Magister*, Latin 'Master of Theology'.

thp thrust horsepower.

THR total hip replacement.

THT Terence Higgins Trust.

TI Textile Institute; Toastmasters International; thermal imaging.

Ti titanium (chemical element).

TIA Telecommunications Industry Association.

TIB Tourist Information Bureau.

TIBOR Tokyo Inter-Bank Offered Rate.

TIC Timber Industries Confederation; Tyre Industry Council; tourist information centre.

TICCIH The International Committee for the Conservation of the Industrial Heritage.

tid *ter in die*, Latin 'three times a day'.

TIF Theatre Investment Fund.

tif telephone interference factor.

Tiff tagged-image file format.

TIG tungsten inert gas.

TIH Their Imperial Highnesses.

TIIAL The International Institute of Applied Linguistics.

TILS Technical Information and Library Service.

TIM time is money.

TIMS The Institute of Management Science.

TIP terminal interface processor.

TIR *Transports Internationaux Routiers*, French 'International Road Transport'.

TIRC Tobacco Industry Research Committee.

TIS Technical Information Service.

TIU Telecommunications International Union.

TJ triple jump (athletics).

TJA Table Jellies Association.

TKO technical knockout (boxing).

TL thermoluminescent.

Tl thallium (chemical element).

tl total loss.

TLA Toy Libraries Association.

TLC tender loving care; thin-layer chromatography; total lung capacity.

TLG Theatrical Ladies' Guild.

TLMI The Leprosy Mission International.

TLO Technical Liaison Officer.

tlo total loss only.

TLR twin-lens reflex (camera).

TLRS Tramway and Light Railway Society.

TLS Times Literary Supplement.

TLU table look-up.

TM Their Majesties; tactical missile; technical manual; trade mark; transcendental meditation; trench mortar.

Tm thulium (chemical element).

tm true mean.

TMA Telecommunications Managers' Association; Theatrical Management Association.

TMBA Teacher Member of the British Arts; Twins and Multiple Births Association.

TMC Tourism Ministers Council.

TMD theatre missile defence.

TML three-mile limit.

TMO telegraphic money order.

TMPDF Trade Marks, Patterns and Designs Federation.

TMS The Minerals, Metals and Materials Society; Tramway Museum Society.

tmv true mean value.

TN trade name; true north.

tn telephone number.

TNC transnational corporation.

TNF transnecrosis factor.

TNIMBM Technicians of the Institute of Maintenance and Building Management.

TNM tactical nuclear missile.

TNPG The Nuclear Power Group.

TNT trinitrotoluene (explosive).

TNTC too numerous to count.

TNW tactical nuclear warfare; theatre nuclear weapon.

TO Tax Officer; Transport Officer; telegraph office; turn over.

t/o take off; turnover.

ToB Tour of Britain (cycling).

Toc H Talbot House (originally telegraphic code for TH, Talbot House being the London headquarters of the charity).

tod time of delivery.

TOE Theatre of Everything.

TOEFL Test of English as a Foreign Language.

ToL Tower of London.

TOL Tree of Life.

TOM Troops Out Movement.

TOO time of origin; to order only.

TOP temporarily out of print; termination of pregnancy.

TOPIC Teletext Output Price Information Computer.

TOPS Theatre Organ Preservation Society; Training Opportunities Scheme.

tor time of receipt.

tos temporarily out of stock; terms of service.

Toshiba *Tokyo Shibaura Denki KK*, Japanese 'Tokyo Shibaura Electrical Corporation'.

tot time over target.

TOW tug of war.

TOWA Tug of War Association.

TP to pay; third party.

tp target practice; teaching practice.

T/P title page.

TPA Taiwan Pineapple Association; Tea Packers' Association; Tea Producers' Association; The Pizza Association; Turkish Peace Association.

tPA tissue plasminogen activator.

TPAS Tenant Participation Advisory Service.

TPC Tall Persons Club of Great Britain.

tpd tons per day.

tph tons per hour.

TPI Town Planning Institute; tax and prices index.

tpi teeth/tracks/turns/threads per inch.

tpm tons per minute.

TPN total parenteral nutrition.

TPO Tree Preservation Order.

TPR Trust for the Protection of Reptiles; temperature, pulse, respiration.

TPS Tax Payers' Society; Thomas Paine Society.

TQM total quality management.

TR Territorial Reserve; transmit-receive.

T/R transmitter-receiver.

TRA The Reclamation Association; Thoroughbred Racing Association (USA).

Trace test equipment for rapid automatic check-out evaluation (prior to take-off).

TRC Thames Rowing Club.

TRDA Timber Research and Development Association.

trem transport emergency.

TRF Trail Riders Fellowship.

trf tuned radio frequency.

TRFA Trussed Rafter Fabricators' Association.

TRG Tertiary Research Group; Tory Reform Group.

TRH Their Royal Highnesses; thyrotrophin-releasing hormone.

TRI Thrombosis Research Institute; Tin Research Institute.

TRM trademark.

tRNA transfer ribonucleic acid.

TRNC Turkish Republic of Northern Cyprus.

TRO Temporary Restraining Order.

TROBI Tree Register of the British Isles.

TRRL Transport and Road Research Library.

TRSR taxi and runway surveillance radar.

TRSSGM tactical range surface-to-surface guided missile.

TS Television Society; Theosophical Society; Tolkien Society; Tourism Society; Training Ship; transsexual; typescript.

ts tensile strength.

t/s transshipment.

TSA The Securities Association; Tourette Syndrome Association; Training Services Agency; Trust for the Study of Adolescence Limited; Tuberous Sclerosis Association of Great Britain; tumour-specific antigen.

TSB Textile Statistics Bureau; Trustee Savings Bank.

TSBA Teeswater Sheep Breeders' Association; Trustee Savings Banks Association.

TSE transmissible spongiform encephalopathy.

TSFA The Securities and Futures Authority.

TSG Tibet Support Group.

TSgt Technical Sergeant.

TSH Their Serene Highnesses; thyroid-stimulating hormone.

TSH-RF thyroid-stimulating-hormone-releasing factor.

tsi tons per square inch.

TSO Trading Standards Officer; town sub-office.

TSP textured soya protein.

TSR Trans-Siberian Railway; tactical strike reconnaissance; terminate and stay resident.

TSRB Top Salaries Review Body.

TSS Turner's Syndrome Society; time-sharing system; toxic shock syndrome.

TSSA Transport Salaried Staffs Association.

TSU this side up.

tsvp *tournez, s'il vous plaît*, French 'please turn over'.

TSW Television South West.

TT Tourist Trophy (motor cycling); Transport Trust; teetotal; telegraphic transfer; time trial (cycling); tuberculin tested.

TTAW Table Tennis Association of Wales.

TTBT Threshold Test Ban Treaty.

TTF Timber Trade Federation.

TTFN ta-ta for now.

TTL through the lens.

TTNS The Times Network Systems (database system for schools).

TTRA Tourist Trophy Riders' Association.

TTS Transport Ticket Society; teletypesetting.

TTT Tyne Tees Television; team time trial (cycling).

TTTA Timber Trade Training Association.

TU Tupolev, Soviet aircraft manufacturer; trade union; transmission unit.

TUA Telecommunications Users' Association; Tractor Users Association.

TUBCS Trade Union Badge Collectors' Society.

TUBE The Union of Bookmakers' Employees.

TUC Trades Union Congress.

TUCC Trades Union Congress General Council.

TUG Telephone Users' Group.

TUI Trade Unions International of Public and Allied Employees.

TUIAFPW Trade Unions International of Agricultural, Forestry and Plantation Workers.

TUIREG Trade Unions International Research and Education Group.

TUIWC Trade Unions International of Workers in Commerce.

TUIWE Trade Unions International of Workers in Energy.

turp trans-urethral resection of the prostate.

TV television; transvestism; transvestite.

TVA *taxe sur la valeur ajoutée*, French 'value-added tax'.

TVE Television Trust for the Environment.

TVEI Technical and Vocational Education Initiative.

TVP textured vegetable protein.

TVRO television, receive only (type of aerial).

TVU Thames Valley University.

TWA Tibetan Women's Association; Trans-World Airlines (USA).

TWh terawatt hour.

TWIF Tug of War International Federation.

TWIMC to whom it may concern.

TWOC taking without owner's consent.

TWR Trans World Radio.

TWS Tasmanian Wilderness Society; The Wilderness Society; The Wildlife Society.

TWU Theatre Writers' Union; Tobacco Worker's Union.

TYC Thames Yacht Club.

U

U Universal (film censorship classification); uranium (chemical element); union; unionist; united; university; upper-class.

u united atomic mass unit; unit; upper.

UA United Artists; Urostomy Association.

ua unauthorised absence; under age.

UAC Ulster Automobile Club.

UAE United Arab Emirates.

UAM underwater-to-air missile.

u & lc upper and lower case.

u & o use and occupancy.

UAR United Arab Republic.

UAS Ulster Archaeological Society; Union of African States.

uas upper air space.

UAU Universities Athletic Union.

uAwg *um Antwort wird gebeten*, German 'reply requested'.

UB40 Unemployment Benefit Form 40 (card held by the unemployed which gives entitlement to state benefits, etc).

UBF Union of British Fascists.

UBKA Ulster Bee Keepers Association.

UBR Uniform Business Rate.

UBS United Bible Societies.

UC University College.

Uc Universal, especially suitable for children (film censorship classification).

uc *una corda*, Italian 'one string' (direction to depress the left-hand pedal of piano); upper case.

u/c undercharge.

UCA Ulster Chemists Association; Ulster Curers Association.

UCAR Union of Central African Republics.

UCAS Universities and Colleges Admissions Service.

UCATT Union of Construction, Allied Trades and Technicians.

UCC Ulster Countryside Commission; Union Carbide Corporation; Universal Copyright Convention; Univeristy College Cork.

UCCA Universities' Central Council on Admissions.

UCI *Union Cycliste Internationale*, French for International Cycling Union.

UCL University College London.

UCLA University of California at Los Angeles.

UCM University Christian Movement.

UCR unconditioned reflex.

UCS unconditioned stimulus.

UCSW Union of Country Sports Workers.

UCW Union of Communication Workers.

UCWRE Underwater Countermeasures and Weapons Research Establishment.

UD United Dairies.

ud unfair dismissal; *ut dictum*, Latin 'as said'.

UDA Ulster Defence Association.

UDC Universal Decimal Classification; Urban Development Corporation; Urban District Council.

UDF Ulster Defence Force; United Democratic Front (South Africa).

UDHR Universal Declaration of Human Rights.

UDI Universal Declaration of Independence.

UDM Union of Democratic Mineworkers.

UDR Ulster Defence Regiment.

UDT United Dominions Trust.

UDUP Ulster Democratic Unionist Party.

UEA Universal Esperanto Association; University of East Anglia.

UEFA Union of European Football Associations.

UEL United Empire Loyalists.

UEPS United Elvis Presley Society.

UER university entrance requirements.

UF United Free Church.

u/f unfurnished.

UFAW Universities Federation for Animal Welfare.

UFC United Free Church (Scotland); Universities Funding Council.

UFF Ulster Freedom Fighters; Ulster Furniture Federation.

UFO unidentified flying object.

UFORA Unidentified Fying Objects Research Association.

u/g underground.

UGC University Grants Committee.

UHF Ulster Historical Foundation; ultra-high frequency.

UHT ultra-heat-treated; ultra high temperature.

UHV ultra high vacuum.

UI Understanding Industry.

ui *ut infra*, Latin for as below.

UIA Ultrasonic Industry Association.

UJD *Utriusque Juris Doctor*, Latin 'Doctor of Both Laws' (canon and civil).

UK United Kingdom.

UKA Ulster King of Arms.

UKADGE United Kingdom Air Defence Ground Environment.

UKAEA United Kingdom Atomic Energy Authority.

UKAFFP United Kingdom Association of Frozen Food Producers.

UKAFMM United Kingdom Association of Fish Meal Manufacturers.

UKASS United Kingdom Association of Suggestion Schemes.

UKCC United Kingdom Central Council for Nursing, Midwifery and Health Visiting.

UKCTA United Kingdom Commercial Travellers Association.

UKCVCC United Kindom Computer Virus Control Centre.

UKFA United Kingdom Fellmongers Association.

UKFC United Kingdom Fortifications Club.

UKFFCA United Kingdom Freight Forwarders Container Association.

UKFR United Kingdom Feline Register.

UKgal United Kingdom gallon.

UKHA United Kingdom Harp Association; United Kingdom Housekeepers Association.

UKIAS United Kingdom Immigrants' Advisory Service.

UKJGA United Kingdom Jute Goods Association.

UKJSA United Kingdom Jet Ski Association.

UKPA United Kingdom Pilots' Association.

UKPIA United Kingdom Petroleum Industry Association Limited.

UKPMA United Kingdom Preserves Manufacturers Association.

UKSCC United Kingdom Spoon Collectors Club.

UKSIA United Kingdom Sugar Industry Association.

UKTA United Kingdom Tea Association.

UKWGF United Kingdom Wool Growers Federation.

UKWWA United Kingdom Wood Wool Association.

UL university library.

ul upper limit.

ULA Ulster Launderers Association; uncommitted logic array.

ULCC ultra-large crude carrier (oil tanker).

ULF ultra-low frequency.

ULM universal logic module.

ULMS underwater long-range missile system.

ULS unsecured loan stock.

ult. ultimate/ly; *ultimo*, Latin 'in the last' (month).

ULTRA Unrelated Live Transplant Regulatory Authority.

ULV ultra low volume.

UMDS United Medical and Dental Schools.

UMFC United Methodist Free Churches.

UMIST University of Manchester Institute of Science and Technology.

UN United Nations.

UNA United Nations Association.

UNBRO United Nations Border Relief Operation.

UNCAST United Nations Conference on the Applications of Science and Technology.

UNCED United Nations Conference on Environment and Development.

UNCITRAL United Nations Commission on International Trade law.

UNCLS United Nations Conference on the Law of the Sea.

UNCSTD United Nations Conference on Science and Technology for Development.

UNCRO United Nations Confidence-Restoring Operation (in Croatia).

UNCTAD United Nations Conference on Trade and Development.

UNDCP United Nations International Drug Control Programme.

UNDOF United Nations Disengagement Observer Force.

UNDP United Nations Development Programme.

UNDRO United Nations Disaster Relief Organization.

UNEF United Nations Emergency Force.

UNEP United Nations Environment Programme.

UNESCO United Nations Educational, Scientific and Cultural Organization.

UNFAO United Nations Food and Agriculture Organization.

Unficyp United Nations Force in Cyprus.

UNFPA United Nations Fund for Population Activities.

ung. *unguentum*, Latin 'ointment'.

UNGA United Nations General Assembly.

UNHCR United Nations High Commission for Refugees; United Nations High Commissioner for Refugees.

UNHQ United Nations Headquarters.

Unicef United Nations Children's Fund, formerly United Nations International Children's Emergency Fund.

UNIDO United Nations Industrial Development Organization.

UNIFIL United Nations Interim Force in Lebanon.

UNIKOM United Nations Iraq-Kuwait Observation Mission.

UNITA *União Nacional por Independência Total de Angola*, Portuguese 'National Union for the Total Independence of Angola'.

UNMOGIP United Nations Military Observer Group in India and Pakistan.

UNO United Nations Organization.

Unosom United Nations Operation in Somalia.

Unprofor United Nations Protection Force (in Bosnia, Croatia, etc).

UNREF United Nations Refugee Emergency Fund.

UNRFNRE United Nations Revolving Fund for Natural Resource Exploration.

UNRRA United Nations Relief and Rehabilitation Administration.

UNRWA United Nations Relief and Works Agency (for Palestinian refugees).

UNSC United Nations Security Council; United Nations Social Commission.

UNSCOM United Nations Special Commission.

UNSG United Nations Secretary General.

UNTC United Nations Trusteeship Council.

UNTT United Nations Trust Territory.

UNWCC United Nations War Crimes Commission.

UNSC United Nations Security Council.

UNTSO United Nations Truce Supervision Organization.

UNY United Nations of Yoga.

UP Union Pacific; United Presbyterian; United Press; University Press.

up under proof (alcohol).

UPA United Printers Association.

UPC United Presbyterian Church; Universal Postal Convention; Universal Product Code.

UPI United Press International.

UPNI Unionist Party of Northern Ireland.

UPOA Ulster Public Officers Association.

UPOW Union of Post Office Workers.

UPS uninterruptible power supply.

UPU Universal Postal Union.

UPUP Ulster Popular Unionist Party.

uPVC unplasticised polyvinyl chloride.

UPW Union of Post Office Workers.

UQ University of Queensland.

UR unconditioned reflex.

URA Urban Regeneration Agency.

URBM ultimate-range ballistic missile.

URC United Reformed Church.

URF uterine relaxing factor.

URI upper respiratory infection.

URL uniform resource locator, World Wide Web.

URT upper respiratory tract.

URTI upper respiratory tract infection.

URTU United Road Transport Union.

US Under-Secretary; United Service; United States; unconditioned stimulus.

us *ut supra*, Latin 'as above'.

u/s unserviceable; useless.

USA United State of America; United States Army.

USAB United States Animal Bank.

USAF United States Air Force.

USBA United States Badminton Association; United States Brewers Association.

USC Ulster Special Constabulary.

USCL United Society for Christian Literature.

USDA United States Department of Agriculture.

USDAW Union of Shop, Distributive and Allied Workers.

USec Under-Secretary.

usf *und so fort*, German 'and so on'.

USFA Ulster Sea Fishermen's Association.

USFWS United States Fish and Wildlife Service.

USG United States Government.

USGA United States Golf Association.

USI United Service Institution; Union of Students in Ireland.

USIA United State Information Agency.

USM underwater-to-surface missile; unlisted securities market.

USN United States Navy.

USNG United States National Guard.

USPG United Society for the Propagation of the Gospel.

USS Under-Secretary of State; United Seamen's Service (USA); United States Ship; Universities Superannuation Scheme; ultrasound scanning.

USSC United States Supreme Court.

USSR Union of Soviet Socialist Republics.

USW ultrashort waves; ultrasonic waves.

usw *und so weiter*, German 'and so forth'.

USWD Undersurface Warfare Division.

UT University of Tasmania; unit trust; urinary tract.

UTA Ulster Transport Authority; Unit Trust Association.

UTC Unitary Tax Campaign; Universal Time Coordinates; University Training Corps.

UTI urinary tract infection.

UTS ultimate tensile strength.

UU Ulster Unionist.

Uub ununbium (chemical element).

UUM underwater to underwater missile.

UUP Ulster Unionist Party.

UUUP United Ulster Unionist Party.

Uun unununnium (chemical element).

Uuu unununium (chemical element).

uuV *unter üblichem Vorbehalt*, German 'errors and omissions excepted'.

UV ultraviolet.

UVA ultraviolet radiation A.

UVAF Unemployed Voluntary Action Fund.

UVB ultraviolet radiation B.

UVC ultraviolet radiation C.

UVF Ulster Volunteer Force.

UVL ultraviolet light.

UVR ultraviolet radiation.

U/w underwriter.

u/w underwater; unladen weight.

UWA University of Western Australia.

UWC Unemployed Workers' Charter.

UWCE Underwater Weapons and Countermeasures Establishment.

UWE University of the West of England.

UWEAMA Under Water Equipment & Apparel Manufacturers' Association.

UWIST University of Wales Institute of Science and Technology.

UWRA Urban Water Research Association.

UWT Urban Wildlife Trust.

UXB unexploded bomb.

V

V vanadium (chemical element); 5 in Roman numerals; victory; volt.

v vacuum; *vel*, Latin 'or'; velocity; verb; verse; verso; versus; vertical; very; *vide*, Latin 'see'; violin; *voce*, Italian 'voice'; volume; *von*, German 'of'; vowel.

VA Vicar Apostolic; Vice-Admiral.

va verb active; verbal adjective.

v/a voucher attached.

va & i verb active and intransitive.

VAB Voluntary Agencies Bureau.

VAD Voluntary Aid Detachment.

VAdm Vice Admiral.

VAMH Voluntary Association for Mental Health.

VAMW Voluntary Association for Mental Welfare.

VAN Voluntary Arts Network; value-added network.

V & A Victoria and Albert Museum.

v & l vodka and lime.

v & t vodka and tonic.

V & V verification and validation.

VANS value-added network service.

VARS Visual Artists Rights Society.

VAS Vasectomy Advancement Society of Great Britain.

VASCAR visual average speed computer and recorded (speed-trap device).

VAT Value Added Tax.

VBBA Vietnam-British Business Association.

VBF Vinegar Brewers Federation.

VBRA Vehicle Builders and Repairers Association.

VC Vatican City; Vickers Commercial (used in names of aircraft manufactured by them, e.g. VC10); Victoria Cross; Viet Cong; vice-chairman; vice-chancellor; vice-consul.

VC&GCA Victoria Cross and George Cross Association.

VCA Vehicle Certification Association.

VCAA Veteran and Clasic Aeroplane Association.

VCC Veteran Car Club of Great Britain.

VCH Victoria County History.

VCPA Vintage and Classic Power Craft Association.

VCPS Video Copyright Protection Society.

VCR video cassette recorder.

VCRA Veterans Cycle Racing Association.

VCSA Vintage & Classic Sailing Association.

VCT Vintage Charities Trust.

VD Volunteer Decoration; venereal disease.

VDH valvular disease of the heart.

VDI virtual device interface.

VDJ video disk jockey.

VDQS *vin délimité de qualité supérieure*, French for quality wine from a specified region.

VDR video-disk recording.

VDRL Venereal Disease Reference Laboratory Test.

VDS Volunteer Development Scotland.

VDT video display terminal.

VDU visual display unit.

VE Victory in Europe (at the end of World War II); vaginal examination.

VEGA Vegetarian Economy and Green Agriculture.

verb. sap. *verbum sapienti sat est*, Latin 'a word is sufficient to the wise'.

vers versed sine.

VES Voluntary Euthanasia Society.

VetMB Bachelor of Veterinary Medicine.

VF ventricular fibrillation; video frequency; voice frequency.

VFM value for money.

VG Vicar-General.

vg very good.

VGA video graphics array.

VGC Vintage Glider Club of Great Britain.

VGSOH very good sense of humour.

vhc very highly commended.

VHD video high density.

VHE very high energy.

VHF very high frequency.

VHS video home system.

VHT very high temperature.

VI *virgo intacta*, Latin for a virgin.

vi verb intransitive; *vide infra*, Latin 'see below'.

VIA Values into Action Scotland; Visually Impaired Association.

VID virtual image display.

VIP very important person.

VIR *Victoria Imperatrix Regina*, Latin 'Victoria, Empress and Queen'.

VIS Veterinary Investigation Service.

vix. *vixit*, Latin 'lived'.

viz. *videlicet*, Latin 'namely'.

VJ Victory over Japan (at the end of World War II); video jockey.

vl *varia lectio*, Latin for variant reading.

VLBC very large bulk carrier (ship).

VLBW very low birth weight.

VLCC very large crude carrier (oil tanker).

VLCD very low calorie diet.

VLDB very large database.

VLDL very low density lipoprotein.

VLF very low frequency.

VLLW very low level waste (nuclear).

VLSI very large scale integration.

VM Virgin Mary; virtual machine.

VM/CMS Virtual Machine, Conversational Monitor System.

VMD *Veterinariae Medicinae Doctor*, Latin 'Doctor of Veterinary Medicine'; Veterinary Medicines Directorate.

VMG Voluntary Movement Group.

VMH Victoria Medal of Honour.

VMM Volunteer Missionary Movement.

VMS Virtual Machine System.

vmt very many thanks.

VNA Vietnam News Agency.

VO Veterinary Officer; voice over.

VOA Voice of America (radio station of the US Information Agency).

VOCA Visiting Orchestras Consultative Association.

VOP very oldest procurable (of spirits).

VOSCO Vietnam Ocean Shipping Company.

VP Vice-President; verb phrase.

vp vanishing point; verb passive.

VPA Vegetable Protein Association.

VPC *vente par correspondance*, French 'mail order'.

vpd vehicles per day.

vph vehicles per hour.

VPO Vienna Philharmonic Orchestra.

vps vibrations per second.

VR *Victoria Regina*, Latin 'Queen Victoria'; Volunteer Reserve; virtual reality; vulcanised rubber.

vr variant reading; verb reflexive.

VRAM video random-access memory.

VRH Volunteer Reading Help.

VRI *Victoria Regina et Imperatrix*, Latin 'Victoria, Queen and Empress'; viral respiratory infection.

VRO vehicle registration office.

VRS Virtual Reality Society.

VS The Victorian Society; Vegetarian Society; Veterinary Surgeon.

vs *vide supra*, Latin 'see above'; *volti subito*, Italian 'turn over quickly' (music).

VSAM virtual storage access method.

VSCC Vintage Sports Car Club.

VSD ventricular septal defect.

VSI Vegetarian Society of Ireland.

VSL Venture Scout Leader.

VSO Vienna State Opera; Voluntary Service Overseas; very superior old (of spirits).

VSOP very superior old pale (brandy, etc.).

VSR very special reserve (of wine, etc.).

VSS vital signs stable.

VSTOL vertical and short take-off and landing.

VSUK Vegetarian Society of the United Kingdom Limited.

VT ventricular tachycardia.

vt verb transitive.

VTO vertical take-off.

VTOHL vertical take-off, horizontal landing.

VTOL vertical take-off and landing.

VTOVL vertical take-off, vertical landing.

VTR videotape recorder.

VU varicose ulcer; volume unit.

vv vice versa.

VVO very, very old (of brandy, etc.).

VW Very Worshipful; *Volkswagen*, German 'People's Car'.

vy various years.

W

W tungsten (chemical element); Wales; Wednesday; Welsh; watt; west; western; white; winter; women; women's (clothing size).

w week; weight; wicket; wide; widow; width; wife; with; won; word.

WA West Africa; Western Australia; Will-writers Association.

WAA Women's Auxiliary Association.

WAAA Women's Amateur Athletic Association.

WAAE World Association for Adult Education.

WAAF Women's Auxiliary Air Force.

WAB Wales Advisory Body for Local Authority Higher Education.

WABA Welsh Amateur Basketball Association; Welsh Amateur Boxing Association.

WACA World Airlines Clubs Association.

WACCC Worldwide Air Cargo Commodity Classification.

WAD World Association of Detectives.

waf with all faults.

WAFA World Association of Flower Arrangers.

WAFB Workers Aid for Bosnia.

WAfr West Africa.

WAG Writers' and Artists' Guild.

WAGA Welsh Amateur Gymnastic Association.

WAGBI Wildfowl Association of Great Britain and Ireland.

WAGC World Amateur Golf Council.

WAGGGS World Association of Girl Guides and Girl Scouts.

WAIA World Association of Introduction Agencies.
WAIF World Adoption International Fund.
WAJ World Association of Judges.
WAM Working Association of Mothers.
WAMF Welsh Amateur Music Federation.
WAMS World Association of Military Surgeons.
WAMT Women and Manual Trades.
wan wide-area network.
W & M William and Mary.
w & s whisky and soda.
w & t wear and tear.
WAO World Association for Orphans and Abandoned Children.
WAPC Women Against Pit Closures.
WAR Women Against Rape; Workers Against Racism.
WARC Women's Amateur Rowing Council; World Administrative Radio Conference; World Alliance of Reformed Churches.
WAS World Aquaculture Society; World Archaeological Society; World Association for Sexology.
WASA Welsh Amateur Swimming Association.
WASAC Welsh Association of Sub Aqua Clubs.
WASH Women Against Sexual Harassment.
WASP white Anglo-Saxon Protestant.
WASWC World Association of Soil and Water Conservation.
WATA World Association of Travel Agents.
WATCH Watch Trust for Environmental Education.
WAVA World Association of Veteran Athletes.
WAYC Welsh Association of Youth Clubs.
WB Warner Brothers; Weather Bureau; World Bank; World Brotherhood.
Wb weber (physics).
WBA West Bromwich Albion; World Boxing Association; World Bowling Association; whole body activity.
WBC World Boxing Council; white blood cell.
WBCS Welsh Black Cattle Society.
WBF World Bridge Federation.
wbi will be issued.
WBO World Boxing Organisation.

WBR whole body radiation.
WBS whole body scan.
WBU Welsh Badminton Union; Welsh Baseball Union.
WC West Central; water closet.
wc without charge.
W/C Wing Commander.
WCA Wholesale Caterers' Alliance; Women's Cricket Association; Wood Carvers Association; World Calendar Association.
wca worst-case analysis.
WCC Wales Craft Council; War Crimes Commission; Welsh Consumer Council; World Cheerleader Council (USA); World Council of Churches; World Cultural Council.
WCCL Welsh Council for Civil Liberties.
W/Cdr Wing-Commander.
WCF World Congress of Faiths; World Curling Federation.
WCMMF World Congress of Man-Made Fibres.
WCP World Council of Peace; World Court Project.
WCRA Women's Cycle Racing Association.
WCS Wilkie Collins Society.
WCT Women Caring Trust; World Championship Tennis.
WCU Welsh Chess Union; World Conservative Union.
WD War Department; Works Department.
2-w/d two-wheel drive.
4-w/d four-wheel drive.
WDA Well Drillers Association; Welsh Development Agency; World Dredging Association.
WDC Woman Detective Constable; World Darts Council; World Disarmament Campaign.
WDS Woman Detective Sergeant.
w/e weekend; week ending.
WEA Workers's Educational Association.
WEAN Women's Earth Action Network.
WEDA Wholesale Egg Distributors Association; Wholesale Engineering Distributors Association.
wef with effect from.
WEN Women's Environmental Network.
WES Western Equestrian Society; Women's

Engineering Society; Writing Equipment Society.

WET Western European Time.

WEU Western European Union.

wf wing forward; wrong fount.

WFA White Fish Authority; Women's Football Association; Workers' Film Association.

WFAS World Federation of Acupuncture Societies.

WFB World Fellowship of Buddhists.

WFC World Feminist Commission; World Food Council.

WFD World Federation of the Deaf.

WFE Women for Freedom in Europe.

WFEO World Federation of Engineering Organizations.

WFH Wages for Housework; World Federation of Healing.

WFLOE Women For Life On Earth.

WFP World Food Programme.

WFS Wild Flower Society; Women for Socialism; World Food Security.

WFSS Welsh Folk Song Society.

WFT Winged Fellowship Trust.

WFTT World Federation of Twinned Towns.

WFTU World Federation of Trade Unions.

WFU Women's Farming Union.

WG Welsh Guards.

wg water gauge; wire gauge.

WGAS Wholesale Grocers Association of Scotland.

WGer West Germany.

WGF Women's Gas Federation and Young Homemakers.

WGGB Writers Build of Great Britain.

WGU Welsh Golfing Union.

Wh watt-hour.

wh wing half.

WHA Welsh Hockey Association; Western Horsemen's Association of Great Britain.

WHAM Women, Heritage and Museums.

whb wash-hand basin.

WHC Women's Health Concern.

WHI Welsh Hearing Institute.

WHL World Hypertension League.

WHML Wellcome Historical Medical Library.

WHO World Health Organization.

WHPU Welsh Homing Pigeon Union.

WHRA Welwyn Hall Research Association.

WHS Wesley Historical Society.

WHSC West Highland Steamer Club.

WI West Indies; Women's Institute.

WIA Willow Importers Association; World Interfaith Association; wounded in action.

WIAC Women's International Art Club.

WIBA Welsh Indoor Bowls Association.

WIGS Women in German Studies.

WIL Workers International League.

WILD International Wilderness Leadership Foundation.

WIM Women in Management; Women in Media; Women in Medicine.

WIMA Women's International Motorcycle Association; World International Medical Association.

wimp windows, icons, menus, pointer.

WING Work Injured Nurses Group.

WIP work in progress.

WIPO World Intellectual Property Organization.

WIR White Irish Resistance.

WISA West Indies Sugar Association; West Indies Shipping Corporation.

WITA Women's International Tennis Association.

WJC World Jewish Congress.

WJCB World Jersey Cattle Bureau.

WJEC Welsh Joint Education Committee.

WJFITB Wool, Jute and Flax Industry Training Board.

WKA Warp Knitters Association.

WL waiting list, wavelength.

WLA Welsh Lacrosse Association; Women's Land Army; World Literary Academy.

WLF Women's Liberal Federation.

WLM Women's Liberation Movement.

WLR Weekly Law Reports.

WLS Welsh Language Society.

WLSS Wheelchair Loan Service Scotland.

WLTM would like to meet.

WM well maintained; white male.

WMA Wallcovering Manufacturers Association; Waterheaters Manufacturers Association; Weather Modification Association; Workers' Music Association; Working Mothers' Association; World Media Association.

WMAC West Midlands Advisory Council for Further Education.

WMC Working Men's Club; World Methodist Council; World Mining Congress.

WMCCSA World Masters Cross Country Ski Association.

WMCIU Working Men's Club and Institute Union Limited.

WMF Waste Management Forum; World Memorial Fund for Disaster Relief.

WMM World Movement of Mothers.

WMO World Meteorological Organization.

wmp with much pleasure.

WMS Welsh Mines Society.

WNA Welsh Netball Association.

WNB weekly news bill.

WNCCC Women's Nationwide Cancer Control Campaign Limited.

wndp with no down payment.

WNE Welsh National Eisteddfod.

wnl within normal limits.

WNO Welsh National Opera.

WNP Welsh National Party.

WNW west-northwest.

WO War Office; warrant officer; wireless operator.

wo walkover; written order.

w/o without; written off.

WOAR Women Organized Against Rape.

woc without compensation.

wocs waiting on cement setting.

WoO *Werke ohne Opuszahl*, German 'works without an opus number' (Beethoven's unpublished works).

Wormt write once, read many times.

Wosac worldwide synchronisation of atomic clocks.

WOSB War Office Selection Board.

WOW War on Want; Wider Opportunities for Women; Women Against the Ordination of Women; World of Water; waiting on weather.

WP Warsaw Pact; Workers Party (Ireland); word processing; word processor.

wp weather permitting.

WPA Water Polo Association; Wire Products Association; World Pheasant Association; World Presbyterian Alliance.

wpb wastepaper basket.

WPBS Welsh Plant Breeding Station.

WPBSA World Professional Billiards and Snooker Association.

WPC Welsh Pricing Committee; Woman Police Constable; World Print Council.

WPCS Welsh Pony and Cob Society; White Park Cattle Society.

WPG Workers Power Group.

WPGA Women's Professional Golf Association.

WPI wholesale price index.

WPM World Presbyterian Missions.

wpm words per minute.

WPMSF World Professional Marathon Swimming Federation.

WPO World Ploughing Organization.

WPRA Waste Paper Recovery Association.

WPS Wireless Preservation Society and National Wireless Museum.

WR Western Region; West Riding (former part of Yorkshire); *Wilhelmus Rex*, Latin 'King William'.

WRA Windsurfing Retailers Association.

WRAC Women's Royal Army Corps.

WRAAC Women's Royal Australian Army Corps.

WRAAF Women's Royal Australian Air Force.

WRAC Women's Royal Army Corps.

WRAF Women's Royal Air Force.

WRAG Welsh Railways Action Group.

WRB Water Resources Board.

WRBS Wholesale and Retail Bakers of Scotland.

WRC Water Research Centre; Women's Resource Centre.

WRDC White Rose Dollmakers' Circle; Wool Research and Development Corporation.

WRF World Rehabilitation Fund; World Runner Foundation.

WRG Waterway Recovery Group.

WRI Women's Rural Institute; war risks insurance.

WRM World Rainforest Movement.

WRN Woman Returners Network.

WRNR Women's Royal Naval Reserve.

WRNS Women's Royal Naval Service.

WRO war risks only.

WRP Workers' Revolutionary Party.

WRRA Women's Road Records Association (cycling).

WRSA World Rabbit Science Association.

WRST World Rainforest Survival Trust.

wrt with respect to.

WRU Welsh Rugby Union.

WRVS Women's Royal Voluntary Service.

WS The Wilderness Society; Web Society; Writer to the Signet.

WSA Water Services Association; West of Scotland Agricultural College; Wine & Spirit Association of Great Britain and Northern Ireland; Women Sport Australia; World Service Authority.

WSAS Wine and Spirit Association of Scotland.

WSAVA World Small Animal Veterinary Association.

WSB World Scout Bureau.

WSBA Welsh Schools Basketball Association.

WSC Welfare State Campaign; Western Sahara Campaign; World Series Cricket; World Spiritual Council.

WSCA Welsh Schools Cricket Association.

WSF Women's Sports Foundation; World Scout Foundation.

WSGF Welsh Seed Growers Federation.

WSJ Wall Street Journal.

WSO World Sikh Organisation; World Simulation Organization.

WSPA World Society for Protection of Animals.

WSRS Wildlife Sound Recording Society.

WSS World Ship Society.

WSSA Weed Science Society of America; Welsh Secondary Schools Association.

WSW west-south-west.

WT weekly takings.

w/t wireless telegraphy.

WTA Women's Tennis Association.

WTB Wales Tourist Board.

WTN Worldwide Television News.

WTO Warsaw Treaty Organization.

WToO World Tourism Organization.

WTrO World Trade Organization.

WTT World Team Tennis.

WTUC World Trade Union Conference.

WU Women's Union.

WUR World University Roundtable.

w/v weight in volume.

WVRSC Wholesale Vegetable and Root Seeds Committee.

WVS Women's Voluntary Service.

WW world war.

w/w wall to wall; weight for weight.

WWA War Widows Association of Great Britain; Welsh Water Authority; Woven Wire Association.

WWF Worldwide Fund for Nature (previously World Wildlife Fund); World Wrestling Federation.

WWGBP World Working Group on Birds of Prey and Owls (Germany).

WWHA Welsh Women's Hockey Association.

WWO Wing Warrant Officer.

WWOOF Working Weekends on Organic Farms.

WWP World Wide Peace.

WWSU World Water Ski Union.

WWT Wildfowl & Wetlands Trust.

WWTA Welsh Weight Training Association; Woollen and Worsted Trades Association.

WWW Women Welcome Women; World Weather Watch; World Wide Web (Internet).

WWWC World Without War Council.

WX Women's Extra (clothing size).

WYC World Youth Choir.

WYSA Woollen Yarn Spinners Association.

WYSIWYG what you see is what you get.

WZO World Zionist Organization.

XYZ

X Christ (from the shape of chi, the Greek capital initial letter of *Christos*); former film censorship classification which limited viewing to those over 16.

x-c cross-country (skiing).

xd ex-dividend.

XDR extended dynamic range (cassettes).

Xe xenon (chemical element).

xi ex interest.

xlwb extra long wheelbase.

Xmas Christmas.

xn ex new (without the right to new shares).

XR X-ray.

xr ex rights.

XRT X-ray therapy.

XS cross-section.

xs expenses.

xw ex warrants.

Y yttrium (chemical element); yen, Japanese currency; yuan, Chinese currency.

y yard; year.

YAA Yachtsmens Association of America.

YAF Young Americans for Freedom.

YAPLO Yorkshire Association of Power Loom Workers.

YAR Yemen Arab Republic.

YASGB Youth Association of Synagogues in Great Britain.

YB Year Book.

Yb ytterbium (chemical element).

YC Young Conservative; yacht club; youth club.

YC & UO Young Conservation and Unionist Organization.

YCA Yacht Charter Association; Yacht Cruising Association.

YCF Yacht Club de France.

YCND Youth Campaign for Nuclear Disarmament.

YD Youth Defence.

YDS Yorkshire Dialect Society.

YE Your Excellency.

YES Youth Employment Service; Youth Enterprise Scheme; Young Entomologists Society.

YET Young Explorers Trust.

YFC Young Farmers' Club.

YFCU Young Farmers' Clubs of Ulster.

YH youth hostel.

YHA Yacht Harbour Association; Youth Hostels Association.

YHAFHE Yorkshire and Humberside Association for Further and Higher Education.

YHANI Youth Hostels Association of Northern Ireland.

YHC Young Herpetologists Club.

YJA Yachting Journalists' Association; Young Journalists' Association.

Y2K Year 2000.

YLGN Young Labour Green Network.

YMBA Yacht and Motor Boat Association.

YMCA Young Men's Christian Association.

YMCU Young Men's Christian Union.

YMFS Young Men's Friendly Society.

YMHA Young Men's Hebrew Association.

yo year old.

yob year of birth.

yod year of death.

yom year of marriage.

YOP Youth Opportunities Programme.

YPTES Young People's Trust for Endangered Species.

YRC Youth Rights Campaign.

YSA Young Socialist Alliance.

YSAU Young Swimmers Athletic Union.

YT Yukon Territory.

YTA Young Theatre Association.

ytd year to date.

YTS Youth Training Scheme.

YTV Yorkshire Television.

YU Yale University.

yuppy young urban professional.

YWCA Young Women's Christian Association.

YWHA Young Women's Hebrew Association.

z zenith; zero; zone.

ZAAA Zambia Amateur Athletics Association.

ZADCA Zinc Alloy Die Casters' Association.

ZANU Zimbabwe African National Union.

ZAPU Zimbabwe African People's Union.

ZB Zen Buddhism.

zB *zum Beispiel*, German 'for example'.

ZCCT Zoo Check Charitable Trust.

ZDA Zinc Development Association.

zeg zero economic growth.

Zift zygote intrafallopian transfer.

ZIP Zone Improvement Plan.

Zn zinc (chemical element).

ZO Zionist Organization.

ZPDA Zinc Pigment Development Association.

zpg zero population growth.

Zr zirconium (chemical element).

ZS Zoological Society.

ZSI Zoological Society of Ireland.

ZSL Zoological Society of London.

ZST Zone Standard Time.

ZTDC Zimbabwe Tourist Development Corporation.

ZUM Zimbabwe Unity Movement.